MODERN HUMANITIES RESEARCH ASSOCIATION

TUDOR & STUART TRANSLATIONS

VOLUME 22

General Editors
ANDREW HADFIELD
NEIL RHODES

AN APOLOGY OR ANSWER IN DEFENCE OF THE CHURCH OF ENGLAND: LADY ANNE BACON'S TRANSLATION OF BISHOP JOHN JEWEL'S *APOLOGIA ECCLESIAE ANGLICANAE*

AN APOLOGY OR ANSWER IN DEFENCE OF
THE CHURCH OF ENGLAND:
LADY ANNE BACON'S TRANSLATION OF
BISHOP JOHN JEWEL'S
APOLOGIA ECCLESIAE ANGLICANAE

Edited by

Patricia Demers

MODERN HUMANITIES RESEARCH ASSOCIATION
2016

Published by
The Modern Humanities Research Association
Salisbury House
Station Road
Cambridge CB1 2LA
United Kingdom

© The Modern Humanities Research Association, 2016

Patricia Demers has asserted her right under the Copyright, Designs and Patents Act 1988 to be identified as the author of this work.

Parts of this work may be reproduced as permitted under legal provisions for fair dealing (or fair use) for the purposes of research, private study, criticism, or review, or when a relevant collective licensing agreement is in place. All other production requires the written permission of the copyright holder who may be contacted at rights@mhra.org.uk

First published 2016

ISBN 978-1-78188-127-9 (pbk)
ISBN 978-1-78188-126-2 (hbk)

Copies may be ordered from www.tudor.mhra.org.uk

MHRA TUDOR AND STUART TRANSLATIONS

GENERAL EDITORS

Andrew Hadfield (University of Sussex)
Neil Rhodes (University of St Andrews)

ASSOCIATE EDITORS

Guyda Armstrong (University of Manchester)
Fred Schurink (University of Manchester)
Louise Wilson (Liverpool Hope University)

ADVISORY BOARD

Warren Boutcher (Queen Mary, University of London); Colin Burrow (All Souls College, Oxford); A. E. B. Coldiron (Florida State University); Patricia Demers (University of Alberta); José Maria Pérez Fernández (University of Granada); Robert S. Miola (Loyola College, Maryland); Alessandra Petrina (University of Padua); Anne Lake Prescott (Barnard College, Columbia University); Quentin Skinner (Queen Mary, London); Alan Stewart (Columbia University)

For details of published and forthcoming volumes please visit our website:

www.tudor.mhra.org.uk

TABLE OF CONTENTS

General Editors' Foreword viii

Preface ix

Editorial Conventions xi

Introduction 1

Further Reading 35

AN APOLOGY OR ANSWER IN DEFENCE OF 41
THE CHURCH OF ENGLAND

    Prefatory Letter from Archbishop Matthew Parker 43

    Part I 45

    Part II 60

    Part III 83

    Part IV 94

    Part V 130

    Part VI 151

Glossary 187

Writers 191

Bibliography 195

Index 207

GENERAL EDITORS' FOREWORD

The aim of the *MHRA Tudor & Stuart Translations* is to create a representative library of works translated into English during the early modern period for the use of scholars, students and the wider public. The series will include both substantial single works and selections of texts from major authors, with the emphasis being on the works that were most familiar to early modern readers. The texts themselves will be newly edited with substantial introductions, notes, and glossaries, and will be published both in print and online.

The series aims to restore to view a major part of English Renaissance literature which has become relatively inaccessible and to present these texts as literary works in their own right. For that reason it will follow the same principle of modernisation adopted by other scholarly editions of canonical literature from the period. The series will have a similar scope to that of the original *Tudor Translations* published early in the last century, and while the great majority of the works presented will be from the sixteenth century, like the original series it will not be rigidly bound by the end-date of 1603. There will, however, be a very different range of texts with new and substantial scholarly apparatus.

The *MHRA Tudor & Stuart Translations* will extend our understanding of the English Renaissance through its representation of the process of cultural transmission from the classical to the early modern world and the process of cultural exchange within the early modern world.

Andrew Hadfield
Neil Rhodes

PREFACE

Editing Anne Cooke Bacon's *An Apology or Answer* has involved a series of discoveries. Although I thought I was familiar with Lady Anne's work, I soon found myself surprisingly immersed in the tangled webs of the controversy between John Jewel and Thomas Harding during which her English translation was always cited by both 'sides' as the clear evidentiary proof of correct or mangled, acceptable or perverse interpretation of religious practice. I started to tread more warily in what became the tulgey wood of this dispute. For all the display of arcane erudition and knowledge of past councils and Church Fathers, how could religion be at the root of this venom and backbiting, these *ad hominem* attacks? Anne Bacon, I understood, provided ammunition for both disputants, yet she herself remained squarely on team Jewel.

The use of a sports metaphor is not entirely inappropriate, since the sense of competitive one-upmanship was the most startling feature of the controversy. These ordained religious were competing for adherents, scoring points on theological knowledge, and relying on Lady Anne's translation to secure their arguments. The time of the appearance of *An Apology or Answer* was still a raw period of transformation, with the Articles of Convocation clashing with the documents of the Council of Trent. As I uncovered more and more of the layers of meaning, allusion, and potentially inflammatory response in the scanty marginalia, I realized that this embedded context, captured with such succinct accuracy in Lady Bacon's translation, needed some fleshing out to capture the heat of the quarrel and the intellectual stakes for which the battle was being fought. As the footnotes kept growing, I came to understand how much religion can reveal about the ways people think and live.

Anne Bacon's acute intelligence shines through her work as a translator — from Italian and Latin — and its strategies of meaning-making. The availability of a substantial portion of her extant letters now enlarges the view of her shrewd judgment and sharp tongue. I found myself toggling back and forth between admiration for her boldness and accomplishment, her unwavering commitment to reform, and sympathy for her apparent isolation in the last decade of her life. Of course the silence of that decade remains a mystery: have letters been lost or did Anne Bacon decline? There is a certain irony surrounding this silence, too. For a woman who was so blunt, vocal, and straightforward in her Protestant and then Puritan loyalties, a quiet diminuendo seems unthinkable.

I want to express my deep thanks to those who have made the Bacon project and its discoveries possible. In the first instance I am very grateful to MHRA general editors Neil Rhodes and Andrew Hadfield for inviting me to prepare this edition, to Louise Wilson for helpful advice about formatting, and to Simon Davies for sharp-eyed editing. Scholarly work always involves lessons learned from generous colleagues and debts incurred. Among the scholars whose encouragement, questions, and remarks have buoyed me up at different times, I want to thank especially Judith Rice Henderson, Brenda Hosington, Joseph Khoury, Jeanine Landtsheer, Elizabeth McCutcheon, Elizabeth Popham, and Micheline White. Wayne Hammond of the Chapin Library at Williams College kindly supplied the cover image; this engraving by Henry R. Cook (active 1800–1845) is the frontispiece of their copy of the first edition. Librarian services throughout the University of Alberta system, and particularly in the Bruce Peel Special Collections Library, have been outstanding. My special thanks go to Peter Box, Robert Desmarais, Jeff Papineau, and Linda Quirk. Brianna Erban, my indefatigable and always upbeat research assistant, has helped to chart pathways through classical, patristic, and conciliar texts with sanity-preserving wit and tremendous good humour.

EDITORIAL CONVENTIONS

The copy text for this edition is the first edition, *An Apologie or answere in defence of the Churche of Englande* (printed by Reginald Wolfe, 1564, STC 14591). Following the conventions of MHRA editions, marginalia and explanations appear in footnotes. Because Lady Bacon's text is so tessellated with biblical phrases and allusions, and so reliant on precise knowledge of conciliar debates and Church Fathers, the extent of these footnotes differs from the norm. Another factor influencing the size and range of the footnotes is the extensive controversy that erupted between Jewel and Harding based on Lady Bacon's text. To savour the character and feel the heat of this fray it seems necessary to me to enter and discuss the thorny arguments themselves. Biblical quotations are based on *The Geneva Bible* (1560), a copy of which Lady Bacon most certainly owned since she used its chapter and verse divisions in her letters.

The marginalia in John Jewel's *Apologia Ecclesiae Anglicanae* (1562) and Anne Bacon's *An Apologie or answere*, both printed by Reginald Wolfe, are identical. Most but not all the marginalia in this edition derive from these original texts. To illustrate the intensely biblical matrix of Bacon's translation, unmarginated biblical allusions and quotations are noted, some (marked L) derived from John Ayre's edition of the *Apologia Ecclesiae Anglicanae* included in the *Works of John Jewel* for the Parker Society (1845–1850).

Lady Bacon's much-lauded translation disappeared from print acknowledgement for almost two centuries. Bacon's text, without the prefatory letter by Archbishop Matthew Parker and without any acknowledgement of Anne Cooke Bacon, appeared in Thomas Chard's printing for James Roberts of *The Apologie of the Church of England [...] by the most reuerend Father in God, Iohn Iuell, Bishop of Sarisbury* (1600); Peter Martyr's congratulatory greeting to his old pupil John Jewel replaced Parker's letter to Anne Cooke. Segments of Bacon's *An Apology or Answer* as cited in Jewel's *Defence of the Apology* were included in the first edition of Jewel's *Works* (1609, reprinted 1611). By 1635 the edition of *The Apology of the Church of England* printed by John Beale used Bacon's unacknowledged translation and again replaced the commendation of Archbishop Parker with

Peter Martyr's letter to Jewel. Later translations by clergymen — Thomas Cheyne (1720), A. C. Campbell (1813), Stephen Isaacson (1825), William Rollinson Whittingham (1831), and William Withers Ewbank (1839) — do not match the pungent, idiomatic clarity of Lady Bacon. Parker's letter and Anne Bacon's acknowledged translation re-appeared in Ayre's Parker Society edition, William Jelf's S.P.C.K. edition of *An Apologie or Answere* (1849), and John Booty's edition of *An Apology of the Church of England* (1963) for the Folger Shakespeare Library.

Fidelity to Lady Bacon's text assumed more and more significance as I realized the scale of its neglect. Along with its interjections and summative, credal additions, her translation conveys the sense of listening to an informed speaker. Presuming an eagerness to listen and learn on the part of her audience, Bacon included long complex sentences alongside simple parataxis to drive home a point. It is important to note that she did not include any punctuation marks to designate quoted speech or strong feeling. There are no exclamation or quotation marks in her text: she expected her readers to follow and understand without intrusive signposting. Although MHRA texts usually rely on modern punctuation, in this instance I am following Lady Bacon's practice and identifying quoted passages in footnotes. Only where colons in Bacon's text obscured the meaning have semi-colons been inserted. The text is inconsistent in its capitalisation of proper nouns, another feature which is reproduced in this edition.

INTRODUCTION

The history of the composition and reception of Bishop John Jewel's *Apologia Ecclesiae Anglicanae* (1562) and of Lady Anne Cooke Bacon's translation, *An Apology or Answer in Defence of the Church of England* (1564), reveals 'the creatively interacting intellectual currents'[1] of Reformation culture. The official defence of the Elizabethan Settlement, *An Apology* is at once an explanation and vindication of the establishment of the English Church and an attack on the perceived failings of the Church of Rome. It embodies the tensions of 'an age of polemic', which Patrick Collinson diagnosed as 'a fissiparous pandemic'; 'thanks to the new technology of print', he remarked, 'polemic became a dominant force in European culture.'[2] In sixteenth-century England, 'an age still impressed by the intricacies of scholarly debate'[3] when spiritual discourse and denominational loyalties were literally matters of life and death, politics and religion were inextricably entwined in early printed books. The two principal figures in the creation and dissemination of this text — both complex, determined personalities devoted to reform — moved in elite and connected circles. Their individual stories reflect and share such Reformation fluctuations as ecclesiastical favour and ostracism, polemical notoriety and neglect. Recognized as 'one of England's greatest Protestant names',[4] Bishop John Jewel of Salisbury needs to be considered alongside his learned and accomplished translator Lady Anne Bacon, whose 'intelligence was equal to that of any man among her contemporaries'[5] and whose text is 'the most significant translation by a woman in this

---

[1] Alister McGrath, *The Intellectual Origins of the European Reformation* (Oxford: Basil Blackwell, 1987), p. 197.
[2] Patrick Collinson, *Richard Bancroft and Elizabethan Anti-Puritanism* (Cambridge: Cambridge University Press, 2013), p. 13.
[3] Wyndham Southgate, *John Jewel and the Problem of Doctrinal Authority* (Cambridge, Mass.: Harvard University Press, 1962), p. 51.
[4] Diarmaid MacCulloch, *Reformation: Europe's House Divided 1490–1700* (London: Allen Lane, 2003), p. 503.
[5] William Urwick, *Nonconformity in Herts: Being Lectures upon the Nonconforming Worthies of St. Albans* (London: Hazell, Watson, and Viney, 1884), p. 96.

period'.[6] This edition aims to explore the interlaced careers of these two formidable proponents of the Church of England.

An Apology marshals its argument to take full advantage of the opportunities for cross-linguistic instruction and proselytizing afforded by print culture. Giving the lie to the old claim 'that translating was a safe and silent task particularly suited to women', the circulation of this text discloses 'how the ideologies of religion and the marketplace meet and influence the production of books'.[7] In light of its vast reaches of church history, patristic writing, and biblical allusion, as well as its apologetic purpose, *An Apology* clearly illustrates how 'printing and translation animated both the recovery of the past and the creation of the future'. Making the past and the foreign 'available and legible', *An Apology* united 'the pan-European community of Latinate readers' with a 'vernacular print readership'.[8] Although Anne Coldiron argues convincingly that one point of the 'learned and secondary mode of expression' of Latin was 'to transcend local expressive differences, not to encourage them', Lady Bacon's translation riffs on the colloquial, giving full rein to the aural qualities of everyday language. Bacon's vivid, idiomatic prose succeeds in creating a form of cross-vernacularization which actually does imagine 'a different sort of English relation to the foreign and the past'.[9] Of course this entangled and in many ways arcane past of classical and patristic writing, histories of councils and heresies, and warnings of major and minor prophets may be as distant to today's readers as to large portions of Lady Bacon's Elizabethan audience. Jewel and Bacon knew their sources and understood the pathways of argument and allusion. This edition,

---

[6] Neil Rhodes, Introduction, *English Renaissance Translation Theory*, ed. by Neil Rhodes with Gordon Kendal and Louise Wilson (London: Modern Humanities Research Association, 2013), p. 48.

[7] Brenda M. Hosington, 'Women Translators and the Early Printed Book', in *A Companion to the Early Printed Book in Britain 1476–1558*, ed. by Vincent Gillespie and Susan Powell (Cambridge: D. S. Brewer, 2014), 248–271 (pp. 248, 266). Hosington notes that over one thousand translations by men and just over forty by women from 1504 to 1557 render the claim absurd. See also *Renaissance Cultural Crossroads: An Online Catalogue of Translations in Britain 1473–1640*, ed. by Brenda M. Hosington et al. at: www.hrionline.ac.uk/rcc.

[8] Anne E. B. Coldiron, *Printers Without Borders: Translation and Textuality in the Renaissance* (Cambridge: Cambridge University Press, 2015), pp. 2, 3, 8, 9.

[9] Coldiron, *Printers Without Borders*, p. 9.

therefore, also aims to elucidate the cryptic marginal citations, thus supplying the explanation and 'ocular proof' of the authors' humanistic learning.

Reference to the translator as an author entails an examination of the early modern translator's role in exercising 'a new subtler freedom', using 'domestication' rather than inattention to herald the sixteenth-century 'modern "stylistic" translation'.[10] The act of translation, we understand, is 'always a reconstitution of values as much as language and a reconstruction of meaning as well as words'.[11] Yet specific expectations surround a religio-political treatise like the *Apology*. Jaime Goodrich notes that 'the practical habitus of the religious translator generally operated between the poles of faithfulness and freedom, depending on the translator's views of the source text's orthodoxy.'[12] Such a bi-polar project did, however, offer real advantages. As Lady Bacon's being enlisted 'to combat the criticism of "hotter" Protestants and English Catholics' and her like-mindedness with her source testify, the translation of Jewel's text was an ideal opportunity: 'female translators — like their male counterparts — found the authorial multiplicity of translation a productive means of assuming authorial poses that established their personal credibility and advanced larger political and religious agendas.'[13] For royal and theological reasons both Bishop Jewel and Bacon were invested in justifying the validity of the Elizabethan Settlement: Jewel addressing lettered or Latinate readers and Bacon 'reaching an audience that lacks more than a smattering of Latin, that has considerable confidence in deciphering alphabetic letters in the vernacular, and that needs to be persuaded that it would benefit from further education in the form of a book'.[14] Both were composing at a defining, foundational juncture. Not only was the

---

[10] Massimiliano Morini, *Tudor Translation in Theory and Practice* (Aldershot: Ashgate Publishing Limited, 2006), p. 29.

[11] Kevin Sharpe, *Selling the Tudor Monarchy: Authority and Image in Sixteenth-Century England* (New Haven: Yale University Press, 2009), p. 325.

[12] Jaime Goodrich, *Faithful Translators: Authorship, Gender, and Religion in Early Modern England* (Evanston, Illinois: Northwestern University Press, 2014), p. 14.

[13] Goodrich, *Faithful Translators*, pp. 13, 25.

[14] Margaret W. Ferguson, *Dido's Daughters: Literacy, Gender and Empire in Early Modern England and France* (Chicago: University of Chicago Press, 2003), p. 87.

number of printing presses increasing, along with the sales of such reform-minded printers as John Day, William Seres, and Edward Whitchurch, Bacon and Jewel's contemporaries were also becoming accustomed to 'intensive reading and re-reading of the same few books, usually devotional ones'[15] in contrast to our own extensive reading — superficial, quick, erratic. Aware as she was of the mode of reading in her day, Bacon made her prose resonate with allusiveness and learning. In fact, as Neil Rhodes observes, 'in a culture in which literary excellence is as likely to be defined by successful assimilation as by originality', translated Renaissance texts 'have to be understood as a dialogue with their sources'.[16]

If we envision translation as a carrying across, a form of bridge, a portrait painted or an exercise in movement and relocation, we also need to acknowledge the realities of the intensely surveillant moment of English Reformation culture. 'The notion of translation has significant metaphorical and conceptual parameters that go beyond mere transfer', indicating 'a specified, limited and controlled type of transfer with religious overtones and political or ideological pretensions.'[17] The exchanges involved in *An Apology* are actually multi-level. In the first instance, we can imagine Bishop Jewel accumulating text and evidence for its defence: referencing volumes of early Church Fathers, relying on his prodigious memory, drawing on his Oxford studies and on the intensive reading he undertook while living with his reformist mentor Peter Martyr Vermigli in Zurich during the Marian reign, and as Bishop with a staff to command, having 'collections systematically made and secretaries copying these into notebooks'.[18] Jewel's library, as purchased by Magdalen College, discloses his method of coding through marginated numbers and underlined passages 'which allow a copyist to make an anthology by subjects'.[19] Lady Bacon's dialogue with Jewel's text combines

---

[15] Franco Moretti, *Distant Reading* (London: Verso, 2013), p. 174.
[16] Rhodes, Introduction, *English Renaissance Translation Theory*, p. 1.
[17] Maria Tymoczko, 'Western Metaphorical Discourses Implicit in Translation Studies', in *Thinking through Translation with Metaphors*, ed. by James St. André (Manchester: St. Jerome Publishing, 2010), 109–43 (pp. 127, 129).
[18] F. J. Levy, *Tudor Historical Thought* (San Marino, California: The Huntington Library, 1967), p. 107.
[19] Neil Ker, 'The Library of John Jewel', *Bodleian Library Record*, 9.5 (1977), 256–65 (p. 263).

INTRODUCTION

her elite Protestant humanist education in languages, rhetoric, and philosophy with her experience as a translator of the sermons of the firebrand preacher Bernardino Ochino from the Italian. Moreover, as the wife of the Lord Keeper of the Great Seal and Privy Councillor Sir Nicholas, and sister-in-law of William Cecil, Lord Burghley, Elizabeth's Principal Secretary, she was 'fully informed of the political intrigues of her day'[20] through this insiders' network, and of the strategies and debates surrounding the establishment of the English Church.

Another perspective to be pursued in the discussion of exchanges and dialogues between the texts of Jewel and Bacon emerges from criteria proposed by a contemporary known to both of them. The President of Magdalen College, Laurence Humphrey, who was to be appointed Jewel's official biographer in 1571, had published in Basel one of the first treatises on translation in the English Renaissance, *Interpretatio Linguarum* (1559). This three-book work, 'stimulated by the Protestant experience of exile', is 'the most comprehensive account of the theory and practice of translation written by an Englishman in the sixteenth century'.[21] Humphrey proposes these criteria for judging the value of a translation: 'it should be comprehensive [*plena*], naturally appropriate [*propria*], attractive [*pura*], and aptly suited [*apta*].'[22]

This edition undertakes to present a double perspective on Lady Bacon and Bishop Jewel then and now, as they were both recognized and judged in their day and our own. With the aim of showcasing Lady Bacon's accomplishment as a translator of Jewel, and the reception of her work, the introduction discusses the writing careers of these two committed reformers. An analysis of the structure of the *Apology* and the lengthy, painstaking, often vitriolic controversy which erupted around it situates the work in the sixteenth century and helps to elucidate its importance. The vast field of translation theory, early modern and contemporary, supplies another angle for grasping the challenges and successes of Lady Bacon's project.

---

[20] Muriel St Clare Byrne, 'The Mother of Francis Bacon', *Blackwood's Magazine* 236 (December 1934), 758–771 (p. 766).
[21] Rhodes, Introduction, *English Renaissance Translation Theory*, pp. 40, 37–38.
[22] Gordon Kendal, trans., in *English Renaissance Translation Theory*, pp. 263–94 (p. 268).

2. 'ONE OF THE LIUELY STONES, & THEREFORE ONE OF THE ELECTE'[23]

The second of the five daughters and four sons of Sir Anthony Cooke and Lady Anne (Fitzwilliam), Anne Cooke (*c.* 1528–1610) was born and educated at the family seat of Gidea Hall in Essex. Sir Anthony, who was largely self-taught, oversaw his children's education in languages (Latin, Greek, French, Italian) and the far-reaching *studia humanitatis*, a Renaissance movement based on the recovery of ancient pagan and Christian texts emphasizing skill in communication in the world; for the Cooke children this study included traditional grammar and rhetoric, history, and moral philosophy.[24] Devoted to Protestant reform, Sir Anthony himself translated and dedicated to King Henry a Latin sermon by St Cyprian; he also served as an unofficial tutor to Henry's successor, reading 'good literature with Edward VI'.[25] The Cooke sisters were hailed in their day, as early as William Barker's *The Nobility of Women* (1559) where 'espestially the daughters of Syr Anthony Cooke' were included 'wch for greke & lattyn be not inferior to any', and John Harrington's translation of Ariosto (1591) identifying these 'three or foure in England out of one famelie' as deserving 'no lesse commendation' than the poet Vittoria Colonna, and citing one sister's verse which he doubted 'if Cambridge or Oxford can mend'.[26] 'Esteemed the most learned

---

[23] Anne Cooke, trans., The Fyfte Sermon, *Fouretene Sermons of Barnardine Ochyne, concernyng the predestinacion and eleccion of God* (London: John Day, 1551), STC 121:14, sig. D2^r, image 26. Cooke's translation of Prediche XXXII, '*Se per salvarsi è necessario credere, che siamo degl'etti*', is a precise rendering of '*vna delle sue viue pietre pero vno degl'eletti*', *La seconda parte delle Prediche, di Mess. Bernardino Ochino Senese, acuratamente castigate* (Geneva, *c.* 1550).

[24] See Paul Oskar Kristeller, *Renaissance Thought II: Papers on Humanism and the Arts* (New York: Harper Torchbooks, 1965), p. 178; Gemma Allen, *The Cooke Sisters: Education, piety and politics in early modern England* (Manchester: Manchester University Press, 2103), pp. 35–44.

[25] M. K. McIntosh, 'Sir Anthony Cooke: Tudor humanist, educator, and religious reformer', *Proceedings of the American Philosophical Society*, 119 (1975), 233–50 (p. 233).

[26] William Barker, *The Nobility of Women (1559)*, ed. by W. Bond, Roxburghe Collection 142 (London: Chiswick Press, 1904), p. 155; Barker's manuscript, which was first published in 1904, adapts and extends Henry Cornelius Agrippa's *De Nobilitate et Praecellentia foemenei sexus* (1529) and Lodovico Domenichi's *La nobilta delle donna* (1549). 'Allusion, The Thirty-Seventh Book', *Ludovico*

women in Europe',[27] many of the Cooke sisters were translators of religious works. The eldest, Mildred Cooke Cecil, Lady Burghley, dedicated her translation of St Basil's homily on Deuteronomy to the Duchess of Somerset (BL, MS Royal 17 B. XVIII). The second youngest, Elizabeth Cooke Hoby Russell, chose John Ponet's *Diallacticon*, a work on the nature of the divine presence in the Eucharist, which she translated as *A Way of Reconciliation* (1605) and published several decades after its composition to honour the memory of her father. In addition she composed funerary epitaphs in three languages, which were engraved upon tombs she designed and commissioned for members of the Cooke, Hoby, and Russell families.

Unlike her sisters, Anne Cooke began her translating career before marriage. As a young woman of nineteen or twenty, she published anonymously five sermons by Bernardino Ochino, ex-General of the Capuchins. In 1547 Archbishop Cranmer had invited Ochino, who had apostatized in 1542, to England and installed him the next year as rector of the London Strangers' Church ministering to Italians, and prebendary of Canterbury. A zealous preacher, like all mendicants, Ochino was nevertheless eager to leave the Empire after the Battle of Mühlberg in Saxony, when the Spanish Imperial forces under Holy Roman Emperor Charles V had defeated the Lutheran Schmalkaldic league of Protestant princes. Cooke's *Sermons of Barnardine Ochine of Sena godlye, frutefull, and uery necessarye for all true Christians* (1548) dwells on the theme of readiness for death. In the prefatory epistle, 'The Interpretour to the gentle reader', she begged pardon for the 'grosse tearmes of a begynner' and promised 'when god geveth better knowledge (according as my talēt wyll extende) to turne mo godly sermōs of the sayde mayster Barnardine into englishe for the enformacion of all that desire to know the truth'; she closed with the reformist pledge that these sermons 'truly conteyne moch to the defacing of papistrie, and hipocrysie, and to the aduancement of the glorye of god'.[28] Homiletic poise and anti-Rome sympathies are uppermost as Anne fulfilled her

---

Ariosto's Orlando Furioso, trans. by Sir John Harrington (1591), ed. by Robert McNulty (Oxford: Clarendon Press, 1971), p. 434.
[27] Urwick, *Nonconformity in Herts*, p. 84.
[28] *Sermons of Barnardine Ochine of Sena* (London: R. Carr for W. Reddell, 1548), STC 997:14, sig. A4r, image 4.

promise in 1551, publishing fourteen sermons on the topics of election and predestination, with her initials on the title page and including a dedication to her mother, 'To the right worshypful and worthily beloved mother, the Lady F'.[29] The address is as rhetorically adroit as her reinforcements of Ochino's preaching. The skill with which she disarms and dispenses with maternal objection to her study through this proof of its usefulness is a remarkable blend of filial duty and singlemindedness. Skirting any mention of disobedience she credits her success to her mother's will.

> [I]t hath pleased you oftē, to reproue my vaine studye in the Italyan tonge, accompting the sede thereof, to haue bene sowen in barayne, unfruitful grounde (syns God thereby is no whytte magnifyed) I haue at the last, perceiued it my duty to proue howe muche the understandynge of youre wyll, could worcke in me towardes the accomplyshynge of the same.

She also closes the address with a contrastive bookending reference to fruitfulness, 'as yeldyng some parte of the fruite of your motherly admonitions, in this my wyllinge servyce'. *Fouretene Sermons* appeared in the same year as a composite volume, *Certayne Sermons of the Ryght Famous and Excellent Clerk* (STC 18766), containing nineteen translations by Anne and six by Richard Argentine, which had originally been published in 1548.

What was the appeal of Ochino? Louise Schleiner notes his 'particular style of individual subjectivity' combined with a 'tall and winning' presence, 'full hair and beard' and vigour in the pulpit 'even after fasting'.[30] 'Ochino's 259 *Prediche* had been very

---

[29] *Fouretene sermons of Barnardine Ochine* (1551), sigs A3ʳ–A4ᵛ. Reproduced in *The Letters of Lady Anne Bacon*, ed. by Gemma Allen (London: Royal Historical Society, Cambridge University Press, 2014), pp. 51–53.

There are some dissenting (and mistaken) views about the identity of 'Lady F'. John King and Mark Rankin, along with Mary Erler, opt for Lady Elizabeth Fane, ardent promoter of the reformed religion and widow of Sir Ralph Fane, who was executed for his allegiance to Edward Seymour in 1552. See John N. King and Mark Rankin, 'Print, Patronage, and the Reception of Continental Reform: 1521–1603', *Yearbook of English Studies*, 38 (2008), 49–67 (p. 60); Mary Erler, *Reading and Writing during the Dissolution: Monks, Friars and Nuns 1530–1558* (Cambridge: Cambridge University Press, 2013), p. 82.

[30] Louise Schleiner, *Tudor and Stuart Women Writers* (Bloomington: Indiana University Press, 1994), p. 35.

successful on the Continent, appearing in Geneva in five installments starting in 1543.'[31] Although 'he was probably the least learned of Cranmer's exiles', in contrast to Peter Martyr and Martin Bucer, M. Anne Overell suggests that 'the stationers knew he would sell'. And although he was later banished from Zurich in 1563 for his failure to condemn polygamy, dying in solitude in Moravia the next year, his vogue in England — lasting to the reissue of *Certayne Sermons* in 1570 (STC 18768) — was due, Overell posits, 'to a generously wide view of Protestantism'.[32] By the time of the reissue of the twenty-five sermons, only Anne Cooke's initials appeared, possibly both the result of this wide view and an acknowledgement of Lady Bacon's accomplishment as the translator of Bishop Jewel. By 1570 reference to Argentine had vanished. Schoolmaster, clergyman, and doctor of medicine, Richard Argentine [*formerly* Sexton] (1510/11–1568) seems to have been a religious opportunist: a reformer during Edward's reign, an ordained priest during Mary's reign, and a 'perfect Protestant' upon Elizabeth's accession.[33]

Anne Cooke's translation itself discloses the attraction of notions about justification, righteousness, and predestination to a serious young woman who was also keen to underscore the moral urgency of Ochino's preaching. Far from being 'deprived of any original voice' and devoting herself to much more than 'a way of keeping busy',[34] she approached translation as an undertaking quite beyond 'the most subordinately paratextual mode of writing'.[35] Justification and righteousness are difficult, often misunderstood, concepts, relying on the conviction that God is righteous and through his grace justifies sinful man. Alister McGrath sketches the full scope of the doctrine of justification as

---

[31] Hosington, 'Women Translators and the Early Printed Book', p. 263.
[32] M. Anne Overell, 'Bernardino Ochino's Books and English Religious Opinion, 1547–80', in *The Church and the Book*, ed. by R. N. Swanson (Woodbridge, Suffolk: The Boydell Press, 2004), pp. 201–11 (pp. 203, 204, 210).
[33] See J. M. Blatchly, 'Argentine, R', *Oxford Dictionary of National Biography*, ed. by H. C. G. Matthew and Brian Harrison (Oxford: Oxford University Press, 2004), online edition, ed. by Lawrence Goldman, January 2008.
[34] Mary Ellen Lamb, 'The Cooke Sisters: Attitudes toward Learned Women in the Renaissance', in *Silent But for the Word: Tudor Women as Patrons, Translators, and Writers of Religious Works*, ed. by Margaret P. Hannay (Kent, Ohio: Ohio State University Press, 1985), pp. 125, 124.
[35] Schleiner, *Tudor and Stuart Women Writers*, p. 51.

it 'encompasses the whole of Christian existence from the first moment of faith, through the increase in righteousness before God and man, to the final perfection of that righteousness in the eschatological city.'[36] The English Reformers, he explains, with 'the strongly political cast' of their theology, 'appear to have worked with a doctrine of justification in which man was understood to be *made* righteous *by faith only*'.[37] Anne Cooke's translation of a total of nineteen sermons reveals her understanding of being elect and her desire to leave a personal mark on this project. 'G.B.', 'Guilielmus (William) Baldwin, a corrector employed by another evangelical printer',[38] supplied *Fouretene Sermons* with a prefatory epistle 'To the Christen Reader' in which feminized dandies or nit-picking critics of 'the honest trauel of a wel occupied gentelwoman' are challenged: 'prety pryckemydantes shal happen to spy amote in thys godly labour [...] seynge it is meter for Docters of divinitye to meddle wyth such matters then Meydens.' Ultimately though, G.B. offers faint praise, reminding such nay-sayers, 'If ought be erred in the translacion, remember it is a womās yea, a gentyl womās, who cōmenly art wonted to lyue idelly, a maidens that neuer gaddid farder thē hir fathers house to learne the language.'[39]

Massimo Sturiale's grammatical analysis of this language, its '*modalità deontica*', or the way the world ought to be according to Ochino and Cooke, substantiates his view of Anne Cooke as '*una donna determinata*' whose talent added '*una interpretazione personale e di conseguenza ad una manipolazione volontaria dell'originale*'.[40] He illustrates this personal interpretation and deliberate manipulation of the original through the instances in which Cooke does not choose such conditional auxiliaries

---

[36] Alister McGrath, *Iustitia Dei: A History of the Christian Doctrine of Justification*, second edition (Cambridge: Cambridge University Press, 1998), p. 36.
[37] McGrath, *Iustitia Dei*, pp. 285, 288.
[38] Hosington, 'Women Translators and the Early Printed Book', p. 264.
[39] Ochino, *Fouretene Sermons of Barnardine Ochyne concerning the predestinacion and eleccion of god. Translated out of Italian in to oure native tounge by A. C.* (London: John Day, 1551), STC 121:14, sig. A2^{r-v}, images 2–3. 'Pryckemydantes' means literally prick-me-dainties.
[40] Massimo Sturiale, *I Sermons di Anne Cooke: Versione "riformata" delle Prediche di Bernardino Ochino* (Catania: Quaderni del Dipartimento di Filologia Moderna, Università degli Studi di Catania, 2003), pp. 71, 65.

combining volition and deference as 'would' and 'should', but rather the more imperative 'must' and 'ought' to reinforce a sense of obligation lacking in Ochino, 'un senso di obbligo che manca invece in Ochino'. Notice how, for example, in her earliest publication, in the fourth of the five *Sermons of Barnardine Ochine of Sena* (1548), Cooke stresses a moral obligation. Ochino's statement on the Christian's otherworldly life — '*Però con Paulo dice, Il mondo è crocifisso a me, & io a lui. Resuscita anco con Christo in nouita di vita*' — becomes 'wherefore he *must* saye with Paul, the world is crucyfyed to me, and I to the worlde. He besyde thys *must* ryse with Christe in newnes of lyfe.'[41] As for errant curiosity, Cooke underlines the words of Ochino, '*Bisognarebbe metterla da canto*' to insist 'It *must* be put aside' in favour of scriptural learning, with '*Doveremo ricordarcidi quello che è scritto*' becoming 'We *oughte* to remember that which is writtē.'[42] In this same sermon, the first of her fourteen, Cooke is even more forceful than her source in foregounding the importance of justification. Ochino's explanation, '*La verità dispiace à falsi Christiani. Si scandalezano dell'Euangelio & della giustificazione per Christo, adunque dovrebbe tacersi*,' becomes an interrogative challenge to those offended by justification: 'The trueth is dyspleasaunt to the false Christians, they fynde offence of the gospel, and Justification by Christe, shoulde it then be kepte in silence?' Ochino's testimony of election, '*Immo debba predicarsi, che Dio alcuni ha eletti, & alcuni nò*', is presented as a straightforward, curt reality: 'Yea, it oughte to be preached that God hathe elected some, and not other some.' The seventh and eighth sermons underscore the responsibilities of election. Although 'our eleccion is al in the hands of God', the seventh sermon clarifies diverse responses to this fact, as 'is evident bi the sun, which hardeneth mire, and melteth waxe'.[43] While the ungodly perceive only partiality and injustice, the elect, sure of their salvation,

---

[41] *Prediche di Bernardino Ochino da Siena* (1542), sig. X2ʳ. Sermon IV, 'By what meane to come to heauen', *Sermons of Barnardine Ochine of Sena* (1548), STC 997:14, sig. E3ʳ, image 35. Italics added.

[42] *Prediche* XXVII; The Fyrst Sermon, *Fouretene Sermons* (1551), STC 121:14, image 6. Subsequent quotations from the same prediche and sermon (images 6 and 7).

[43] 'Of the diverse effects that it worketh in man to beleue that our eleccion is all in the handes of God', *Fouretene Sermons* (1551), STC 121:14, image 31.

know that they are justified through the sacrifice of Christ, their singular judge. Faith, as the ladder metaphor of the eighth sermon indicates, furnishes access to this 'intelligence of the secretes of God.'[44]

The Ochino project was an instructive apprenticeship for Anne Cooke. As well as securing the recognition of ever-canny publishers, she must have experienced the pleasure of extending the audience of this charismatic preacher, the satisfaction of displaying her linguistic skills, and the freedom to emphasize elements of moral obligation in her own text. Although no mention of Ochino occurs in Jewel's Latin or Bacon's *Apology or Answer* or in Jewel's lengthy dispute with Catholic exile Thomas Harding, she established herself, at this early stage in her career, as a compelling voice for reform-minded clergy and their principles.

Convinced of being a member of the elect through the vigour of her faith, Anne Cooke — capable, acknowledged, connected — married lawyer and administrator Nicholas Bacon, recently widowed father of six children, in 1553. With the accession of Mary in July, Anne, a lady-in-waiting who had 'probably been in Mary's service in the immediate past',[45] rushed to greet the new monarch at Kenninghall palace in Norfolk and assure her of the loyalty of her husband and brother-in-law, William Cecil, both of whom had strong connections to Edwardine reform. She was thus critically important in salvaging their careers at court.[46] Despite multiple pregnancies, only two sons, Anthony (b. 1558) and Francis (b. 1561), survived. From the evidence of Sir Nicholas's poem to Anne when they were living in seclusion during the last year of Mary's reign and his prayer when he was elevated to Lord Keeper of the Great Seal of England, it was a happy marriage. To Anne he wrote:

Calleinge to mynde my wyfe moste dere
How ofte you have in sorrowes sadde
My dropeinge lookes turned into gladde,

---

[44] 'Howe it ought to be answered to thē yᵉ lamente that God hath created them foreseyng theyr dampnaciō', *Fouretene Sermons*, image 36.
[45] David Loades, *Mary Tudor: A Life* (Oxford: Basil Blackwell, 1989), p. 192. Loades calls the centre of political power and intrigue 'a glorified boudoir', with seven ladies, thirteen gentlewomen and three chamberers.
[46] For Anne's political roles, see Allen, *The Cooke Sisters*, pp. 124–25, 141–56.

How ofte you have my moodes to badde
Borne patientlye with a mylde mynde,
Asswageinge them with wordes righte kynde.[47]

For both of them he prayed 'soe to endewe me and AB uxor with thy grace and favor that we maye by the remembraunce of theis they benefittes of our creatyon, redemptyon, parentes, byrthe, Education, state of lyfe, and forgivenes of synnes breede suche a love in our hartes towardes thee, and by thy remembraunce of thy iustice suche a feare, as from henceforthe all our thoughts, speakinges, and doeings maye be to the honor and glorye of thy holye name.'[48] Anne and Nicholas read Cicero and Seneca to one another; according to Archbishop of Canterbury Matthew Parker, she was Nicholas's *alter ipse*, for they were *unus spiritus, una caro*.[49] It was while Lady Anne was the mother of an extended family of eight children that she undertook the translation of *Apologia Ecclesiae Anglicanae*.

Since this introduction aims to consider Lady Bacon alongside Bishop Jewel, it is time to address the background of the *Apologia*'s writer. Born near Berrynarbor, Devonshire, and educated locally at Barnstaple school before going up to Merton College and then Corpus Christi College, Oxford, John Jewel (1522–1571) matured as a Protestant during Edward's reign. When Peter Martyr was appointed Regius Professor of Divinity at Oxford, Jewel attached himself to this Continental reformer, auditing his lectures and becoming ordained under Cranmer's rite in 1551. As it did for Nicholas and Anne Bacon, Mary's reign complicated Jewel's fate. He was expelled from Corpus Christi on account of 'his association with Peter Martyr, his preaching of heresy at St Mary's, his failure to attend Mass, and his ordination'.[50] Jewel's service as notary at the disputations of Oxford martyrs Nicholas Ridley and Thomas Cranmer may have

---

[47] Sir Nicholas Bacon, 'Made at Wymbleton in his Lo: greate sickenes in the laste yeare of Quene Marye', *The Recreations of His Age* (Oxford, 1919), p. 26.
[48] Sir Nicholas Bacon, *The Recreations of His Age*, pp. 39–40.
[49] Matthew Parker to Anne Bacon, 6 February 1568, *The Letters of Lady Anne Bacon*, ed. by Gemma Allen (London: Royal Historical Society, Cambridge University Press, 2014), p. 68; *alter ipse*: other self; *unus spiritus, una caro*: one spirit, one heart.
[50] Gary W. Jenkins, *John Jewel and the English National Church: The Dilemmas of an Erastian Reformer* (Aldershot: Ashgate Publishing Limited, 2006), p. 37.

'triggered his forced subscription'[51] to the tenets of Roman doctrine, an action which was followed shortly by his departure for the Continent. He regretted the decision to subscribe almost immediately, publicly confessed his fault at Frankfort 'in the midst of the congregation', and as he later explained such expediency in the controversy with Doctor Henry Cole, Dean of St Paul's, 'I confess I should have done otherwise; but, if I had not done as I did, I had not been here now to encounter with you.'[52] With Martyr he moved from Frankfort to Strasbourg, where he encountered likeminded exiles from the Edwardine circle, 'many of them Jewel's equals as scholars but worldly in a sense quite foreign to him',[53] among whom was Sir Anthony Cooke. He followed Martyr, now Professor of Hebrew at Zurich, as his assistant. With Elizabeth's accession and his return to England, Jewel became a major figure in the consolidation of the Elizabethan Settlement. 'He was an ecclesiastical commissioner, Bishop of Salisbury, member of the House of Lords, justice of the peace, and one who had the confidence and trust of the chief persons of the realm.'[54]

The Act of Supremacy (1559) installed Elizabeth as the spiritual and ecclesiastical as well as temporal governor of the realm, severing ties with the Church of Rome and assigning to the Imperial Crown the role of 'reformation, order and correction [...] of all manner of errors, heresies, schisms, abuses, offences, contempts and enormities'.[55] It also required this oath of all ecclesiastical persons:

> I do utterly testify and declare in my conscience, that the queen's highness is the only supreme governor of this realm, and of all other her highness's dominions and countries, as well in all spiritual or ecclesiastical things or causes, as temporal,

---

[51] Jenkins, *John Jewel and the English National Church*, p. 39.
[52] John Jewel, 'The True Copies of the Letters between the Reverend Father in God John Bishop of Sarum and D. Cole', 1560, *Works*, ed. by John Ayre, 4 vols (Cambridge: Cambridge University Press, 1845–1850), I, 61.
[53] Southgate, *John Jewel and the Problem of Doctrinal Authority*, p. 21.
[54] John E. Booty, *John Jewel As Apologist of the Church of England* (London: S.P.C.K., 1963), p. 7.
[55] Act of Supremacy (I Elizabeth, *Cap.* 1), *Doctrines Illustrative of English Church History*, ed. by Henry Gee and William John Hardy (New York: Macmillan, 1896), pp. 447–48.

and that no foreign prince, person, prelate, state or potentate, has, or ought to have, any jurisdiction, power, superiority, preeminence, or authority ecclesiastical or spiritual, within this realm; and therefore I do utterly renounce and forsake all foreign jurisdictions, powers, superiorities, and authorities, and do promise that from henceforth I shall bear faith and true allegiance to the queen's highness, her heirs and lawful successors, and to my power shall assist and defend all jurisdictions, pre-eminences, privileges, and authorities granted or belonging to the queen's highness, her heirs and successors, or united and annexed to the imperial crown of this realm.

The Act of Uniformity (I Elizabeth, *Cap.* 2, 1559) abolished the Mass, re-introduced a modified *Book of Common Prayer* as an official text, and mandated attendance at Sunday service. Although this transition away from Marian Catholicism signalled the beginning of a new era for Jewel and Bacon, traditionalists 'did not abandon hope of the continuance of something of the old order', a hope 'inhering in the physical remains of Catholic cult, "the monuments of superstition"'.[56] Elizabeth's accession was a historical moment poised in two directions. From the point of view of print culture, it was a richly productive and polemical time of catechisms, sermons, disputations, and refutations. As well as the eleven separate editions of the *Apologia* in a hundred-year span, Ian Green tabulates 'at least a dozen and in some cases a score of treatises' on the Creed, Decalogue, prayer, and sacraments, all of which contributed to 'the gradual growth of lay acquiescence in the new religion [...] and the emergence of a nation that was at least outwardly Protestant'.[57] In material terms the need to extirpate images of the old meant that parishioners would once again bear the brunt and enormous costs of demolition and destruction. As Eamon Duffy itemizes, 'the newly acquired Roods and patronal statues, the untarnished latten pyxes and paxes and holy-water stoups, the missals and manuals still smelling of printer's ink, which Marian archdeacons had demanded, were to be once more pitched into wheelbarrows and trundled to the fire.'[58]

---

[56] Eamon Duffy, *The Stripping of the Altars: Traditional Religion in England 1400–1580* (New Haven: Yale University Press, 1992), pp. 566, 569.
[57] Ian Green, *Print and Protestantism in Early Modern England* (Oxford: Oxford University Press, 2000), pp. 633, 223, 555.
[58] Duffy, *The Stripping of the Altars*, p. 571.

Jewel heralded the new dispensation by inaugurating a full decade of intense publication — from the *Challenge Sermon* at Paul's Cross (1559) and its repetition at court (1560) published as *The Copie of a Sermon*, his extended controversy with the Dean of St Paul's, Dr Cole (1560), a Latin *Epistola* ostensibly written by an Englishman to his old friend living in Paris (1561), the *Apologia Ecclesiae Anglicanae* (1562), his *Replie* (1565) to Thomas Harding's *Answere to Maister Iuelles chalenge*, and his *Defence of the Apology* (1567), to his enlarged edition of the *Defence* (1570) in response to Harding's *Detection of sundrie foule errours* (1568). The fifteen and subsequent twelve propositions of Jewel's *Challenge Sermon*, first delivered in the open-air pulpit in the grounds of St Paul's Cathedral on 26 November 1559, served as a draft of the argument of the *Apologia*. His challenge to Catholics is to present scriptural or patristic proof of the validity of their doctrinal positions, which would lead to his re-conversion. Forecasting the astringent tone of the *Apologia*, the *Sermon* undertakes to uproot what is presumed to be the traditional or historical validity of Catholic (that is, recently Marian) Eucharistic practice about the Real Presence, reception in one kind, and elevation at the Consecration. By citing the absence of patristic or scriptural precedent, Jewel also questions the setting up of images and the prohibition of reading the Word of God in one's own tongue. Jewel's epistolary controversy with Dr Cole, which followed, illustrates the intense nature of Reformation debate, with each sentence in this back-and-forth volley spreading to pages of contestatory sources and citations — a preview of the vitriolic exchanges to come between Jewel and Harding. At the request of Secretary Cecil and using the pseudonym 'Nicholaus. N. Anglus', Jewel composed the *Epistola*, which was printed in France under the supervision of Nicholas Throckmorton, the English ambassador in Paris. John Booty clarifies that 'it was propaganda inspired and executed under the authority of the Government.'[59] In addressing the 'cold-blooded distortion' of those who attacked reformers, the letter writer poses questions of pastoral care:

Was this the way theologians ought to behave? Was this the way to feed the people? Was this the way to ascend to a high

---

[59] Booty, *John Jewel as Apologist of the Church of England*, p. 45.

place, and to proclaim the gospel to Sion? [...] Did they learn this from Occam, from Scotus, from Benedict, and from Francis?[60]

Although 'Nicholaus' asserts that 'our preachers' have never mentioned such shameful acts in the pulpit and does not 'deny that all these things are true', he nevertheless details 'that your monks sometimes made a great number of plots against noble girls and raped them in the very churches themselves and under the eyes of their idols, and in a horrible way subjected them to the passion of each one, and finally, to keep from exposing the crime, killed them.' While indicting his opponents who 'speak not from the heart but like pythons from the belly', he also alludes revealingly to the state of the Church in England 'scarcely put[ting] themselves together again, as after a shipwreck'. The *Epistola* and *Challenge Sermon* together point to the need for the *Apologia*, for an affirming statement of English belief and practice as conveyed by a trusted, informed ecclesiastical figure. There is an ironic element in these preliminaries, too. Questions about the way theologians ought to behave and remarks about speaking like pythons resound throughout the extensive controversy surrounding the defence of the *Apologia*.

3. 'FEW *PRECLARAE FEMINAE MEAE SORTIS* ARE ABLE OR BE ALYVE TO SPEAK AND JUDG OF SUCH PROCEADINGS'[61]

'Among the official Reformations of sixteenth-century Europe', the unprecedented feature of the Elizabethan Settlement, as Diarmaid MacCulloch views it, is that 'it was planned and executed entirely by former Nicodemites, Protestants who had nevertheless conformed outwardly to the Roman Church from the moment Mary had secured her throne.'[62] To bolster his

---

[60] Booty, Appendix, *Epistola*, trans. by J. Booty, *John Jewel As Apologist of the Church of England*, pp. 210–25 (p. 213). Subsequent quotations from this translation.
[61] Anne Bacon to Anthony Bacon, 12 May 1595, *The Letters of Lady Anne Bacon*, p. 217.
[62] Diarmaid MacCulloch, *Silence: A Christian History* (New York: Viking, 2013), pp. 174–75.

argument he cites William Cecil, Nicholas Bacon, and his 'emphatically Protestant wife [who] had been among Queen Mary's ladies-in-waiting'. Jewel's Marian exile had confirmed and enhanced his Reform allegiance; Lady Bacon's service to Queen Mary, about which we know very little, in no way diminished her aspirations for an English Church. Both were equipped and ready for the challenge of the early years of Elizabeth's reign, when there was need for an *Apologia* to reassure a Latinate, Reform-minded, Continental readership of ecclesiastical stability in England and for *An Apology* to do the same for an English audience.

In both Latin and English the *Apology* was originally printed as a continuous text. One way in which it was made more accessible was through the demarcation of parts or chapters. This segmentation was first presented in Jewel's *Defence*, as it was included in early editions of the *Works of John Jewel* (1609, reprinted 1611). *An Apology* appeared with divisions into parts in 1635, with most subsequent editions following this pattern.[63] Because the separation into parts makes the intense exercise of grappling with the argument of this treatise more feasible, this edition includes the designation of parts as breathing spaces and as comparative guides in annotating the sparsely marginated text. Six parts or chapters also help us to follow the direction and, at times, divagations of the argument. Although Gary Jenkins maintains that 'Jewel's *oratio* hobbled his *theologica*,'[64] the purposefulness of Jewel's text is apparent. Part I introduces the often-slandered and opposed figure of Truth as an overarching value which accounts for Protestant perseverance in the face of what is perceived as Catholic arrogance and malice. Part II, in outlining the key tenets of Reformation belief, explains the existence of the two sacraments, Baptism and the Eucharist, and

---

[63] Separation into parts occurs in *An Apology of the Church of England* (London: John Beale, 1635); *An Apology of the Church of England*, trans. by Thomas Cheyne (London: Jonah Bowyer, 1720); *An Apology for the Church of England*, trans. by A.C. Campbell (Pontefract: B. Boothroyd, 1813); *An Apology for the Church of England*, trans. by S. Isaacson (London: John Hearne, 1825); *An Apology of the Church of England*, trans. by W.R. Whittingham (New York: Protestant Episcopal Press, 1831); *Works*, ed. by John Ayre, vols 3–4; *An Apology of the Church of England*, ed. by R. W. Jelf (London: S.P.C.K., 1849); *An Apology of the Church of England*, ed. by J. E. Booty (Ithaca: Cornell University Press, 1963).

[64] Jenkins, *John Jewel and the English National Church*, p. 135.

of married clergy, and opposes concepts of transubstantiation and purgatory. Part III explores the origins of heresy, defending the English Church against the persecutions and false charges it has endured, and upholding unity as the way to know the church of God. Part IV takes aim at Roman adversaries, outlining their descent from the ideals of the primitive Church. Part V continues the history of loss through citing Church Fathers and Council decrees to underscore that the Church of Rome may err. Possibly added as a response to the Council of Trent (1545–1563), Part VI challenges the roles of papal and conciliar authority, recapitulating the belief that Truth and Peace will prevail.

Because the *Apology*'s rejection of transubstantiation, a critical doctrine confirmed at Trent, crystallizes one of the key differences between Reformers and Roman traditionalists, it is worth pausing to consider why this understanding was such a salient Reformation flashpoint. The Eucharist was the climax of the Mass, as Miri Rubin explains, since 'the transcendent was thus made to seem mundane by turning the sacrament of the altar into a meal. [...] Meaning often relied', she notes, 'on the existence of paradox.'[65] This intermingling of the domestic and the sacred in the central attraction structured one's devotional identity. Although the term *transubstantio* first appeared in a work by English theologian Robert Pullen (d. 1146), the opening creed of the Fourth Lateran Council (1215) used transubstantiation 'to describe the means by which the Real Presence occurred in the Mass'.[66] With the corroborating argument of Thomas Aquinas in his commentary on the *Sentences* of Peter of Lombard and in the *Summa theologiae* that 'the body and blood of Christ could be present without being sensed', Aquinas insisted 'that the metaphysics of the Eucharist outweigh the importance of the intentionality of the believer' and hence that 'transmutation was the only acceptable understanding of transubstantiation.'[67] This

---

[65] Miri Rubin, 'Popular Attitudes to the Eucharist' in *A Companion to the Eucharist in the Middle Ages*, ed. by Ian Christopher Levy, Gary Macy, Kristen van Ausdall (Leiden: Brill, 2012), 448–68 (pp. 450, 467).
[66] Gary Macy, 'Theology of the Eucharist in the High Middle Ages' in *A Companion to the Eucharist in the Middle Ages*, 355–97 (p. 375).
[67] Macy, 'Theology of the Eucharist in the High Middle Ages', pp. 377, 389. He cites *Summa theologiae*, ed. by P. Caramello (Rome: Marietti, 1956), 3. 80, pp. 488–91.

was the centuries-old belief that was being questioned and negated throughout *An Apology*.

Though initially published anonymously, the *Apologia* was recognized as Jewel's work. Having received a gift of the *Apologia* from the Archbishop of Canterbury, Peter Martyr wrote to congratulate Bishop Jewel, declaring himself 'absolutelie satisfied' with 'this felicitie of your wit, this reedification of the Church of God, this singular ornament of the estate of England'. To his unmarried, childless disciple Martyr expressed 'joy that I have lived to see that day wherein you have been the father of such a famous and renowned child.'[68] With editions of *An Apology or Answer* from 1600 on, Peter Martyr's congratulatory letter regularly replaced Matthew Parker's commendation of Lady Bacon. Her much-praised translation of Bishop Jewel was no doubt, as Alan Stewart argues, 'an official, commissioned work'.[69] The superior conciseness and idiomatic flair of *An Apology or Answer* over the first anonymous English translation produced two years earlier, at the time of Jewel's original, underline the apt choice of Lady Bacon. In fact, the Victorian editor of Jewel's works, John Ayre, goes as far as to suggest that the initial translator may have been the Archbishop of Canterbury, Matthew Parker himself.[70] Archbishop Parker's prefatory letter addressed to 'the right honorable learned and virtuous Ladie A. B.' makes it clear that both he and Jewel vetted this translation 'and have without alteration allowed of it'. Mentioning 'modestie' three times in his opening commendation of Bacon's exemplary, publicly beneficial, and precedent-setting accomplishment, he praises her 'cleare translation' which has delivered the Latin book 'from the perils of ambiguous and doubtful constructions'.[71]

If Jewel can be construed as the father of this text, we might feasibly consider Anne Bacon to be its mother. In what her contemporary Laurence Humphrey would recognize as a

---

[68] *The Apologie of the Church of England* (London: Thomas Chard, 1600), STC 423:07, image 2. The Latin letter from Peter Martyr, 'D. Ionni Ivello, Episcopo Sarisburiensi P. Martyr S.D' first prefaced the *Apologia Ecclesiae Anglicanae* (London: Thomas Vautrollier, 1581), STC 251:08 , sigs A2r–A3r.

[69] Alan Stewart, 'The Voices of Anne Cooke, Lady Anne and Lady Bacon', in *'This Double Voice': Gendered Writing in Early Modern England*, ed. by Danielle and Elizabeth Clarke (Basingstoke: Macmillan, 2000), pp. 88–102 (p. 88).

[70] See *Works*, ed. by J. Ayre, IV, xxvii.

[71] Reproduced in this edition and in *The Letters of Lady Anne Bacon*, pp. 59–61.

comprehensive, appropriate, attractive, and aptly suited style, Bacon's *An Apology or Answer* fulfils 'a credal function' at the same time as it demonstrates 'awareness of a potential oral dissemination'.[72] Knowing even at this stage in her life that there were indeed few distinguished women (*preclarae feminae*) of her sort, and embracing what Lynne Magnusson calls 'a sense of vocation', she illustrated the shaping influences of 'her education of civic humanism' through 'her rare stylistic ability'.[73] Even though Philip Hughes found the criticism of the old religion 'negative, destructive, and disingenuous', he judged the text to be 'brilliantly written, in the style of the classic oratory [by] a contemporary translator of genius'.[74] Here we see Lady Bacon's graceful ease of *sprezzatura* adding value and wide intelligibility to Jewel's text. She is, in this sense, a visible translator contributing to the revaluation of visibility 'in the early modern world for its guarantees of a pleasing innovation that showed itself engaged with the literary past'.[75]

Her style has a provocative directness, best apprehended in the contrasts with the 'anonymous' 1562 translation.[76] Where the latter translated '*sacrificuli*'[77] with colourless literalism as 'sacrificing Preestes' (C4ʳ), Lady Bacon adds a deflating reference to 'common Massing priests' who listen to 'whisperings' [*murmura*] in the confessional (Part II). The consumed host does not end up in 'the withdrawing place' (D3ʳ) but goes 'into the

---

[72] Gemma Allen, '"a briefe and plaine declaration": Lady Anne Bacon's 1564 translation of the *Apologia Ecclesiae Anglicanae*', in *Women and Writing, c. 1340–c. 1650: The Domestication of Print Culture*, ed. by Anne Lawrence-Mathers and Phillipa Hardman (York: York Medieval Press, 2010), pp. 62–76 (p. 70). See also Allen, *The Cooke Sisters: Education, piety and politics in early modern England*, pp. 65–71.

[73] Lynne Magnusson, 'Imagining a National Church: Election and Education in the Works of Anne Cooke Bacon', in *The Intellectual Culture of Puritan Women, 1558–1680*, ed. by Johanna Harris and Elizabeth Scott-Baumann (London: Palgrave Macmillan, 2011), pp. 42–56 (pp. 42–44).

[74] Philip Hughes, *The Reformation in England*, revised edition, three vols in one (New York: Macmillan, 1963), III, 66, 97.

[75] A. E. B. Coldiron, 'Visibility now: Historicizing foreign presences in translation', *Translation Studies*, 5.2 (2012), 191–200 (p. 192).

[76] John Jewel, *An Apologie or Aunswer in Defence of the Church of England 1562* (Menston: The Scolar Press). Quotations will be based on this facsimile edition and to parts of Lady Bacon's translation in this edition.

[77] *Apologia Ecclesiae Anglicanae* (London, 1562), STC 555:02, image 11.

belly, and is cast out into the privy' (Part II). When dealing with the account of Pope Joan, Bacon bypasses the genteel euphemism of 'she had applied her selfe in ye holy seat unto other mens lustes' (F4^r) and resorts to the colloquial term for a promiscuous woman, 'she had played the naughty Pack' (Part IV) as a colourful rendering of *'aliorūi libidini exposuisset'*.[78] Instead of characterizing clerical gluttony and excess with 'their minde is upon their platters' (S1^r), she particularizes *'hinc illae lachrymae, animus est in patinis'*[79] with 'Hence cometh their whining, their heart is on their halfpenny' (Part IV).

An opportunity for re-creative cultural transfer for Bacon, her language of translation has a timely resonance, whether narrating an ancient trial or defining such terms as heresy or creed.[80] Her report on the accusation of Sophocles by his own sons at the close of Part I not only exposes the irony of the accusation but conveys her insight into the parallels between the familial betrayals in ancient Greece and the violation of trust among the reform-minded faithful in Elizabethan England. She extends the Latin to ensure that her text is a communal statement of belief, adding her own hinging summation, 'This therefore is our Belief', to conclude Part I. Core elements of that belief reside in the work of early Church Fathers and the canons of early Councils. Bacon conveys a passionate intensity when she magnifies Jewel's interrogation, *'Cur tam vetus causa iacet sine patrono? Ferrum quidem & flammam semper habuerunt ad manum de Cōciliis vero antiquis & Patribus magnum silentium.'*[81] In contrast to the earlier translation's tepid observations about 'a cause abandoned so longe tyme' with 'no worde at all' (L2^r), she colours the sense of antiquity, alliterates the neglect, and adds an everyday jab at this great silence: 'Why lieth so ancient a cause thus long in the dust destitute of an Advocate? Fire and sword they have had always ready at hand, but as for the old Councils and the fathers, all Mum, not a word' (Part V). After a fusillade of questions about

---

[78] *Apologia Ecclesiae Anglicanae*, image 22.
[79] *Apologia Ecclesiae Anglicanae*, image 60.
[80] See Patricia Demers, '"Nether bitterly nor brablingly": Lady Anne Cooke Bacon's Translation of Bishop Jewel's *Apologia Ecclesiae Anglicanae*', in *English Women, Religion, and Textual Production, 1500–1625*, ed. by Micheline White (Farnham: Ashgate, 2011), pp. 205–17.
[81] *Apologia Ecclesiae Anglicanae*, image 37.

the authority of the pope and the power of recent councils, she extends Jewel's reiterated statement of lack, '*Non habent, ô Deus bono, non habent ea, quae habere gloriantur: non antiquitatem, non universalitatem, non locorum, non temporum omnium consensum*',[82] into a series not just of repeated objects, but of full accusatory statements about hypocrisy along with an emphatic interjection: 'They have not, good Lord, they have not (I say) those things which they boast they have: they have not that antiquitie, they have not that universalitie, they have not that consent of all places, nor of all times' (Part V).

Responses to the recently-concluded third period (1562–1563) of the Council of Trent, the Council's twenty-five sessions which leaders of the English Church did not attend, and its positions on universality and inerrancy, percolate throughout *An Apology*. Pope Pius IV's letter to Queen Elizabeth (5 May 1560) inviting her to send bishops and envoys was expectedly unsuccessful. 'In May 1561, the nuncio Girolamo Martinengo, bearing the invitation to the council for Queen Elizabeth, was denied entrance to the kingdom on the grounds that the presence of a nuncio in England was illegal and could give rise to unrest.'[83] Although *An Apology or Answer* 'says nothing about predestination' and 'little even upon the doctrine of justification by faith',[84] these subjects, both central preoccupations of reformers and of Bacon's translation of Ochino, were discussed at Trent, along with complete conviction in regards to transubstantiation and the salvific nature of seven sacraments. The Council declared that the gift of faith 'is the first stage of human salvation, the foundation and root of all justification, without which *it is impossible to please God.*' On the topic of predestination, the Council warned against presumption since 'it is impossible to know whom God has chosen for himself.' Announcing its aim as 'the removal of errors and the rooting out of heresies, which have arisen at the present

---

[82] *Apologia Ecclesiae Anglicanae*, image 40.
[83] John W. O'Malley, *Trent: What Happened at the Council* (Cambridge, Mass.: Harvard University Press, 2013), p. 170. O'Malley cites the letter of May 1560 from *Concilium Tridentinum. Diariorum, Actorum, Epistularum, Tractatuum nova collectio* (Freiburg i/Br,: Herder, 1901–2001), VIII, 17.
[84] Peter White, *Predestination, Policy and Polemic: Conflict and Consensus in the English Church from the Reformation to the Civil War* (Cambridge: Cambridge University Press, 1992), p. 71.

time concerning the most holy sacraments', the Council treated the sacraments as the 'means by which all true justness either begins, or once received gains strength, or if lost is restored'. It also reiterated the understanding that at the Consecration 'there takes place the change of the whole substance of the bread into the substance of the body of Christ our Lord, and of the whole substance of the wine into the substance of his blood.'[85]

Challenging Trent's avowed adherence to the teaching of scripture, the apostolic traditions, and the opinion of previous councils and Church Fathers, Jewel asked pointed questions about the appropriated authority of the Council:

> *Postremò quid si nō dissimulāter, aut obscurè, sed perspicuè & apertè decernant, contra expressum verbū Dei? An quicquid isti dicūt, statim erit Evangeliū? An iste erit exercitus Dei? An ibi istorū linguis natabit spiritus sanctus, aut illi possunt vere dicere, Visum est spiritui sancto, & nobis?*[86]

Bacon captures the animus of the questions.

> Shortly, what though they make Decrees expressly against God's Worde, and that not in hucker mucker or covertly but openly & in the face of the world: must it needs yet be Christ be at hand among them there? Shall the holy Ghost flow in their tongues: or can they with truth say, We and the holy Ghost have thought so? (Part VI)

Meeting the boldness of the Council's public declaration with this interrogation, she not only drums on the implausibility of these positions but allows for the swelling chorus of negative answers.

A vocal chorus of Continental Catholic opposition was quickly heard,[87] but Jewel directed his response to one opponent, Catholic exile Thomas Harding (1516–1572). The controversy between these two Devon natives had all the elements of a verbal pitched battle — duelling patristic citations, events in Church history, and definitions from Greek and Latin. They had both been students

---

[85] Council of Trent, Sessions 6, 7, 13, *Decrees of the Ecumenical Councils*, ed. by Norman P. Tanner, 2 vols (London: Sheed and Ward, 1990), II, 674, 676, 684, 695.

[86] *Apologia Ecclesiae Anglicanae*, image 47.

[87] See Jenkins, 'The Catholic Reaction to Jewel', *John Jewel and the English National Church*, pp. 115–154.

at Barnstaple; Harding had proceeded to Winchester before going up to New College, Oxford, where he rose to become Regius Professor of Hebrew. Both were committed to Edwardine reform, and both subscribed to the Marian Articles in the fall of 1554. While Jewel recanted, Harding did not. With Elizabeth's accession and the return of Jewel, Harding (who had previously deprived Jewel) lost his professorship and position as Treasurer of Salisbury Cathedral. On the Continent he assisted William Allen in the founding of the English College at Douai, and lived the remainder of his years in Louvain. Predictably, Jewel scholars support their man, with Wyndham Southgate declaring 'that Jewel was the better scholar as well as the abler controversialist.'[88] John Booty laments the 'futility' of their controversy, 'known by the fact that both men entered the contest with the conviction that religion is "an absolute thing" and that "only one religion can be right"'.[89] Gary Jenkins' nuanced treatment of Jewel finds him 'the defender of an imprecisely constructed ecclesiastical communion', an Erastian who upheld 'the primacy of the prince and the primacy of Scripture', with 'faulty' logic and 'flawed' theology.[90] But because of their intensive, layered and, yes, virulent scrutiny, often sentence by sentence, word by word, the battle between Jewel and Harding illuminates the world of sixteenth-century religious polemic. It also widens our understanding of the significance of many of the obscure and elliptical allusions in *An Apology or Answer*. The ease and frequency with which Lady Bacon's brisk translation captures the sense of an arcane Latin or Greek phrase reflect the breadth of her knowledge. Significantly, too, the standard English text cited by both parties throughout this prolonged dispute was Lady Bacon's.

The importance of the controversy was recognized in their own day. William Whitaker translated into Latin Jewel's *Replie unto Mr Hardinges Answeare* (1565), which was the second volley between the disputants about Jewel's *Challenge Sermon*; as Whitaker explained, it was 'most worthy of being read, not only by Englishmen, but of being [...] shared with foreign peoples too'.[91]

---

[88] Southgate, *John Jewel and the Problem of Doctrinal Authority*, p. 89.
[89] Booty, *John Jewel as Apologist of the Church of England*, p. 205.
[90] Jenkins, *John Jewel and the English National Church*, pp. 241, 243, 245.
[91] J. W. Binns, *Intellectual Culture in Elizabethan and Jacobean England: The Latin Writings of the Age* (Leeds: Francis Cairns, 1990), p. 243.

Archbishop Parker was convinced of the value of the second version of the *Defence*. He wrote to Bishop Parkhurst of Norwich (24 February 1572) to 'commend the late Bp of Sarum's last book to be had in the rest of the parish churches within your diocese, wherein they be not'.[92] Although Parkhurst judged the text too inflammatory, the account books of other parishes provide 'evidence that the *Apologia* and *Defence* were treated as official and necessary together with the Bible, the *Book of Common Prayer*, and the Homilies'.[93] A subsequent Archbishop of Canterbury and chief overseer of the King James Bible, Richard Bancroft, recognizing that there were 'more recusants now', wanted 'every parish to buy one of the works of bishop Jewel', a wish he fulfilled by ordering copies of the 1609 *Works* from the printer John Norton 'that hereby the said parishes may have those books near at hand, which will the better encourage them to buy them'.[94] His entrepreneurial directive must have paid off: in 1938 Henry J. Cowell reported the existence of Jewel's *Defence* and *Works*, which included Lady Bacon's translation, along with Erasmus's *Paraphrases* and Foxe's *Actes and Monuments* 'chained in thirteen different cathedrals and parish churches in England'.[95]

4. 'A CŌMOCION WITHIN THE VERY BOWELS OF THE SOULE'[96]

Because Archbishop Parker's prefatory letter addressed to Ladie A. B. disappeared from editions from 1600 on, only to reappear in John Ayre's Parker Society edition of the *Works of John Jewel* (1845–1850), Richard William Jelf's S.P.C.K. edition

---

[92] Archbishop Parker to Bishop Parkhurst of Norwich, *The Correspondence of Matthew Parker, Archbishop of Canterbury*, ed. by John Bruce and Thomas Thomason Perowne (Cambridge: Cambridge University Press, 1853), p. 417.
[93] Booty, *John Jewel as Apologist of the Church of England*, pp. 6–7.
[94] Edward Cardwell, *Documentary Annals of the Reformed Church of England*, 2 vols (Oxford: Oxford University Press, 1839–1844), II (1844), 160.
[95] John Booty, Introduction, *An Apology of the Church of England by John Jewel*, ed. by J. Booty (Ithaca: Cornell University Press, 1963), p. xliii. He cites Henry J. Cowell, *The Four Chained Books* (London: Kingsgate Press, 1938), p. 35.
[96] Bernardino Ochino, *Fouretene Sermons of Barnardine Ochyne*, trans. by A. C. (London: John Day, 1551), STC 121:14, image 62, 'Of the effects wrought bi the spirite of god when it entrethe into the soule: the xiiii Sermon'.

of *An Apologie or Answere* (1849), and John Booty's edition of *An Apology of the Church of England* for the Folger Shakespeare Library (1963), it is easy enough to understand why Anne Cooke Bacon, if mentioned at all, was relegated to the role of wife and mother. Early feminist reclamation of Renaissance women's writing in the work of Mary Ellen Lamb and Louise Schleiner contributed to her re-discovery.[97] Gemma Allen's fine edition of her letters, released from their almost-impenetrable italic, reveals the articulate determination of a learned woman and lauded translator, the concerns of a vigilant matriarch throughout her lengthy widowhood, and a lifelong dedication to reform.

Translations and letters together illustrate the different senses and roles of holy commotion in the life of Lady Bacon. The bustle and stir of the Ochino project and especially the sermon about the effect of the spirit on the soul precede the polemical tumult of *An Apology or Answer* as it was volleyed back and forth by Jewel and Harding. The deliberate challenge to the ecclesiastical hierarchy along with the sharp reprimands and judgments of her letters lead to the question mark of her final decade of silence, possibly brought on by another form of commotion, mental perturbation. Although this silence may be the result of the loss of letters or a decline in powers, Gemma Allen cautions against putting 'undue weight' on the testimony of one of Anthony Bacon's servants, Edward Spencer, that she was "'little better than frantic in her age'" since Lady Bacon had described Spencer as 'but an irefull peevish fellow yf he be looked into and checked for his loose demeanour'.[98] About Lady Bacon's final state of commotion, perhaps her mind remained unaffected and perhaps it is condescending to speculate.

The letters supply a private view of the intellect and personality of Anne Cooke Bacon. There is a good deal of confirmation of her reformist sympathies, but there are also strong indications that she favoured a more concerted, godly reformation. Such a distinction between Bacon the apologist and Bacon the correspondent suggests an additional link with Bishop John Jewel. In his examination of 'the difference between the public

---

[97] See notes 30 and 34.
[98] Allen, *The Letters of Lady Anne Bacon*, Anne Bacon to Anthony Bacon, 25 May 1593, pp. 33, 128 (hereafter, *Letters*).

and private Jewel' particularly in the aftermath of the controversy about the wearing of vestments, Gary Jenkins comments: 'Though worried about the sad condition of religion within England, and though cassock and surplice troubled his conscience, nonetheless Jewel saw England's need for order outweighing any concern that may have troubled him about things not materially pertinent to the Faith.'[99] In the decades following Jewel's death in 1571 and that of her husband in 1579, Lady Bacon was less willing to temporize. A display of learning and insight, her correspondence boldly questions the established church order outlined in *An Apology* and declares her loyalties to suppressed Puritan preachers.

The exchange with French theologian and Calvinist disciple Théodore de Bèze, who dedicated his commentary on the Penitential Psalms to Anne Bacon, indicates the extent of her reputation. At the beginning of her son Anthony's twelve-year stay on the Continent, Lady Bacon, writing in Latin as a widow and weak woman ('*mulierem viduam et imbecillem*'), had asked Bèze in Geneva to act as a father ('*loco patris*').[100] Within three months Bèze presented his dedicated book, expressing confidence in and reverence for her learning: '*vous y trouverez quelque consolation après la lecture de ces grands et saincts docteurs Grecs et Latins qui vous sont familiers, pour vous confermer de plus en plus en la meditation des choses spirituelles, et en ceste constance et patience Chrestienne de laquelle le Seigneur vous a tellement ornee, qu'en vous est vrayement recognue ce chrestiennement magnanime courage.*'[101] Five of her letters are in Latin; to guard against being read by untutored gossips, some conveyed information about names and dates in Greek and, to remind recipients of the intellectual pedigree of the sender, others have snippets of Hebrew and Greek, particularly the signature of 'widow' χηρα in ten letters.

---

[99] Jenkins, *John Jewel and the English National Church*, pp. 156, 160.
[100] *Letters*, Anne Bacon to Théodore de Bèze, 24 July 1581, pp. 82–83.
[101] *Letters*, Théodore de Bèze to Anne Bacon, 1 November 1581, p. 85. You will find here some comfort after reading these great and holy Greek and Latin doctors with whom you are familiar to strengthen you more and more in meditating on spiritual things and in that Christian constancy and patience with which the Lord has gifted you, that in you is truly recognized this Christianly noble courage.

INTRODUCTION

The godly concerns of the Ochino sermons and the antipapistry of *An Apology* are consistent features. The letters have the intensity of listening to an emphatic voice with a stress on moral obligation reminiscent of both the Ochino project and the colloquial immediacy so prominent in her translation of Jewel. Gemma Allen notes the 'striking' amount of 'reported speech' in Anne's correspondence. 'She has a particular awareness,' Allen remarks, 'of the gap between the spoken word and action. [...] Anne's reportage of speech-acts, the testimony of her witnesses, is another technique designed to persuade her reader that her epistolary advice was based on strong, incontrovertible evidence.'[102] Katy Mair sees the correspondence 'structured by maternal authority and filial obedience', with Anne's censoriousness expressed in 'an unusually candid voice', exacerbating 'the existing distrust and suspicion within the relationship'.[103]

Her greatest energies were expended for her sons when they were adults. 'They feel the smarting want of a father now in their ripe age', she admitted to her nephew.[104] She must have known of Anthony's imprisonment in Montauban in Picardie for sodomy, a capital crime in France. Anthony was released by the intervention of Henri de Navarre. In Anthony's 'endless cycle of borrowing, debt, court cases and communication problems with England', she refused 'the necessary injection of cash' and went as far as to utter some reportedly vile threats about wishing his imprisonment and death to Anthony's Catholic servant, Thomas Lawson, who was presenting his case at Gorhambury and whom Lady Anne had thrown in prison with Lord Burghley's compliance.[105] Although the messenger Captain Francis Allen remarked that Lady Bacon 'repented immediately her words' wishing for Anthony's death, he noted that she foresaw a similar fate for her misbehaving son: 'She is resolute to procure her majesty's letter for to force you to return and when that shall be if her Majesty gave you your right or desert, she should clap you

---

[102] *Letters*, pp. 19–20.
[103] Katie Mair, 'Material Lies: Anxiety and Epistolary Practice in the Correspondence of Anne, Lady Bacon and Anthony Bacon', *Lives and Letters* (2012), pp. 59–74 (pp. 62, 74).
[104] *Letters*, Anne Bacon to Robert Cecil, 13 July 1594, p. 188.
[105] Lisa Jardine and Alan Stewart, *Hostage to Fortune: The Troubled Life of Francis Bacon 1561–1626* (London: Victor Gollancz, 1998), p. 111.

up in prison'.[106] She laments not becoming a grandmother: 'I shulde have ben happy to have seen chylder's chylder but Frannce spoyled me and myne'.[107]

Throughout her widowhood, support for godly clergymen and antipathy towards Catholics fuelled her passions. Following the hastily convened Lambeth Conference in 1584 and the suspension of clergy who did not subscribe to Archbishop Whitgift's Three Articles (1583) enshrining loyalty to the sovereignty of the Queen, the *Book of Common Prayer* and the Articles of Convocation (1563) reiterated in *An Apology*, she wrote to her brother-in-law Burghley, who had tried to moderate Whitgift's insistence on surveillance with minimal success. She complained:

> Yf it may like your goode Lordship, the report of the late coonference at Lambath hath ben so handled to the discrediting of those learned that labour for right reformation in the ministry of the gospell, that it is no small greff of mynde to the faythfull preachers, becaus the matter is thus by the othersyde caried away as thowgh their cawse cowlde not sufficiently be warranted by the worde of God.

For Lady Bacon, the suspended were among the most effective and rewarding preachers.

> For myn own part, my goode Lorde, I wyll not deny but as I may I heare them in their publyck exercyses, as a cheff duty commanded by God to weedoes, and also I confess, as one that hath fownde mercy, that I have profyted more in the inwarde feeling knowledg of God his holy wyll, thowgh but in a small measure, by such syncere and sownde opening of the scrypture by an ordinary preaching, within these 7 or 8 yeres then I dyd by hearing odd sermons at Powles well nigh 20 yeres together.[108]

Whitgift, it is worth noting, had been tutor and mentor to Anthony and Francis at Cambridge. Lady Anne continued to exhort Anthony about his Catholic associates. She called his servant Lawson 'that foxe [...] he will prye and prattle'; as for his friend, the double agent Anthony Standen, Lady Bacon was

---

[106] Jardine and Stewart, *Hostage to Fortune*, p 114; they cite Francis Allen to Anthony Bacon, 17 August 1589.

[107] *Letters*, Anne Bacon to Anthony Bacon, 25 January 1597, p. 280.

[108] *Letters*, Anne Bacon to William Cecil, 26 February 1585, pp. 87, 88.

blunt: 'Be not to frank with that papist. Such have seducing spirits to snare the godly'.[109] Her likely patronage of the surreptitious and threatening publication, *A Parte of a Register* (1593), which documented persecutions and publicized Puritan arguments, was 'aimed at Archbishop Whitgift's despotic exercise of power' and performed, in Lynne Magnusson's estimate, 'a bold form of political action'.[110] While Lady Bacon attempted to heal the rift with the Cecils which Anthony's associations abroad had created, she also warned him against the Catholic loyalties of Henry Howard, Earl of Northampton, in advising Anthony 'to avow your Christian estimation of the godly preachers before ευρι οουαρδ, τεχνησ πληρον [Henry Howard, full of skill]'.[111]

For his part, Anthony addressed Lady Bacon, who was still a benefactor of sorts, with respectful caution. Although his letters pledge 'dewtyfull intente' and 'filliol respecte', he is 'imboldened [...] to remonstrate' with his 66-year-old mother 'with a most dewtyfull minde and tender care of your Ladyship's soule and reputation'. Citing the treatment of Lawson, he accuses her of 'a souveraigne desire to overrule your sonnes in all thinges, how litle soever you understande eyther the grounde or the circumstances of their proceedings, or els from want of charety, abandoninge your minde continuallie to most strange and wrongfull suspitions'.[112] Mother and son, however, continued to correspond until at least two years before Anthony's death in 1601.

She worries about her sons' spiritual and physical health (kidney stones, clouded urine, gout), their sexual preferences of male bedchamber companions, their late rising, their luxurious ways. She reminds Anthony, 'I have continually kept howse and lyved owt of dett'.[113] She also continues to send them supplies and gifts along the 25-mile route from Gorhambury to London; at his request she forwards plate and a bed to Francis, and to Anthony at different times, carpet and pictures, pewter candlesticks, three quarters of wheat, hogsheads of beer, partridges, pigeons, a boiled pig's head, strawberries, and plums. She delivers

---

[109] *Letters*, Anne Bacon to Anthony Bacon, 3 February 1592, p. 100; Anne Bacon to Anthony Bacon, 26 June 1593, p. 137.
[110] Magnusson, 'Imagining a National Church', p. 48.
[111] *Letters*, Anne Bacon to Anthony Bacon, 20 January 1597.
[112] *Letters*, Anthony Bacon to Anne Bacon, 12 July 1594, pp. 186–187.
[113] *Letters*, Anne Bacon to Anthony Bacon, *c.* 23 September 1593, p. 150.

advice to prominent contemporaries, too. Terrified to hear Robert Devereux, Earl of Essex, described as 'a terrible swearer', she is convinced this habit is the result of 'no catechizing in coorte' and steps in to remind the Earl of injunctions against swearing in specific biblical passages.[114] Although she broaches the topic of 'carnall dalyance' with Essex, he assures her almost immediately that this recent charge is 'falce and unjust' and that he is 'free from taxation of incontinentcy withe anie woman that lives'. In the midst of this very personal correspondence, she discloses her own circumstances, in her late sixties, to Essex whom she addresses 'from the confines of ruinated Verulam', confessing '*beinge* sicklie and weake manie waies', 'as one almost forgotten in the worlde'.[115]

Lady Bacon's print capital, previously limited to her translations of the understudied Ochino sermons and Bishop Jewel's *Apologia*, has expanded from manuscript to print thanks to Allen's edition of her letters. In this further illumination of Lady Bacon's story, poise, triumphalism, and plaudits co-exist with suspicion, neglect, and sadness. The funeral of the 82-year-old matriarch was a quiet affair with no feast, Francis asking an old friend Sir Michael Hickes to join him for the mournful occasion. Lisa Jardine and Alan Stewart see a strange vulnerability in Francis's request, adding that 'for a man who never missed an opportunity for ostentatious public display when occasion required, the absence of any funeral feast is significant'.[116] Francis's trajectory was on the rise; he was soon to become Attorney General, Lord Keeper of the Privy Seal, Baron Verulam of Verulam, and Viscount St Alban's. This statesman, scientist, and philosopher requested to be buried in the same churchyard as his mother.

---

[114] *Letters*, Anne Bacon to Robert Devereux, 23 December [1595], pp. 236–37.
[115] *Letters*, Anne Bacon to Robert Devereux, 1 December 1596; Robert Devereux to Anne Bacon, 1 December 1596; Anne Bacon to Robert Devereux, 23 December [1595], pp. 238, 263, 266–267.
[116] Jardine and Stewart, *Hostage to Fortune*, p. 322.

INTRODUCTION

5. 'IN THE LORD, UNFEYNEDLIE ALLWAYES, ABACON. LATE LORD KEPER'S WIDOW.'[117]

Translator, matriarch, and champion of reform, Anne Cooke Bacon reminds us of the ways that religion, alongside politics, economics, and culture, was an integral component of individual and communal identity. The centrality of *An Apology or Answer* throughout the extended Jewel-Harding controversy and as a baseline of all subsequent editions of and commentary on the *Apologia* reveals the power of Bacon's writing to substantiate or inflame. Her 'highly responsible and significant undertaking' shows how 'the precise meaning of each word' can be 'of the highest importance'.[118] Bacon's 'humanistic' rather than 'technical' translation, always reflective of an engaged, learned intelligence, highlights what Lawrence Venuti calls the 'double writing' aspect of translation 'as both communication and interpretive transcription'.[119]

What does this exercise of translation disclose about Lady Bacon? In what ways does it reveal the Christian within the woman? Speculations about a writer's interiority are fraught undertakings, often revealing more about the analyst than the writer. However, I want to offer my own sense of this talented woman emerging from close contact with her work. For Anne Bacon the categories of Christian and woman were not actually distinct. As an elite young Protestant she translated Ochino, and as a privileged wife and mother she took up the challenge of making Bishop Jewel available in English. As his approved voice, *An Apology* — whether acknowledged as her translation or not — was the medium for the wide distribution of Jewel's most famous and influential work. Even in the senior and less public years of her widowhood, she was an unflinching supporter of reform, a disposition that could combine virulent criticism of the Church of Rome as well as sharp rebuke of preaching failures within the Church of England. While rapprochement and

---

[117] *Letters*, Anne Bacon to William Cecil, Lord Burghley, 10 March 1597, p. 285.
[118] Jane Stevenson, *Women Latin Poets: Language, Gender, and Authority from Antiquity to the Eighteenth Century* (Oxford: Oxford University Press, 2005), p. 267.
[119] Lawrence Venuti, *The Translator's Invisibility: A History of Translation*, second edition (New York: Routledge, 2008), pp. 34, 276.

conciliation were not features of her style, neither was guile or masking. With a lifetime of passionate, intimate devotion to matters of belief she remained 'in the Lord, unfeynedlie allwayes'.

Her work throbs with the meaning of religion for historical actors and, in this way, challenges our quickness to reduce it to its lowest common denominator. Words such as 'truth', 'church', 'sacrifice', and 'sacrament' ground Lady Bacon's understanding and orient her concepts of unity and memory. Reading *An Apology or Answer* in the twenty-first century causes us to rethink the 'master narrative of secularization' and the 'overly simple divide between the secular and the religious'. As Andrea Sterk and Nina Caputo contend, 'despite the tendency of many historians to interpret religious beliefs primarily as symptoms of a particular sociopolitical or cultural climate or to view religion as another component of a more tangible matrix of power or identity, religion can be a cause as much as an effect of social, economic, or political change'.[120] Throughout her life as ardent student of languages, self-possessed parent, and vigilant reformer, Lady Bacon experienced and expressed the interanimation of religious and political change. Moreover, her comprehensive, appropriate, attractive, and aptly suited translation of Jewel invites us 'to weigh and consider' *An Apology or Answer* so that it can be 'read wholly, and with diligence and attention'.[121]

---

[120] Andrea Sterk and Nina Caputo, 'Introduction: The Challenge of Religion in History', in *Faithful Narratives: Historians, Religion, and the Challenge of Objectivity*, ed. by Andrea Sterk and Nina Caputo (Ithaca: Cornell University Press, 2014), pp. 6, 9.
[121] Francis Bacon, 'Of Studies', *Essays or Counsels Civil and Moral*, ed. by Charles W. Eliot (New York: P. F. Collier & Son, 1909), p. 128.

FURTHER READING

Allen, Gemma, '"a briefe and plaine declaration": Lady Anne Bacon's 1564 translation of the *Apologia Ecclesiae Anglicanae*', in *Women and Writing, c. 1340–c. 1650: The Domestication of Print Culture*, ed. by Anne Lawrence-Mathers and Phillipa Hardman (York: York Medieval Press, 2010), pp. 62–76

——, *The Cooke Sisters: Education, piety and politics in early modern England* (Manchester: Manchester University Press, 2013)

André, James St, ed., *Thinking through Translation with Metaphors* (Manchester: St. Jerome Publishing, 2010)

Apologia Ecclesiae Anglicanae (London, 1562), STC 555:02

Bacon, Lady Anne, *The Letters of Lady Anne Bacon*, ed. by Gemma Allen (London: Royal Historical Society, Cambridge University Press, 2014)

Bacon, Sir Nicholas, *The Recreations of His Age* (Oxford, 1919)

Binns, J. W., *Intellectual Culture in Elizabethan and Jacobean England: The Latin Writings of the Age* (Leeds: Francis Cairns, 1990)

Booty, John E., *John Jewel as Apologist of the Church of England* (London: S.P.C.K., 1963)

Byrne, Muriel St Clare, 'The Mother of Francis Bacon', *Blackwood's Magazine* 236 (December 1934), 758–771

Clarke, Danielle and Elizabeth Clarke, eds, *'This Double Voice': Gendered Writing in Early Modern England* (Basingstoke: Macmillan, 2000)

Coldiron, A. E. B., 'Visibility now: Historicizing foreign presences in translation', *Translation Studies*, 5.2 (2012), 191–200

——, *Printers Without Borders: Translation and Textuality in the Renaissance* (Cambridge: Cambridge University Press, 2015)

Collinson, Patrick, *Godly People: Essays on English Protestantism and Puritanism* (London: The Hambledon Press, 1983)

——, *Richard Bancroft and Elizabethan Anti-Puritanism* (Cambridge: Cambridge University Press, 2013)

Cowell, Henry J., *The Four Chained Books* (London: Kingsgate Press, 1938)

Demers, Patricia, '"Nether bitterly nor brablingly": Lady Anne Cooke Bacon's Translation of Bishop Jewel's *Apologia Ecclesiae Anglicanae*', in *English Women, Religion, and Textual Production, 1500–1625*, ed. by Micheline White (Farnham: Ashgate, 2011), pp. 205–17

Duffy, Eamon, *The Stripping of the Altars: Traditional Religion in England 1400–1580* (New Haven: Yale University Press, 1992)

Ferguson, Margaret W., *Dido's Daughters: Literacy, Gender and Empire in Early Modern England and France* (Chicago: University of Chicago Press, 2003)

Goodrich, Jaime, *Faithful Translators: Authorship, Gender, and Religion in Early Modern England* (Evanston, Illinois: Northwestern University Press, 2014)

Green, Ian, *Print and Protestantism in Early Modern England* (Oxford: Oxford University Press, 2000)

Hermans, Theo, 'Images of Translation: Metaphor and Imagery in the Renaissance Discourse on Translation', in *The Manipulation of Literature: Studies in Literary Translation*, ed. by Theo Hermans (Beckenham, Kent: Croom Helm, 1985), pp. 103–35

Hosington, Brenda M., 'Women Translators and the Early Printed Book', in *A Companion to the Early Printed Book in Britain 1476–1558*, ed. by Vincent Gillespie and Susan Powell (Cambridge: D. S. Brewer, 2014), pp. 248–71

——, ed. et al., *Renaissance Cultural Crossroads: An Online Catalogue of Translations in Britain 1473–1640* <www.hrionline.ac.uk/rcc>

Hughes, Philip, *The Reformation in England*, revised edition, three vols in one (New York: Macmillan, 1963)

Jardine, Lisa and Alan Stewart, *Hostage to Fortune: The Troubled Life of Francis Bacon 1561–1626* (London: Victor Gollancz, 1998)

Jenkins, Gary W., *John Jewel and the English National Church: The Dilemmas of an Erastian Reformer* (Aldershot: Ashgate Publishing, 2006)

Jewel, John, *An Apologie or Aunswer in Defence of the Church of England, concerning the state of Religion used in the same 1562* (Menston, Yorkshire: The Scolar Press, 1969), STC 14590

——, *An Apologie or answere in defence of the Churche of Englande, with a briefe and plaine declaration of the true Religion professed and used in the same* (London: Reginald Wolfe, 1564), STC 14591

Ker, Neil, 'The Library of John Jewel', *Bodleian Library Record*, 9.5 (1977), 256–65

King, John N. and Mark Rankin, 'Print, Patronage, and the Reception of Continental Reform: 1521–1603', *Yearbook of English Studies*, 38 (2008), 49–67.

Kristeller, Paul Oskar, *Renaissance Thought II: Papers on Humanism and the Arts* (New York: Harper Torchbooks, 1965)

Lamb, Mary Ellen, 'The Cooke Sisters: Attitudes toward Learned Women in the Renaissance', in *Silent But for the Word: Tudor Women as Patrons, Translators, and Writers of Religious Works*, ed. by Margaret P. Hannay (Kent, Ohio: Ohio State University Press, 1985), pp. 107–25.

Levy, F. J., *Tudor Historical Thought* (San Marino, California: The Huntington Library, 1967)

Loades, David, *Mary Tudor: A Life* (Oxford: Basil Blackwell, 1989)

MacCulloch, Diarmaid, *Reformation: Europe's House Divided 1490–1700* (London: Allen Lane, 2003)

——, *Silence: A Christian History* (New York: Viking, 2013)

Magnusson, Lynne, 'Widowhood and Linguistic Capital: The Rhetoric and Reception of Anne Bacon's Epistolary Advice', *English Literary Renaissance*, 31 (2001), 3–33

——, 'Imagining a National Church: Election and Education in the works of Anne Cooke Bacon', in *The Intellectual Culture of*

Puritan Women, 1558–1680, ed. by Johanna Harris and Elizabeth Scott-Baumann (London: Palgrave Macmillan, 2011), pp. 42–56

Mair, Katie, 'Material Lies: Anxiety and Epistolary Practice in the Correspondence of Anne, Lady Bacon and Anthony Bacon', *Lives and Letters* (2012), 59–74

McGrath, Alister E., *The Intellectual Origins of the European Reformation* (Oxford: Basil Blackwell, 1987)

——, *Iustitia Dei: A History of the Christian Doctrine of Justification*, second edition (Cambridge: Cambridge University Press, 1998)

McIntosh, M. K., 'Sir Anthony Cooke: Tudor humanist, educator, and religious reformer', *Papers of the American Philosophical Society*, 119 (1975), 233–50

Morini, Massimiliano, *Tudor Translation in Theory and Practice* (Aldershot: Ashgate Publishing, 2006)

Ochino, Bernardino, *Sermons of Barnardine of Sena godly, frutefull, and uery necessarye for all true Christians translated out of Italien into Englishe* (London: R. Carr for W. Reddell, 1548), STC 997:14

——, *Fouretene Sermons of Barnardine Ochyne, concerning the predestinacion and eleccion of god. Translated out of Italian in to our native tounge by A. C.* (London: John Day, 1551), STC 121:14

——, *Certayne Sermons of the right famous and excellente Clerk Master Barnardine Ochine. [...] Faythfully translated into Englyshe* (London: John Day, 1551?), STC 18766

——, *Sermons of Barnardine Ochyne (to the number of 25) [...] Translated out of Italian into our native tongue by A. C.* (London: John Day, 1570), STC 18768

O'Malley, John W., *Trent: What Happened at the Council* (Cambridge, MA: Harvard University Press, 2013)

Overell, M. A., 'Bernardino Ochino's Books and English Religious Opinion, 1547–80', in *The Church and the Book*, ed. by R. N. Swanson (Woodbridge, Suffolk: The Boydell Press, 2004), pp. 201–11

FURTHER READING

Parker, Matthew, *The Correspondence of Matthew Parker, Archbishop of Canterbury*, ed. by John Bruce and Thomas Thomason Perowne (Cambridge: Cambridge University Press, 1853)

Rhodes, Neil, ed., with Gordon Kendal and Louise Wilson, *English Renaissance Translation Theory* (London: Modern Humanities Research Association, 2013)

Schleiner, Louise, *Tudor and Stuart Women Writers* (Bloomington: Indiana University Press, 1994)

Southgate, Wyndham M., *John Jewel and the Problem of Doctrinal Authority* (Cambridge, MA: Harvard University Press, 1962)

Sterk, Andrea and Nina Caputo, eds, *Faithful Narratives: Historians, Religion, and the Challenge of Objectivity* (Ithaca: Cornell University Press, 2014)

Stevenson, Jane, *Women Latin Poets: Language, Gender, and Authority from Antiquity to the Eighteenth Century* (Oxford: Oxford University Press, 2005)

Stewart, Alan, 'The Voices of Anne Cooke, Lady Anne and Lady Bacon', in *'This Double Voice': Gendered Writing in Early Modern England*, ed. by Danielle and Elizabeth Clarke (Basingstoke: Macmillan, 2000), pp. 88–102

Sturiale, Massimo, *I* Sermons *di Anne Cooke: Versione "riformata" delle* Prediche *di Bernardino Ochino* (Catania: Quaderni del Dipartimento di Filologia Moderna, Università degli Studi di Catania, 2003)

Urwick, William, *Nonconformity in Herts: Being Lectures upon the Nonconforming Worthies of St. Albans* (London: Hazell, Watson, and Viney, 1884)

Venuti, Lawrence, *The Translator's Invisibility: A History of Translation*, second edition (New York: Routledge, 2008)

AN APOLOGY OR ANSWER IN DEFENCE OF THE CHURCH OF ENGLAND WITH A BRIEF AND PLAIN DECLARATION OF THE TRUE RELIGION PROFESSED AND USED IN THE SAME

To the right honourable learned and virtuous Ladie A. B.[1] M. C.[2]
wisheth from God grace, honour, and felicity

MADAME, ACCORDING to your request I have perused your studious labour of translation profitably employed in a right commendable work. Whereof for that it liked you to make me a Judge, and for that the thing itself hath singularly pleased my judgment, and delighted my mind in reading it, I have right heartily to thank your Ladyship, both for your own well thinking of me, and for the comfort that it hath wrought me. But far above these private respects, I am by greater causes enforced, not only to show my rejoice of this your doing, but also to testify the same by this my writing prefixed before the work, to the commodity of others, and good encouragement of yourself. You have used your accustomed modesty in submitting it to judgment, but therein is your praise doubled, sith it hath passed judgment without reproach. And whereas the chief author of the Latin work and I, severally perusing and conferring your whole translation, have without alteration allowed of it, I must both desire your Ladyship, and advertise the readers, to think that we have not therein given any thing to any dissembling affection towards you, as being contented to wink at faults to please you, or to make you without cause to please yourself: for there be sundry respects to draw us from so doing, although we were so evil minded, as there is no cause why we should be so thought of. Your own judgment in discerning flattery, your modesty in misliking it, the laying open of our opinion to the world, the truth of our friendship towards you, the unwillingness of us both (in respect of our vocations) to have this public work not truly and well translated, are good causes to persuade, that our allowance is of sincere truth and understanding. By which your travail (Madame) you have expressed an acceptable duty to the glory of GOD, deserved well of this Church of Christ, honourably defended the good fame and estimation of your own native tongue, shewing it so able to contend with a work originally written in the most praised speech: and besides the honour ye have done to the kind of women and

---

[1] Lady Anne Cooke Bacon.
[2] Matthew Cantuariensis, Matthew Parker, Archbishop of Canterbury ('Cantuar').

to the degree of Ladies, ye have done pleasure to the Author of the Latin book, in delivering him by your clear translation from the perils of ambiguous and doubtful constructions: and in making his good work more publicly beneficial: whereby ye have raised up great comfort to your friends, and have furnished your own conscience joyfully with the fruit of your labour, in so occupying your time: which must needs redound to the encouragement of noble youth in their good education, and to spend their time and knowledge in godly exercise, having delivered them by you so singular a precedent. Which your doing good Madame, as God (I am sure) doth accept and will bless with increase, so your and ours most virtuous and learned sovereign Lady and Mistress shall see good cause to commend: and all noble gentlewomen shall (I trust) hereby be allured from vain delights to doings of more perfect glory. And I for my part (as occasion may serve) shall exhort other to take profit by your work, and follow your example; whose success I beseech our heavenly Father to bless and prosper. And now to the end both to acknowledge my good approbation, and to spread the benefit more largely, where your ladyship hath sent me your book written, I have with most hearty thanks returned it to you (as you see) printed; knowing that I have therein done the best, and in this point used a reasonable policy, that is, to prevent such excuses as your modesty would have made in stay of publishing it. And thus at this time I leave further to trouble Your good Ladyship.

M. C.

PART I

It hath been an old complaint, even from the first time of the Patriarchs and Prophets, and confirmed by the writings and testimonies of every age, that the Truth wandereth here and there as a stranger in the world, and doth readily find enemies and slanderers amongst those that know her not.[1] Albeit perchance this may seem unto some a thing hard to be believed, I mean to such as have scant well and narrowly taken heed thereunto, specially seeing all mankind of nature's very motion without a teacher doth covet the truth of their own accord; and seeing our Saviour Christ himself, when he was on earth, would be called the Truth, as by a name most fit to express all his divine power; yet we, which have been exercised in the holy scriptures, and which have both read and seen what hath happened to all godly men commonly at all times, what to the Prophets, to the Apostles, to the holy Martyrs, and what to Christ himself; with what rebukes, revilings, and despites they were continually vexed whiles they here lived, and that only for the truth's sake: we (I say) do see, that this is not only no new thing, or hard to be believed, but that it is a thing already received and commonly used from age to age. Nay truly, this might seem much rather a marvel, and beyond all belief, if the Devil, who is the father of lies and enemy to all truth, would now upon a sudden change his nature, and hope that truth might otherwise be suppressed than by belying it; or that he would begin to establish his own kingdom by using now any other practices, than the same which he hath ever used from the beginning.[2] For since any man's remembrance, we can scant find one time, either when Religion did first grow, or when it was settled, or when it did afresh spring up again, wherein truth and

---

[1] **Marg.** Tertull. in Apolog. [Tertullian (*c.* 160–225), early Roman African apologist and theologian, *Apologia*, 1: 'She [Truth] knows that she is but a sojourner on the earth, and that among strangers she naturally finds foes.' *The Ante-Nicene Fathers*, ed. by Alexander Roberts, James Donaldson, and A. Cleveland Coxe, trans. by Robert Ernest Wallis, 10 vols (Buffalo, NY: Christian Literature Publishing Company, 1885–1896), III (1887), 17.]

[2] **Marg.** John viii. [John 8.44: 'Ye are of your father the devill, and the lusts of your father yee will doe: he hath bene a murtherer from the beginning, and abode not in the trueth, because there is no trueth in him. When he speaketh a lie, then speaketh hee of his owne: for he is a liar, and the father thereof.']

innocency were not by all unworthy means and most despitefully entreated. Doubtless the Devil well seeth, that so long as truth is in good safety, himself cannot be safe, nor yet maintain his own estate.

For, letting pass the ancient patriarchs and Prophets, who, as we said, had no part of their life free from contumelies and slanders. We know there were certain in times past, which said and commonly preached, that the old ancient Jews (of whom we make no doubt but they were the worshippers of the only and true God) did worship either a sow or an ass in God's stead, and that all the same Religion was nothing else, but a sacrilege and a plain contempt of all godliness.³ We know also that the Son of God, our Saviour Jesu Christ, when he taught the truth, was counted a Juggler° and an enchanter, a Samaritan, Beelzebub, a deceiver of the people, a drunkard, and a Glutton.⁴ Again, who wotteth° not what words were spoken against Saint Paul the most earnest and vehement preacher and maintainer of the truth? Sometime that he was a seditious and busy man, a raiser of tumults, a causer of rebellion; sometime again, that he was an heretic; sometime that he was mad; Sometime that only upon strife and stomach he was both a blasphemer of God's law, and a despiser of the fathers' ordinances.⁵ Further who knoweth not how Saint Stephen after he had thoroughly and sincerely embraced the truth, and began frankly and stoutly to preach and set forth the same, as he ought to do, was immediately called to answer for his life, as one that had wickedly uttered disdainful and heinous words against the law, against Moses, against the Temple, and against God?⁶ Or who is ignorant that in times past there were some which reproved

---

³ **Marg.** Corn. Tacit. [Cornelius Tacitus (*c.* 56–117), Roman senator, consul, and historian, *Histories*, v. 5: 'the Jews have purely mental conceptions of Deity, as one in essence.' *Complete Works*, ed. by Alfred John Church, William Jackson Brodribb, and Sara Bryant for Perseus (New York: Random House, 1873, repr. 1942) p. 660.]

⁴ **Marg.** Matt. xi. [Matthew 11.19: 'The Sonne of men came eating and drinking, and they say, Behold a glutton and a drinker of wine, a friend unto Publicans & sinners: but wisdome is justified of her children.']

⁵ **Marg.** Act. xxvi. [Acts 26.24: 'And as he thus answered for himselfe, Festus sayd with a loud voyce, Paul, thou art besides thy selve, much learning doth make thee mad.'] L

⁶ Acts 6:11: 'Then they suborned men, which sayd, We have heard him speak blasphemous words against Moses, and God.'

the holy Scriptures of falsehood, saying they contained things both contrary and quite one against other; and how that the Apostles of Christ did severally disagree betwixt themselves, and that St Paul did vary from them all?⁷ And not to make rehearsal of all, for that were an endless labour: who knoweth not after what sort our fathers were railed upon in times past, which first began to acknowledge and profess the name of Christ, how they made private conspiracies, devised secret counsels against the commonwealth, and to that end made early and privy meetings in the dark, killed young babes, fed themselves with men's flesh, and like savage and brute beasts, did drink their blood? In conclusion, how that after they had put out the candles, they committed adultery between themselves, and without regard wrought incest one with another: that Brethren lay with their sisters, sons with their Mothers, without any reverence of nature or kin, without shame, without difference; and that they were wicked men without all care of Religion, and without any opinion of God, being the very enemies of mankind, unworthy to be suffered in the world, and unworthy of life?⁸

---

⁷ **Marg.** Marc. ex Tertull. Ælius e Lact. [Tertullian, *Adversus Marcionem*, I. 19: 'These are Marcion's *Antitheses*, or contradictory propositions, which aim at committing the gospel to a variance with the law, in order that from the diversity of the two documents which contain them, they may contend for a diversity of gods also.' And IV. 3: 'Well, but Marcion, finding the Epistle of Paul to the Galatians (wherein he rebukes even apostles for "not walking uprightly according to the truth of the gospel," as well as accuses certain false apostles of perverting the gospel of Christ), labours very hard to destroy the character of those Gospels which are published as genuine and under the name of apostles, in order, forsooth, to secure for his own Gospel the credit which he takes away from them.' *The Ante-Nicene Fathers*, III (1887), 285, 348. Tertullian opposed Marcion's dualist, gnostic beliefs depicting the Old Testament God as tyrannical and the New Testament God as superior and forgiving and foregrounding Paul as the primary apostle. Lactantius (*c.* 250–325), Christian advisor to Emperor Constantine: 'He chiefly, however, assailed Paul and Peter, and the other disciples, as disseminators of deceit, whom at the same time he testified to have been unskilled and unlearned.' *Institutiones Divinae* (*Divine Institutes*), V. 2 in *The Ante-Nicene Fathers*, VII (1886), 138. This work was an exposition of Christian theology in an elegant Ciceronian style.]

⁸ **Marg.** Euseb. Lib. v. cap. i.; Tertull. in Apolog. iii.; Idem, i. ii. iii. et vii. viii. ix. [Eusebius (*c.* 260–340), Roman ecclesiastical historian and Bishop: 'And some of our heathen servants also were seized, as the governor had commanded that all of us should be examined publicly. These, being ensnared by Satan, and fearing for themselves the tortures which they beheld the saints endure, and

All these things were spoken in those days against the people of God, against Christ Jesu, against Paul, against Stephen, and against all them whosoever they were, which at the first beginning embraced the truth of the Gospel, and were contented to be called by the name of Christians, which was then a hateful name among the common people.[9] And although the things which they said, were not true, yet the Devil thought it should be sufficient for him, if at the least he could bring it so to pass, as they might be believed for true; and that the Christians might be brought into a common hatred of everybody, and have their death and destruction sought of all sorts.[10] Hereupon kings and princes being led then by such persuasions, killed all the Prophets of God, letting none escape: Isaiah with a saw, Jeremy with stones, Daniel with lions, Amos with an iron bar, Paul with the sword, and Christ upon the cross,[11] and condemned all Christians to imprisonments, to

---

being also urged on by the soldiers, accused us falsely of Thyestean banquets and Œdipodean intercourse, and of deeds which are not only unlawful for us to speak of or to think, but which we cannot believe were ever done by men.' *Church History* (*c.* 324), v. 1, trans. by Arthur Cuhman McGiffert, *Nicene & Post-Nicene Fathers*, ed. by Philip Schaff and Henry Wace, Series II (Buffalo: Christian Literature Publishing Company, 1886–1900), VI (1890), 213. Tertullian, *Apology*, 2: 'Nothing like this is done in our case, though the falsehoods disseminated about us ought to have the same sifting, that it might be found how many murdered children each of us had tasted; how many incests each of us had shrouded in darkness; what cooks, what dogs had been witness of our deeds.' *The Ante-Nicene Fathers*, III (1887), 18. Tertullian disproved the charges of Christians sacrificing infants at the Lord's supper and committing incest.]

[9] **Marg.** Tertull. in Apol. cap. iii. [Tertullian, *Apologia*, 3: 'What are we to think of it, that most people so blindly knock their heads against the hatred of the Christian name; that when they bear favourable testimony to any one, they mingle with it abuse of the name he bears?' *The Ante-Nicene Fathers*, III (1887), 20.] L

[10] **Marg.** Tertull. in Apol. cap. iii. [Tertullian, *Apologia*, 3: 'It is a high offence for anyone to be reformed by the detested name. Goodness is of less value than hatred of Christians.' *The Ante-Nicene Fathers*, III (1887), 20.]

[11] By order of the Jewish king Manasseh Isaiah was sawn though with a wooden saw. Amos was tortured and killed with a staff wielded by the son of Amaziah, the priest at Bethel. Jeremiah was stoned to death by his people at Taphnai in Egypt. Daniel survived the lions' den, died of natural causes, and was buried with great honour in Babylon. Although the New Testament does not record the manner of Paul's death, Christian tradition maintains that he was beheaded in Rome during the rule of Nero (*c.* AD 67). All four gospels recount the crucifixion of Jesus.

AN APOLOGY OR ANSWER IN DEFENCE OF THE CHURCH

torments, to the pikes, to be thrown down headlong from rocks and steep places, to be cast to wild beasts, and to be burnt, and made great fires of their quick bodies, for the only purpose to give light by night, and for a very scorn and mocking stock; and did count them no better than the vilest filth, the offscourings° and laughing games of the whole world.[12] Thus (as ye see) have the authors and professors of the truth ever been entreated.

Wherefore we ought to bear it the more quietly, which have taken upon us to profess the Gospel of Christ, if we for the same cause be handled after the same sort; and if we, as our forefathers were long ago, be likewise at this day tormented, and baited with railings, with spiteful dealings and with lies, and that for no desert of our own, but only because we teach and acknowledge the truth.[13]

They cry out upon us at this present everywhere, that we are all heretics, and have forsaken the faith, and have with new persuasions and wicked learning utterly dissolved the concord of the Church, that we renew, and as it were, fetch again from hell, the old and many a day condemned heresies; that we sow abroad new sects, and such broils as never erst° were heard of; also that we are already divided into contrary parts and opinions, and could yet by no means agree well among ourselves; that we be cursed° creatures, and like the Giants do war against God himself, and live clean without any regard or worshipping of God; that we despise all good deeds; that we use no discipline of virtue, no laws, no customs; that we esteem neither right, nor order, nor equity, nor justice; that we give the bridle to all naughtiness, and provoke the people to all licentiousness and lust; that we labour and seek to overthrow the state of Monarchies and Kingdoms, and to bring all things under the rule of the rash inconstant people and unlearned multitude; that we have seditiously fallen from the Catholic Church, and by a wicked schism and division have

---

[12] **Marg.** Suet Tranq. in Nerone. [Suetonius Tranquillus (70–130), known as Suetonius, second-century Roman historian, *De vita Caesarum, In Nerone* (AD 121), 16.2: 'Punishment was inflicted on the Christians, a class of men given to a new and mischievous superstition.' *Lives of the Caesars*, ed. and trans. by J. C. Rolfe for the Loeb Classical Library 31 and 38, 2 vols (Cambridge, MA: Harvard University Press, 1914), II, 111.]

[13] **Marg.** 1 Tim. iv. [1 Timothy 4.10: 'For therefore wee labour and are rebuked, because we trust in the living God, which is the Saviour of all men, specially of those that beleeve.'] L

shaken the whole world, and troubled the common peace and universal quiet of the church; and that, as Dathan and Abiram conspired in times past against Moses and Aaron,[14] even so we at this day have renounced the Bishop of Rome without any cause reasonable; that we set nought by the authority of the ancient fathers and Councils of old time; that we have rashly and presumptuously disannulled the old ceremonies, which have been well allowed by our fathers and forefathers many hundred years past, both by good customs and also in ages of more purity; and that we have by our own private head, without the authority of any sacred and general Council brought new traditions into the Church, and have done all these things not for Religion's sake, but only upon a desire of contention and strife.

But that they for their part have changed no manner of thing, but have held and kept still such a number of years to this very day all things as they were delivered from the Apostles and well approved by the most ancient fathers.

And that this matter should not seem to be done but upon privy slander, and to be tossed to and fro in a corner, only to spite us, there have been besides wilily procured by the Bishop of Rome, certain persons of eloquence enough, and not unlearned neither, which should put their help to this cause, now almost despaired of, and should polish and set forth the same, both in books and with long tales, to the end, that when the matter was trimly and eloquently handled, ignorant and unskilful persons might suspect there was some great thing in it. Indeed they perceived that their own cause did everywhere go to wrack, that their sleights were now espied and less esteemed, and that their helps did daily fail them, and that their matter stood altogether in great need of a cunning spokesman.

Now as for those things which by them have been laid against us, in part they be manifestly false, and condemned so by their own judgments which spake them, partly again, though they be as false too indeed, yet bear they a certain show and colour of truth, so as the Reader (if he take not good heed) may easily be

---

[14] **Marg.** Num. xvi. [Dathan and Abiram were the sons of Eliab. Numbers 16.3: 'Who gathered themselves together against Moses, and against Aaron, and sayde ynto them, *Ye take* too much vpon you, seeing all the Congregation is holy, every one of them, and the Lord *is* among them: wherefore then lift ye your selves above the Congregation of the Lord?'] **L**

AN APOLOGY OR ANSWER IN DEFENCE OF THE CHURCH

tripped and brought into error by them, specially when their fine and cunning tale is added thereunto; and part of them be of such sort, as we ought not to shun them as crimes or faults, but to acknowledge and profess° them as things well done, and upon very good reason.

For shortly to say the truth, these folk falsely accuse and slander all our doings; yea the same things which they themselves cannot deny but to be rightly and orderly done; and for malice do so misconstrue and deprave all our sayings and doings, as though it were impossible, that anything could be rightly spoken or done by us. They should more plainly and sincerely have gone to work if they would have dealt truly, but now they neither truly nor sincerely, nor yet Christianly, but darkly and craftily charge and batter us with lies, and do abuse the blindness and fondness of the people, together with the ignorance of Princes, to cause us to be hated, and the truth to be suppressed.

This, lo ye, is the power of darkness, and of men which lean more to the amazed wondering of the rude multitude and to darkness, than they do to truth and light; and as St Hierom saith, which do openly gainsay the truth, closing up their eyes, and will not see for the nonce.[15] But we give thanks to the most good and mighty God, that such is our cause, whereagainst (when they would fainest°) they were able to utter no despite, but the same which might as well be wrested against the holy fathers, against the Prophets, against the Apostles, against Peter, against Paul, and against Christ himself.

Now therefore, if it be lawful for these folks to be eloquent and fine-tongued in speaking evil, surely it becometh not us in our

---

[15] Jerome (*c.* 347–420), Latin Christian Doctor of the Church, translator of the Bible from Hebrew and Greek into Latin; *Biblia Sacra Vulgata*, the *Vulgate*, was declared the 'authentic' text at the Council of Trent (session 4, 8 April 1546). Editor John Ayre admits 'it is not easy to say what passage is intended by this vague quotation.' He suggests '*Porro aliud est, si clausis, quod dicitur, oculis mihi volunt maledicere,*' *Contra Rufinum* (*c.* 402), II. Another possibility from the same three-book work: 'They could not bear to hear the truth, and therefore they pierced the tongue that spoke truth with the pin that parted their hair,' III. As annotated in *Apologia* 1562. John Jewel, *Works*, ed. by John Ayre, 4 vols (Cambridge: Cambridge University Press, 1845–50), III (1848), 181. See also *Decrees of the Ecumenical Councils*, ed. by Norman P. Tanner, 2 vols (London: Sheed & Ward, 1990), II, 664. *The Principal Works of St Jerome*, trans. by W. H. Fremantle, *Nicene & Post-Nicene Fathers*, VI (1893), 540.

cause, being so very good, to be dumb in answering truly. For men to be careless what is spoken by them and their own matter, be it never so falsely and slanderously spoken, (especially when it is such, that the Majesty of God and the cause of religion may thereby be damaged), is the part doubtless of dissolute and wretchless persons, and of them which wickedly wink at the injuries done unto the name of God. For although other wrongs, yea oftentimes great, may be borne and dissembled of a mild and Christian man, yet he that goeth smoothly away and dissembleth the matter when he is noted of heresy, Ruffinus was wont to deny that man to be a Christian.[16] We therefore will do the same thing which all laws, which nature's own voice doth command to be done, and which Christ himself did in like case, when he was checked and reviled, to the intent we may put off from us these men's slanderous accusations, and may defend soberly and truly our own cause and innocency.

For Christ verily when the Pharisees charged Him with sorcery as one that had some familiar Spirits, and wrought many things by their help, I, said he, have not the Devil, but do glorify my Father: but it is you, that have dishonoured me, and put me to rebuke and shame.[17] And St Paul when Festus the lieutenant scorned him as a madman: I (said he) most dear Festus, am not mad, as thou thinkest, but I speak the words of truth and soberness.[18] And the ancient Christians, when they were slandered to the people for mankillers, for adulterers, for committers of incest, for disturbers of the commonweals, and did perceive that by such slanderous accusations the Religion which they professed, might be brought in question, namely if they should seem to hold their peace, and in manner to confess the fault; lest this might hinder the free course of the Gospel, they made Orations, they

---

[16] Tyrannius Rufinus (*c.* 345–410), monk and translator mainly of Origen and Eusebius, *Apologiae in S. Hieronymum*, I. Though Rufinus was initially a friend of Jerome, the two differed over their support (Rufinus) or criticism (Jerome) of Origen, as illustrated in their pamphlet war: Jerome's *Contra Rufinum* and Rufinus's *Contra Hieronymum*. Origen (*c.* 185–254), Greek scholar and early Christian theologian, was condemned by the Council of Constantinople (AD 553) for his teaching on the pre-existence of souls and the subordination of the Son of God to the Father.

[17] **Marg.** Joh. viii. [John 8.49: 'Jesus answered, I have not a devill, but I honour my Father, and ye have dishonoured me.'] L

[18] **Marg.** Act. xxvi. [Acts 26.25.]

put up supplications, and made means° to Emperors and Princes, that they might defend themselves and their fellows in open audience.[19]

But we truly, seeing that so many thousands of our brethren in these last twenty years have borne witness unto the truth, in the midst of most painful torments that could be devised; and when Princes desirous to restrain the Gospel sought many ways but prevailed nothing, and that now almost the whole world doth begin to open their eyes to behold the light; we take it that our cause hath already been sufficiently declared and defended, and think it not needful to make many words, since the matter saith enough for itself. For if the popes would, or else if they could weigh with their own selves the whole matter, and also the beginning and proceedings of our Religion, how in a manner all their travail hath come to nought, nobody driving it forward; and how on the other side, our cause, against the will of Emperors, from the beginning, against the wills of so many kings, in spite of the Popes, and almost maugre° the head of all men, hath taken increase, and by little and little spread over into all countries, and is come at length even into kings' courts and palaces. These same things methinketh might be tokens great enough to them, that God Himself doth strongly fight in our quarrel, and doth from heaven laugh at their enterprises; and that the force of truth is such, as neither man's power, nor yet hell-gates are able to root it out. For they be not all mad at this day, so many free Cities, so many Kings, so many Princes, which have fallen away from the Seat of Rome, and have rather joined themselves to the Gospel of Christ.

And although the Popes had never hitherunto leisure to consider diligently and earnestly of these matters, or though some other cares do now let° them, and diverse ways pull them, or though they count these to be but common and trifling studies, and nothing to appertain to the Pope's worthiness, this maketh not why our matter ought to seem the worse. Or if they perchance will not see that which they see indeed, but rather will withstand

---

[19] **Marg.** Quadrat. Justin. Melit. Tertul. alli-que. [All were apologists. Quadratus, a disciple of the apostles, wrote several treatises in defence of the Christian religion (AD 128); Justinus was martyred for his oration (AD 150); Melito, Bishop of Sardis, composed a Christian apology (AD 172); Tertullian published his Apology anonymously in Rome (AD 201).]

the known truth, ought we therefore by and by to be counted heretics, because we obey not their will and pleasure? If so be that Pope Pius were the man (we say not which he would so gladly be called) but if he were indeed a man that either would account us for his brethren, or at least would take us to be men, he would first diligently have examined our reasons, and would have seen what might be said with us, what against us; and would not in his Bull, whereby he lately pretended a council, so rashly have condemned so great a part of the world, so many learned and godly men, so many commonwealths, so many kings, and so many princes, only upon his own blind prejudices and fore-determinations, and that without hearing of them speak or without showing cause why.[20]

But because he hath already so noted us openly, lest by holding our peace we should seem to grant a fault, and specially because we can by no mean have audience in the public assembly of the general Council, wherein he would no creature should have power to give his voice or to declare his opinion, except he were sworn, and straitly bound to maintain his authority.

For we have had good experience hereof in the last conference at the council at Trident, where the ambassadors and divines of the Princes of Germany, and of the free Cities, were quite shut out from their company; neither can we yet forget, how Julius the Third,[21] above ten years past, provided warily by his writ that none of our sort should be suffered to speak in the Council (except there were some peradventure that would recant and change his opinion). For this cause chiefly we thought it good to yield up an account of our faith in writing, and truly and openly to make answer to those things wherewith we have been openly charged, to the end the world may see the parts and foundations of that doctrine, in the behalf whereof so many good men have little regarded their own lives. And that all men may understand what manner of people they be, and what opinion they have of God and of Religion, whom the Bishop of Rome before they were called to tell their tale, hath condemned for heretics, without any good consideration, without any example, and utterly without law

---

[20] **Marg.** Pius IV. [Pope Pius IV (1559–1565) issued *Bulla celebrationis*, in November 1560, convening the third and final period (1562–1563) of the Council of Trent ('Trident').] L

[21] Pope Julius III (1550–1555) convoked the second period (1551–1552) of the Council of Trent.

or right, only because he heard tell that they did dissent from him and his in some point of Religion.

And although St Hierom would have nobody to be patient when he is suspected of heresy, yet we will deal herein neither bitterly nor brablingly,° nor yet be carried away with anger and heat, though he ought to be reckoned neither bitter nor brabler° that speaketh the truth.[22] We willingly leave this kind of eloquence to our adversaries, who whatsoever they say against us, be it never so shrewdly° or despitefully said, yet think it is said modestly and comely enough, and care nothing whether it be true or false. We need none of these shifts which do maintain the truth.

Further, if we do show it plain that God's holy Gospel, the ancient Bishops, and the primitive Church do make on our side, and that we have not without just cause left these men, and rather have returned to the Apostles and old catholic Fathers. And if we shall be found to do the same not colourably or craftily, but in good faith, before God, truly, honestly, clearly, and plainly; and if they themselves which fly our doctrine and would be called Catholics, shall manifestly see how all those titles of antiquity whereof they boast so much, are quite shaken out of their hands, and that there is more pith in this our cause than they thought for; we then hope and trust that none of them will be so negligent and careless of his own salvation, but he will at length study and bethink himself, to whether part he were best to join him. Undoubtedly, except one will altogether harden his heart and refuse to hear, he shall not repent him to give good heed to this our defence, and to mark well what we say, and how truly and justly it agreeth with Christian Religion.

For where they call us heretics, it is a crime so heinous, that unless it may be seen, unless it may be felt, and in manner may be holden with hands and fingers, it ought not lightly to be judged or believed, when it is laid to the charge of any Christian man.[23]

---

[22] Ayre, editor of Jewel's *Works*, suggests that this comes from Jerome's letter to Pammachius against the errors of John of Jerusalem. Jerome had been accused of mis-translating a letter from Epiphanius to John of Jerusalem; in his Letter 57 to Pammachius he repudiates the charge and defends his methods of translating sense for sense not word for word. 'For, though I am called a falsifier, and have my reputation torn to shreds, [...] I am content to repudiate the charge without retaliating in kind.' *Nicene and Post-Nicene Fathers*, VI (1893), 119.

[23] **Marg.** Hæresis quid [What is heresy?] L

For heresy is a forsaking of salvation, a renouncing of God's grace, a departing from the body and spirit of Christ. But this was ever an old and solemn property with them and their forefathers; if any did complain of their errors and faults, and desired to have true Religion restored, straightway to condemn such one for heretics, as men new-fangled and factious.° Christ for no other cause was called a Samaritan, but only for that He was thought to have fallen to a certain new Religion, and to be the Author of a new sect. And Paul the apostle of CHRIST was called before the Judges to make answer to a matter of heresy, and therefore he said: According to this way which they call heresy, I do worship the God of my fathers, believing all things which be written in the law and in the Prophets.[24]

Shortly to speak. This universal religion, which Christian men profess at this day, was called first of the heathen people a Sect and Heresy.[25] With these terms did they always fill princes' ears, to the intent when they had once hated us with a foredetermined opinion, and had counted all that we said to be faction and heresy, they might be so led away from the truth and right understanding of the cause. But the more sore and outrageous a crime heresy is, the more it ought to be proved by plain and strong arguments, especially in this time, when men begin to give less credit to their words, and to make more diligent search of their doctrine than they were wont to do. For the people of God are otherwise instructed now than they were in times past, when all the Bishops of Rome's sayings were allowed for Gospel, and when all Religion did depend only upon their authority. Nowadays the holy scripture is abroad, the writings of the Apostles and Prophets are in print, whereby all truth and Catholic doctrine may be proved, and all heresy may be disproved and confuted.

Sithence° then they bring forth none of these for themselves, and call us nevertheless heretics, which have neither fallen from Christ nor from the Apostles, nor yet from the Prophets, this is an injurious and a very spiteful dealing. With this sword did Christ put off the Devil when he was tempted of him; with these weapons

---

[24] **Marg.** Acts xxiv. [Acts 24.14: 'But this I confesse unto thee, that after the way (which they call heresie) so worship I the God of my fathers, beleeving all things which are written in the Law and the Prophets.'] L

[25] **Marg.** Tertull. in Apolog. [Tertullian, *Apologia*, 10: 'we are accused of sacrilege and treason.' *The Ante-Nicene Fathers*, III (1887), 26.]

ought all presumption which doth advance itself against God, to be overthrown and conquered.[26] For all Scripture, saith St Paul, that cometh by the inspiration of God, is profitable to teach, to confute, to instruct, and to reprove, that the man of God may be perfect, and thoroughly framed to every good work.[27] Thus did the holy fathers always fight against the heretics with none other force than with the holy scriptures. St Augustine when he disputed against Petilian a heretic of the Donatists:[28] Let not these words, quoth he, be heard between us: I say, or you say: let us rather speak in this wise: Thus saith the Lord. There let us seek the Church: there let us boult° out our cause.[29] Likewise St Hierom: All those things (saith he) which without the testimony of the Scriptures are holden as delivered from the Apostles, be thoroughly smitten down by the sword of God's word.[30] St Ambrose also, to Gratian the Emperor: Let the Scripture (saith he) be asked the question, let the Prophets be asked, and let Christ be asked.[31] For at that time made the

360

---

[26] **Marg.** 2 Cor. x. [II Corinthians 10.5: 'Casting downe the imaginations, and every high thing that is exalted against the knowledge of God, and bringing into captivitie every thought to the obedience of Christ.'] L

[27] **Marg.** 2 Tim. iii. [II Timothy 3.16–17: 'For the whole Scripture *is* given by inspiration of God, and *is* profitable to teach, to convince, to correct, *and* to instruct in righteousnesse, That the man of God may be absolute, being made perfect unto all good works.']

[28] The Donatists, followers of Donatus (d. 355), were an ascetic, schismatic sect in North Africa who considered sanctity a requirement for membership and administration of the sacraments.

[29] **Marg.** De Unit. Eccl. cap. iii. Contr. Maxim. Arian. Episc. Lib. iii. cap. xiv. [Augustine (354–430), Roman African Doctor of the Church, theologian, and philosopher, *Ad Catholicos Epistola Contra Donatistas Vulgo De Unitate Ecclesiae, Liber Unus, caput iii. 5: 'sed, ut dicere cœperam, non audiamus, Haec dicis, haec dico, sed audiamus Haec dicit Dominus, Patrologia Latina*, ed. by Jacques-Paul Migne, 221 vols (Petit-Montrouge, Paris, Migne, 1844–1864), XLIII (1841); Augustine, *Contra Maximinum haereticum Arianorum episcopum*, III. 14.]

[30] **Marg.** In prim. cap. Aggae. [Jewel quotes Jerome in his 'Sermon on Haggai I': 'Hierome, writing upon Aggeus, saith: *Quæ absque auctoritate et testimoniis scriptuarum quasi traditione apostolica sponte reperiunt atque confingunt, percutit gladius Dei*: the sword of God striketh those things, which men find out and devise of themselves without the authority and testimonies of the scriptures, and deliver forth as if they came by the tradition of the apostles.' *Works*, II, 991.]

[31] Ambrose (*c*. 340–397), Roman Christian theologian, Doctor of the Church, and Bishop of Milan, hymnist-founder of Ambrosian chant. *De fide ad Gratianum Augustum*, I. 6: 'Let us enquire of the Scriptures, of apostles, of prophets, of Christ.' *Nicene and Post-Nicene Fathers*, Series I, X (1896), 207.

Catholic fathers and Bishops no doubt but that our Religion might be proved out of the holy scriptures. Neither were they ever so hardy as to take any for a heretic, whose error they could not evidently and apparently reprove by the self same scriptures. And we verily do make answer on this wise as St Paul did: According to this way which they call heresy, we do worship God and the Father of our Lord Jesus Christ, and do allow all things which have been written either in the Law or in the Prophets, or in the Apostles' works.[32]

Wherefore, if we be heretics, and they (as they would fain be called) be Catholics, why do they not, as they see the fathers, which were Catholic men, have always done? Why do they not convince and master us by the divine scriptures? Why do they not call us again to be tried by them? Why do they not lay before us how we have gone away from Christ, from the Prophets, from the Apostles, and from the holy fathers? Why stick they to do it? Why are they afraid of it? It is God's cause. Why are they doubtful to commit it to the trial of God's word? If we be heretics, which refer all our controversies unto the holy scriptures, and report us to the self same words, which we know were sealed by God himself, and in comparison of them set little by all other things whatsoever may be devised by men, how shall we say to these folk, I pray you, what manner of men be they, and how is it meet to call them, which fear the judgment of the holy scriptures, that is to say, the judgment of God himself, and do prefer before them their own Dreams and full cold Inventions; and to maintain their own traditions, have defaced and corrupted now these many hundred years the ordinances of Christ and of the Apostles?

Men say that Sophocles the tragical Poet, when in his old days he was by his own sons accused before the Judges for a doting and sottish man, as one that fondly wasted his own substance, and seemed to need a Governor to see unto him; to the intent he might clear himself of the fault, he came into the place of Judgment, and when he had rehearsed before them his Tragedy called OEDIPUS COLONEUS, which he had written at the very time of his accusation, marvellous exactly and cunningly, did of himself ask the judges whether they thought any sottish or doting man could do the like piece of work.[33]

---

[32] **Marg.** Acts xxiv: [See Part I, note 24.] L
[33] **Marg.** Sophocles Poeta. [*Oedipus at Colonus*, one of the seven surviving

AN APOLOGY OR ANSWER IN DEFENCE OF THE CHURCH

410 In like manner, because these men take us to be mad, and appeach° us for heretics, as men which have nothing to do, neither with CHRIST, nor with the Church of GOD, we have judged it should be to good purpose, and not unprofitable, if we do openly and frankly set forth our faith wherein we stand, and show all that confidence which we have in CHRIST JESU, to the intent all men may see what is our judgment of every part of Christian religion, and may resolve with themselves, whether the faith which they shall see confirmed by the words of Christ, by the writings of the Apostles, by the testimonies of the catholic fathers, and by the examples of many ages, be but a certain rage of furious and mad men, and a conspiracy of heretics. This therefore is our Belief.

---

tragedies of the Athenian playwright Sophocles (497–406 BC), dramatizes the feud between Oedipus's two sons which is mirrored in the trumped-up charges against the playwright himself. Bishop Jewel and Anne Bacon were likely familiar with the account of Sophocles in Cicero's *De Senectute*, 7.2: 'when, because of his absorption in literary work, he was thought to be neglecting his business affairs, his sons haled him into court [...] on the ground of imbecility. [...] Thereupon, it is said, the old man read to the jury his play. [...] He was acquitted by the verdict of the jury.' (*Cicero on Old Age*, trans. by W. A. Falconer, Loeb Classical Library, 29 vols (Cambridge, MA: Harvard University Press, 1912–1999), xx (1923).] L

PART II

We believe that there is one certain nature and divine power, which we call GOD: and that the same is divided into three equal Persons, into the Father, into the Son, and into the holy Ghost; and that they all be of one power, of one Majesty, of one eternity, of one Godhead, and of one substance. And although these three persons be so divided, that neither the Father is the Son, nor the Son is the holy Ghost, or the Father; yet, nevertheless, we believe that there is but one very God. And that the same one God hath created heaven and earth, and all things contained under heaven.

We believe that JESUS Christ the only Son of the eternal Father (as long before it was determined before all beginnings) when the fullness of time was come, did take of that blessed and pure Virgin, both flesh and all the nature of man, that he might declare to the world the secret and hid will of his father; which will had been laid up from before all ages and generations. And that he might full finish in his human body the mystery of our redemption, and might fasten to the cross our sins, and also that handwriting which was made against us.[1]

We believe that for our sakes he died, and was buried, descended into hell, the third day by the power of his Godhead returned to life, and rose again; and that the fortieth day after his resurrection, whiles his Disciples beheld and looked upon him, he ascended into heaven to fulfil all things, and did place in majesty and glory the self same body wherewith he was born, wherein he lived on earth, wherein he was jested at, wherein he had suffered most painful torments and cruel kind of death, wherein he rose again, and wherein he ascended to the right hand of the Father,[2] above all rule, above all power, all force, all dominion, and above every name that is named, not only in this world, but also in the world to come. And that there He now sitteth, and shall sit, till

---

[1] **Marg.** Gal. iv. [Galatians 4.4: 'But when the fullnesse of time was come, God sent forth his Sonne made of a woman, *and* made under the Lawe.'] **L**

[2] **Marg.** August. Tract. 50 in Johan. [Augustine, *In Johannis evangelium tractatus*, L. 13: 'of beholding and not of following Him, He ascended into heaven, and is no longer here.' *Nicene and Post-Nicene Fathers*, Series I, VII (1888), 282.]

AN APOLOGY OR ANSWER IN DEFENCE OF THE CHURCH

all things be full perfected.³ And although the Majesty and Godhead of Christ be everywhere abundantly dispersed, yet we believe that his body, as St Augustine saith, must needs be still in one place;⁴ and that Christ hath given majesty unto his body, but yet hath not taken away from it the nature of a body; and that we must not so affirm Christ to be God that we deny him to be man: and, as the Martyr Vigilius saith, that Christ hath left us as touching his human nature, but hath not left us as touching his divine nature.⁵ And that the same Christ, though he be absent from us concerning his manhood, yet is ever present with us concerning his Godhead.⁶ From that place also we believe that Christ shall come again to execute that general judgment, as well of them whom he shall then find alive in the body as of them that be already dead.

We believe that the holy Ghost, who is the third person in the holy Trinity, is very God: not made, not created, not begotten, but proceeding from both the Father and the Son, by a certain mean unknown unto men, and unspeakable; and that it is his property to mollify and soften the hardness of man's heart when

---

³ **Marg.** Acts iii. [Acts 3.21: 'Whom the heaven must containe untill the time that all things be restored, which God had spoken by the mouth of all his holy Prophets since the world began.']

⁴ **Marg.** In Epist. Ad Dard. [Augustine, CLXXXVII. 3: Augustine to Claudius Postumus Dardanus: 'You say that from this we are to know, perhaps, that paradise is established in some part of heaven, or that, because God is everywhere, the man who is in God is also present everywhere.' *Augustine of Hippo, Selected Writings*, ed. by Mary T. Clark (Mahwah: Paulist Press, 1984), p. 404.]

⁵ **Marg.** Contr. Euych. Lib. 1. [Vigilius (n.d.), Bishop of Thapsus and Pope (537–555), *Contra Eutychetem*, I. 6: '*Ut non videant, non intelligant, in Christo aliud divinitati, aliud humanitati ejus congruere, licet sit utrumque commune.*' *Patrologia Latina*, LXII (1847), I, col. 98.]

⁶ **Marg.** Fulgent. Ad Thrasym. [Fulgentius (*c.* 468–533), Roman African theologian and Bishop of Ruspe, *Ad Trasimundum Vandalorum Regem*, II. 17: '*Christus, cum absit a nobis per forman servi, tamen semper est nobiscum per forman Dei.*' (*Patrologia Latina*, LXV, 1847). As Peter Martyr Vermigli commented on and extended this passage from Fulgentius in his *Oxford Treatise and Disputation on the Eucharist* (1549): 'The same individual according to his human substance was absent from heaven while he was on earth, and left the earth when he ascended to heaven. [...] How is he present to his believers unless he is without limits and true God?' *The Oxford Treatise and Disputation on the Eucharist*, trans. and ed. by Joseph C. McLelland, *Sixteenth Century Essays & Studies*, 83 vols (Kirksville: Truman State University Press, 1983–2010), LVI (2000), 117.]

50   He is once received thereunto, either by the wholesome preaching of the Gospel, or by any other way; that he doth give men light, and guide them unto the knowledge of God, to all way of truth, to newness of the whole life, and to everlasting hope of salvation.

We believe that there is one Church of God, and that the same is not shut up (as in times past among the Jews) into some one corner or kingdom, but that it is catholic and universal, and dispersed throughout the whole world. So that there is now no nation which may truly complain that they be shut forth, and may not be one of the Church and people of God; and that this Church is the kingdom, the body and the spouse of Christ; and that Christ alone is the Prince of this kingdom, that Christ alone is the Head of this Body, and that Christ alone is the bridegroom of this spouse.

Furthermore, we believe that there be divers degrees of ministers in the Church, whereof some be deacons, some priests, some Bishops, to whom is committed the office to instruct the people, and the whole charge and setting forth of religion; yet notwithstanding we say that there neither is nor can be any one man, which may have the whole superiority in this universal state, for that Christ is ever present to assist his Church, and needeth not any man to supply his room, as his only heir to all his substance; and that there can be no one mortal creature, which is able to comprehend or conceive in his mind the universal Church, that is, to wit, all the parts of the world, much less able to put them in order, and to govern them rightly and duly. For all the Apostles, as Cyprian saith, were of like power among themselves, and the rest were the same that Peter was, and that it was said indifferently to them all, feed ye: indifferently to them all, Go into the whole world: indifferently to them all, Teach ye the Gospel.[7] And as Hierom saith, all Bishops wheresoever they be, be they at Rome, be they at Eugubium, be they at Constantinople, be they at Rhegium, be all of like pre-eminence, and of like priesthood.[8]

---

[7] **Marg.** De Simplic Prælat. [Cyprian (*c.* 200–258), Roman African theologian, martyr, and Bishop of Carthage, *De unitate ecclesiae*, I. 4: 'Assuredly the rest of the apostles were also the same as was Peter, endowed with a like partnership both of honour and power; but the beginning proceeds from unity.' *The Ante-Nicene Fathers*, v (1868), 380.]

[8] **Marg.** Ad. Evagr. [Jerome, *Epistola Ad Euagrium*. Eugubium, or Gubio, a small town in Urbino, is addressed by Jerome because of its small size as an episcopal see in comparison to Rome.]

And, as Cyprian saith, there is but one Bishopric, and a piece thereof is perfectly and wholly holden of every particular Bishop.[9] And according to the judgment of the Nicene Council we say that the Bishop of Rome hath no more jurisdiction over the church of God than the rest of the Patriarchs, either of Alexandria or Antiochia have.[10] And as for the Bishop of Rome, who now calleth all matters before himself alone, except he do his duty as he ought to do, except he administer the sacraments, except he instruct the people, except he warn them and teach them, we say that he ought not of right once to be called a Bishop, or so much as an elder. For a Bishop, as saith Augustine, is a name of labour, and not of honour: because he will have that man understand himself to be no Bishop, which will seek to have pre-eminence, and not to profit others.[11] And that neither the Pope nor any other worldly creature, can no more be head of the whole Church, or a Bishop over all, than he can be the bridegroom, the light, the salvation, and life of the Church. For these privileges and names belong only to Christ, and be properly and only fit for him alone. And that no Bishop of Rome did ever suffer himself to be called by such a proud name before Phocas the emperor's time, who as we know, by killing his own sovereign Maurice the emperor, did

---

[9] **Marg.** De Simplic. Prælat. [Cyprian, *De unitate ecclesiae*, 5. Thomas Harding and Jewel disagreed on the meaning of Cyprian. Stressing inter-dependency, Harding quoted Cyprian: 'there are many beams of one sun, many boughs of one root, many rivers of one fountain, so there are many bishops of one bishoprick'. Jewel emphasized singularity: '*Ecclesia una est, quae in multitudinem latius incremento fæcunditatis extenditur; quomodo solis multi radii, sed lumen unum; et rami arboris multi, sed robor unum*: the bishoprick is one, a part whereof every several bishop is possessed in whole. The church is one, which by her great increase is extended unto many: as in the sun, the beams be many but the light is one; and in a tree the boughs be many but the body is one.' *Works*, III, 291, 300–01.]

[10] Jewel is alluding to the first four of the major councils, which he mentions throughout the *Apologia*: Nicea (325) condemned Arianism and defined the consubstantiality of God the Father and the Son; Constantinople (381) affirmed the consubstantiality of the Holy Spirit with the Father and the Son; Ephesus (431) declared the divine maternity of Mary as bearer of God, *theotokos*; Chalcedon (451) condemned monophysitism which attributed only one nature to Christ and declared Eutyches a heretic for his assertion that Constantinople was equal to Rome. The Council of Trent (1545–1563), so central to Jewel's argument, was the nineteenth ecumenical council.

[11] **Marg.** 1 ad Tim. iii. [I Timothy 3.1: 'This *is* a true saying, If any man desire the office of a Bishop, hee desireth a worthie worke.'] L

by a traitorous villainy aspire to the empire which was about the six hundredth and thirteenth year after Christ was born. Also the Council of Carthage did circumspectly provide, that no Bishop should be called the highest Bishop or chief priest.¹² And therefore, sithence° the Bishop of Rome will nowadays so be called, and challengeth unto himself an authority that is none of his; besides that he doth plainly contrary to the ancient Councils, and contrary to the old fathers. We believe that he doth give unto himself, as it is written by his own companion Gregory, a presumptuous, a profane, a sacrilegious, and an Antichristian name: that he is also the king of pride, that he is Lucifer, which preferreth himself before his brethren: that he hath forsaken the faith, and is the forerunner of Antichrist.¹³

Further we say, that the minister ought lawfully, duly, and

---

¹² In *The Defence* Jewel quotes from the Council of Carthage: '*Primæ sedis episcopus non appelletur princeps sacerdotum, vel summus sacerdos, vela liquid hujusmodi; sed tantum primæ sedis episcopus. Universalis autem nec etiam Romanus pontifex appelletur*. Let not the bishop of any of the first sees be called the prince of priests, or the highest priest, or by any other like name, but only the bishop of the first see. But let not the bishop of Rome himself be called the first bishop. Concil Carthag. III., cap 26.' Harding clarified that this third council of Carthage was a provincial council. About its 26th canon, 'the decrees of this council pertained but to the province of Afric. By which decree they willed only their primates of Afric to keep themselves within their limits, and not presumptuously to take upon themselves more glorious titles than to them pertained. By this canon the pope's primacy and title is no whit diminished or disproved.' Jewel rebutted that Harding suffered from 'some inordinate passion in your stomach,' but he did not address the provincial nature of the council. Editor Ayre notes that 'the last sentence is not printed in Gratian as a part of the decree of the council. But bishop Jewel asserts that there was MS. authority for its really being so.' *Works*, III, 312–14.

¹³ **Marg.** Greg. Epist. Lib. iv. Epist. 76, 78, 80. Et Lib. VII. epist. 66. [Gregory the Great (*c.* 540–604), Latin Christian theologian, Pope, and Doctor of the Church. In the 27 articles of Bishop Jewel's extensive *A Reply to M. Harding's Answer* (1565), his response to the objections of recusant Thomas Harding (1516–1572), the former canon in residence and treasurer of Salisbury Cathedral, whom Jewel ejected and who was exiled in Belgium, addresses the Bishop of Rome in the fourth article. Jewel cites Gregory, who calls the Pope's 'name of universal bishop [...] vain and hurtful; the confusion, the poison, and utter and universal destruction of the church,' and notes that whoever uses this title 'followeth Lucifer, and is the very forerunner and messenger of antichrist' (Greg. Lib. IV, Epist. 39). Gregory calls this name a type of pride, *typum superbiae* (Lib. VI, Epist. 2), a name of hypocrisy, *nomen hypocriseos* and blasphemy, *nomen blasphemiae* (Lib. IV, Epist. 39). *Works*, I, 345.]

AN APOLOGY OR ANSWER IN DEFENCE OF THE CHURCH

orderly to be preferred to that office of the Church of God, and that no man hath power to wrest himself into the holy ministry at his own pleasure and list. Wherefore these persons do us the greater wrong, which have nothing so common in their mouth, as that we do nothing orderly and comely, but all things troublesomely and without order; and that we allow every man to be a priest, to be a teacher, and to be an Interpreter of the Scriptures.

Moreover, we say that Christ hath given to his ministers power to bind, to loose, to open, to shut, and that the office of loosing consisteth in this point, that the Minister should either offer by the preaching of the Gospel the merits of Christ and full pardon, to such as have lowly and contrite hearts, and do unfeignedly repent them, pronouncing unto the same a sure and undoubted forgiveness of their sins, and hope of everlasting salvation. Or else that the minister, when any have offended their brothers' minds with a great offence, with a notable and open fault, whereby they have as it were banished and made themselves strangers from the common fellowship, and from the body of Christ, then after perfect amendment of such persons, doth reconcile them, and bring them home again, and restore them to the company and unity of the faithful. We say also that the minister doth execute the authority of binding and shutting, as often as he shutteth up the gate of the kingdom of heaven against the unbelieving and stubborn persons, denouncing unto them God's vengeance and everlasting punishment. Or else when he doth quite shut them out from the bosom of the Church by open excommunication. Out of doubt, what sentence soever the Minister of God shall give in this sort, God himself doth so well allow of it, that whatsoever here in earth by their means is loosed and bound, God himself will loose and bind, and confirm the same in heaven.

And touching the keys, wherewith they may either shut or open the kingdom of heaven, we with Chrysostom say, they be the knowledge of the Scriptures:[14] with Tertullian we say, they be the

---

[14] Jewel quotes *Opus imperfectum in Matthaeum*, hom. 16, ch. 33, a work attributed to Saint John Chrysostom (*c.* 349–407), Archbishop of Constantinople and Early Church Father, although it is part of *pseudo-Chrysostomus*: '*Clavis est scientia scripturarum, per quam asperitur janua veritatis*: the key is the knowledge of the scriptures, whereby is opened the gate of the truth.' Harding argued for a larger understanding of keys: 'The holy fathers, for good considerations grounded upon scripture, have divided the keys into the key of order and

interpretation of the law:[15] and with Eusebius, we call them the word of God.

Moreover, that Christ's disciples did receive this authority, not that they should hear the private confessions of the people, and listen to their whisperings, as the common Massing priests do everywhere nowadays, and do it so, as though in that one point lay all the virtue and use of the keys: but to the end they should go, they should teach, they should publish abroad the Gospel, and be unto the believing a sweet savour of life unto life, and unto the unbelieving and unfaithful, a savour of death unto death;[16] and that the minds of godly persons being brought low by the remorse of their former life and errors, after they once began to look up unto the light of the Gospel, and believe in Christ, might be opened with the word of God, even as a door is opened with a key. Contrariwise, that the wicked and wilful folk, and such as would not believe nor return into the right way, should be left still as fast locked and shut up, and as St Paul saith, wax worse and worse.[17] This take we to be the meaning of the keys; and that after this fashion men's consciences either be opened or shut. We say that the priest indeed is Judge in this case, but yet hath no manner of right to challenge an authority or power, as saith Ambrose.[18]

---

the key of jurisdiction. [...] Verily [these keys] be not only the knowledge of the scriptures, nor the interpretation of the law, nor the word of God, [...] but also miracles and plagues and all other things which prepare the will or understanding of man, whereby he may receive the benefit of those most principal keys that now we speak of.' Jewel dismissed his explanation as 'vanities' and asked: 'when the priest hath nothing else but a pretty little key, or no key at all, what authority he hath either to open or to shut.' *Works*, III, 363–65.

[15] Jewel quotes Tertullian, *Adversus Marcionem*, Book IV, sec. 27: '*Quam clavem habebant legis doctores, nisi interpretationem legis?* What key had the doctors of the law, saving the exposition of the law?' *Works*, III, 364.

[16] II Corinthians 2.16: 'To the one *we are* the savour of death, unto death, and to the other the savour of life, unto life: and who is sufficient for these things?'

[17] **Marg.** 2 Tim. iii. [II Timothy 3.13: 'But the evill men and deceivers shall waxe worse and worse, deceiving, and being deceived.']

[18] **Marg.** De Pœnit. Dist 1. Cap. Verb. Dei. [Harding and Jewel conduct a lengthy debate about confession and the remission of sins (*Works*, III, 366–80). Arguing in favour of auricular or private confession, Harding states that 'sins cannot duly be remitted or retained, unless they be known to him that hath authority thereto' (p. 367). Seeing no mention of 'secret confessions in the ancient fathers,' Jewel maintains that 'the priest may be a judge over sin, notwithstanding he never hear private confessions, nor have particular knowledge

AN APOLOGY OR ANSWER IN DEFENCE OF THE CHURCH

And therefore our Saviour Jesu Christ to reprove the negligence of the Scribes and Pharisees in teaching, did with these words rebuke them saying: Woe unto you Scribes and Pharisees, which have taken away the keys of knowledge, and have shut up the kingdom of heaven before men.[19] Seeing then the key whereby the way and entry to the kingdom of God is opened unto us, is the word of the Gospel and the expounding of the Law and Scriptures, we say plainly, where the same word is not, there is not the key. And seeing one manner of word is given to all, and one only key belongeth to all, we say there is but one only power of all ministers, as concerning opening and shutting. And as touching the Bishop of Rome, for all his Parasites flatteringly sing in his ears those words in his ears, To thee will I give the keys of the kingdom of heaven, (as though those keys were fit for him alone, and for nobody else) except he go so to work as men's consciences may be made pliant, and be subdued to the Word of God, we deny that he doth either open or shut, or hath the keys at all.[20] And although he taught and instructed the people (as would to God he might once truly do, and persuade himself it were at the least some piece of his duty) yet we think his key to be never a whit better or of greater force than other men's. For who

---

of every several sin' (p. 374). Placing authority in the word of God, he quotes Ambrose, *De poenitentia*, dist. 1, can. 51, col. 1686: '*Verbum Dei dimittit peccata. Sacerdos est judex. Sacerdos quidem officium suum exhibit; sed nullius potestatis jura exercet*. The word of God forgiveth sins. The priest is the judge. The priest executeth his office; but he exerciseth the right of no power' (p. 379). Harding extends the quotation from Ambrose: 'he meaneth that a priest exerciseth not the right of any his own proper power in remitting sins. [...] He avoucheth that he which receiveth the Holy Ghost (whom priests receive when they be consecrated in the sacrament of order) receiveth also power to loose and bind sins' (p. 379).]

[19] **Marg.** Luke xi. [Luke 11.52: 'Woe *be* to you, Lawyers: for ye have taken away the key of knowledge: ye entred not in your selves, and them that came in, ye forbade.']; Matt. xxiii. [Matthew 23.13: 'Woe therefore *be* unto you, Scribes and Pharisees, hypocrites, because ye shut up the kingdome of heaven before men: for ye your selves goe not in, neither suffer ye them that would enter, to come in.']

[20] **Marg.** Matt. xvi. [Matthew 16.19: 'And I will give unto thee the keyes of the Kingdom of heaven, and whatsoever thou shalt bind upon earth, shall be bound in heaven: and whatsoever thou shalt loose on earth, shall be loosed in heaven.'] **L**

hath severed him from the rest? Who hath taught him more cunningly to open, or better to absolve than his brethren?

We say that matrimony is holy and honourable in all sorts and states of persons, in the patriarchs, in the prophets, in the apostles, in holy martyrs, in the ministers of the Church, and in Bishops, and that it is an honest and lawful thing (as Chrysostom saith) for a man living in matrimony, to take upon him therewith the dignity of a Bishop.[21] And as Sozomenus saith of Spiridion;[22] and as Nazianzen saith of his own father,[23] that a good and diligent Bishop doth serve in the ministry never the worse for that he is

---

[21] **Marg.** Chrysost. In Epist. ad Tit. Hom 2. [John Chrysostom, *Epistolam ad Titum*, hom. II, ch. 1. Chrysostom explains Paul's directive to Titus about ordaining elders: 'To stop the mouths of those heretics, who condemned marriage, showing that it is not an unholy thing in itself, but so far honorable, that a married man might ascend the holy throne; and at the same reproving the wanton, and not permitting their admission into this high office who contracted a second marriage.' Harding and Jewel debate the place and sanctity of marriage. For Harding, 'Chrysostom, well considered, disproveth no part of the catholic doctrine in this behalf, but condemneth both the doctrine and common practice of his companions, these new fleshly gospellers.' Jewel quotes Augustine that 'marriage is not an evil or unlawful thing, but only a burdenous and a grievous thing.' Citing the married state of Tertullian and Gregory of Nyssa, among others, Jewel maintains that 'the clergy of England were never bound to such vow of chastity' and asks 'how is it then that the same priests nevertheless continued still in lawful matrimony for the space of more than a thousand years together after Christ, and that without reproof, and without offence of the church of God?' *Nicene and Post-Nicene Fathers*, XIII, 801. *Works*, III, 386–87, 389, 395.]

[22] Harding quotes and translates the Greek statement by Sozomen (*c.* 400–450), historian of the early church, about Spyridion, Bishop of Trimythun in Cyprus: 'Spiridion was a husbandman, having wife and children, and yet for all that he was never the worse about God's service.' (*Ecclesiastical History*, Book I, ch. 11). Harding asks, 'But how and whereof gather ye that he served God the better, and was more able to do good, because of his marriage?' Jewel observes: 'The whole difference that is between M. Harding and us touching this matter standeth only in these two poor words "rather the better" and "never the worse."' *Works*, III, 412–13.

[23] **Marg.** Nazian. in Monod. De Basil. [Gregory of Nazianzus (*c.* 329–390), Cappadocian Father, Trinitarian theologian, and philosopher, *Oratio XVIII, Funebris in patrem, praesente Basilio*, 18: 'But she who was given by God to my father became not only, as is less wonderful, his assistant, but even his leader, drawing him on by her influence in deed and word to the highest excellence; judging it best in all other respects to be overruled by her husband according to the law of marriage, but not being ashamed, in regard of piety, even to offer herself as his teacher.' *Nicene and Post-Nicene Fathers*, VII, 257.]

married, but rather the better, and with more ableness to do good.[24] Further we say, that the same law which by constraint taketh away this liberty from men, and compelleth them against their wills to live single, is the doctrine of devils, as Paul saith: and that ever since the time of this law, a wonderful uncleanness of life and manners in God's ministers, and sundry horrible enormities have followed, as the Bishop of Augusta, as Faber, as Abbas Panormitanus, as Latomus, as the Tripartite work, which is annexed to the second Tome of the Councils, and other champions of the Pope's band, yea and as the matter itself and all histories do confess.[25] For it was rightly said by Pius the Second a Bishop of Rome, that he saw many causes why wives should be taken away from priests, but that he saw many more, and more weighty causes why they ought to be restored them again.[26]

---

[24] **Marg.** Theophyl. ad. Tit. 10. [Jewel underscores the value of Nazianzen's wife during his conversion and throughout his episcopacy. 'Thus we see her light and ability grew more and more and increased daily.' Jewel argues that by her means Nazianzen 'was the better able to do his office.' *Works*, III, 414.]

[25] **Marg.** 1 Tim. iv. [I Timothy 4.1–3: 'Now the Spirit speaketh evidently, that in the latter times some shall depart from the faith, and shall give heed unto spirits of errour, and doctrines of devils, Which speak lyes through hypocrisy, and have their consciences burned with an hote yron, Forbidding to marry, *and commanding* to abstain from meates which God hath created to be received with giving thanks of them which beleeve and know the trueth.' All of these authorities wrote in favour of priests' marriage: Huldericus, Bishop of Augusta (fl. 860) known for his letter to Pope Nicholas opposing clerical celibacy, *Epistola de cleri cælibatu*; Jacobus Faber or Jacques Lefèvre (*c*. 1455–1536), theologian, whose French New Testament stressed the rule of scripture and justification by faith; Panormitanus or Nicolo de Tudeschi (1386–1445), Benedictine abbot and canonist allied with antipope Felix V and upheld the superiority of the council over the pope; Jacobus Latonus or Jacques Masson (*c*. 1475–1544), Flemish theologian, who criticized Luther and interrogated the imprisoned William Tyndale. Jewel quotes *Opus Tripartitum*, joined with the Council of Lateran (Book III, ch. 7, *Concilia*, II, 1002): '*Tantum immunditia luxuriæ notoria est in multis partibus mundi, non solum in clericis, sed etiam in sacerdotibus, imo, quod horribile est audire, in prælatis majoribus.* Such notorious filthiness of lechery there is in many parts of the world, not only in the inferior clerks, but also in priests, yea, and in the greater prelates too: which thing is horrible to be heard.' *Works*, III, 426.]

[26] **Marg.** Platin. in Vita Pii Secundi. [Bartolomeo Platina (1421–1481), prefect of the Vatican library, reported on the papacy of Pius II in *De vitis ac gestis summorum pontificum*: '*Sacerdotibus magna ratione sublatas nuptias, maiori restituendas videri.*' (p. 295.) Harding translated and commented: 'Marriage was taken from priests with great reason, and that it seemed it were to be restored

We receive and embrace all the Canonical Scriptures, both of the Old and New Testament, giving thanks to our God, who hath raised up unto us that light which we might ever have before our eyes, lest either by the subtlety of man, or by the snares of the Devil we should be carried away to errors and lies. Also that these be the heavenly voices, whereby God hath opened unto us his will, and that only in them man's heart can have settled rest; that in them be abundantly and fully comprehended all things whatsoever be needful for our salvation, as Origen, Augustine, Chrysostom, and Cyrillus have taught: that they be the very might and strength of God to attain to salvation: that they be the foundations of the Prophets and Apostles, whereupon is built the Church of God: that they be the very sure and infallible rule, whereby may be tried whether the Church doth stagger or err, and whereunto all ecclesiastical Doctrine ought to be called to account: and that against these Scriptures neither law nor ordinance, nor any custom ought to be heard, no though Paul his own self or an Angel from heaven should come and teach the contrary.[27]

Moreover, we allow the Sacraments of the Church, that is to say certain holy signs and ceremonies which Christ would we should use, that by them He might set before our eyes the mysteries of our salvation, and might more strongly confirm our faith which we have in his blood, and might seal his grace in our hearts. And those Sacraments together with Tertullian, Origen, Ambrose, Augustine, Hierom, Chrysostom, Basil, Dionysius, and other Catholic fathers do we call figures, signs, marks or badges, prints, copies, forms, seals, signets, similitudes, patterns,

---

again with greater. [...] Not that wives were taken away from priests, neither that wives ought to be restored to priests again. It speaketh only of marriage, which, as before a man enter into holy orders, no vow being made, is lawful; so by orders taken, a vow of chastity being solemnly made, is utterly unlawful.' Jewel responded: 'whereas ye would seem not utterly to condemn the state of matrimony, "but only to set single life before it, as a better thing before a good;" it may please you to understand that, notwithstanding a thing in itself be best, yet is it not therefore universally best for every man.' *Works*, III, 419, 421. Pius II (1405–1464), known as Aeneas Silvius, was a poet, novelist, and playwright; in his *Commentaries*, an early form of autobiography, he admitted to and rejected his earlier immoral conduct.]

[27] Galatians 1.8: 'But thogh that we, or an Angel from heaven preache unto you otherwise, than that which we have preached unto you, let him be accursed.'

representations, remembrances, and memories. And we make no doubt together with the same Doctors to say, that those be certain visible words, seals of righteousness, tokens of grace: and do expressly pronounce, that in the Lord's supper, there is truly given unto the believing, the body and blood of the Lord, the flesh of the Son of God, which quickeneth our souls, the meat that cometh from above, the food of immortality, grace, truth, and life. And the supper to be the communion of the body and blood of Christ, by the partaking whereof we be revived, we be strengthened, and be fed unto immortality, and whereby we are joined, united, and incorporate unto Christ, that we may abide in him, and he in us.

Besides we acknowledge there be two sacraments, which we judge, properly ought to be called by this name, that is to say Baptism and the sacrament of thanksgiving. For thus many we see were delivered and sanctified by Christ, and well allowed of the old fathers Ambrose and Augustine. We say that Baptism is a sacrament of the remission of sins, and of that washing, which we have in the blood of Christ, and that no person which will profess Christ's name, ought to be restrained or kept back therefrom; no not the very babes of Christians, forsomuch as they be born in sin, and do pertain unto the people of God. We say that Eucharistia, the supper of the Lord, is a sacrament, that is to wit, an evident token of the body and blood of Christ: wherein is set as it were before our eyes, the death of Christ and his resurrection, and what act soever he did whilst he was in his mortal body, to the end we may give him thanks for his death, and for our deliverance. And that by the often receiving of this sacrament, we may daily renew the remembrance of that matter, to the intent we being fed with the body and blood of Christ, may be brought into the hope of the resurrection and of everlasting life, and may most assuredly believe, that the body and blood of Christ doth in like manner feed our souls, as bread and wine doth feed our bodies. To this banquet we think the people of God ought to be earnestly bidden, that they may all communicate among themselves, and openly declare and testify both the godly society which is among them, and also the hope which they have in Christ Jesu. For this cause if there had been any which would be but a looker on, and abstain from the holy Communion, him did the old fathers and Bishops of Rome in the primitive Church, before Private mass came up, excommunicate as a wicked person and as a Pagan.[28] Neither was there any Christian at that time which did communicate alone whiles other looked on.[29] For so did Calixtus in times past decree, that after the consecration was finished, all should communicate, except they had rather stand without the Church doors; because thus (saith he) did the Apostles appoint, and the same the holy Church of Rome keepeth still.[30]

---

[28] **Marg.** Chrysost. ad Ephes. Hom. 3. [Chrysostom, *In epistola ad Ephesios*, Hom. 3: 'For every one, that partakes not of the mysteries, is standing here in shameless effrontery. It is for this reason, that they which are in sins are first of all put forth.' *Nicene and Post-Nicene Fathers*, XIII, 64.]

[29] **Marg.** De Consecr. Dist. 1. cap. Omnes. [Harding explains: 'This banquet being thus set forth, if some devout persons think themselves for good causes unworthy to assay thereof, and to receive that heavenly food sacramentally, finding themselves not so well prepared as St Paul requireth in that behalf, yet for love of it desire to be present and behold that table, and spiritually to taste of that healthful dish. [...] Such are not to be condemned as idle lookers on, nor to be driven out of the church. [...] And not seldom the priest at the mass (which for this respect with unreasonable novelty you term private) where none other were disposed to receive with him sacramentally, but spiritually only, hath received alone the holy things which he hath offered. Neither the decree of Anacletus requireth that all the people present should communicate with the priest at the mass, which thing ye should not have objected to the church, seeing that it is not observed by your own new order in your congregations.' *Works*, III, 472–73.] **L**

[30] **Marg.** Dist. 2. Sæculares. De Cons. Dist. ii. cap. Peracta. [Harding cited the decree of Anacletus, the third Bishop of Rome (79–92), '*Peracta autem consecratione &*, and when the consecration is ended let them all communicate that will not be kept without the church doors. [...] Who seeth not this request of receiving the communion to be referred to the priests, deacons, sub-deacons and other ministers, in solemn feasts, serving the bishop at mass? For in that place Anacletus speaketh never a word expressly of the lay-people.' Jewel addressed the error in Gratian, twelfth-century canonist, who had attributed the saying to Callistus, Bishop of Rome (218–233): 'ye confess that Gratian, your great rabbin, might be deceived' and 'instead of one error hath made two: for indeed, as it is true that these words were never written by Calixtus, so of the other side it is likewise true that they were never written by Anacletus, but were manifestly forged and falsified by others.' Jewel maintained that the words do 'touch' the lay people. He offered his own translation and commented: '"Let them all communicate, unless they will be removed out of the church," he setteth thereto this exposition: *Hoc antiquum est; nam hoc hodie relictum videtur arbitrio cujuslibet*: This was the old manner; for now-a-days it is free for every man to do therein what he will.' Gratian's *Concordia discordantium canonum* (c. 1140), known as the *Decretum*, was an early collection of canon law. *Works*, III, 473, 476.]

AN APOLOGY OR ANSWER IN DEFENCE OF THE CHURCH

Moreover, when the people cometh to the holy communion, the Sacrament ought to be given them in both kinds, for so both Christ hath commanded, and the Apostles in every place have ordained, and all the ancient fathers and Catholic Bishops have followed the same. And whoso doth contrary to this, he (as Gelasius saith) committeth sacrilege.[31] And therefore we say, that our Adversaries at this day, who having violently thrust out and quite forbidden the holy Communion, do without the word of God, without the authority of any ancient Council, without any catholic father, without any example of the primitive Church, yea and without reason also, defend and maintain their private Masses and the mangling of the Sacraments, and do this not only against the plain express commandment and bidding of Christ, but also against all antiquity do wickedly therein, and are very Church robbers.

We affirm that bread and wine are holy and heavenly mysteries of the body and blood of Christ, and that by them Christ himself being the true bread of eternal life, is so presently given unto us, as that by faith we verily receive his body and his blood. Yet say we not this so, as though we thought that the nature of bread and wine is clearly changed and goeth to nothing, as many have dreamed in these later times, which yet could never agree among themselves of this their dream. For that was not Christ's meaning, that the wheaten bread should lay apart his own nature, and receive a certain new divinity, but that he might rather change us, (and to use Theophylact's words) might transform us into his

---

[31] **Marg.** De Cons. Dist. 2. Comperimus. [Gelasius (d. 496), Roman African espistolographer and Pope, in *Corpus juris canonici* (Paris 1624), tom. I, Decretum Gratiani, col. 1918. In answer to Harding's explanation that communion under both kinds was not commanded expressly by Christ (John 6.53) nor ordained by the apostles, Jewel quoted Gelasius about the sacrilege of dividing the mystery that must remain one and identical: '*Aut integra sacramenta percipiant, aut ab integris arceantur; quia divisio unius ejusdemque mysterii sine grandi sacrilegio non potest pervenire*: Either let them receive the whole sacraments (in both kinds), or else let them be driven from the whole.' In the early church only the celebrating priest was obliged to receive from the chalice in the person of the apostles and of the whole church; Gelasius could have been condemning heretical priests who abstained from the cup. In contrast to Jewel's charge of 'only a pieced or a half-communion,' Harding maintained the full presence of Christ under both species. *Works*, III, 478, 481. See Part V, note 50.]

body.³² For what can be said more plainly than that which Ambrose saith: Bread and wine remain still the same they were before, and yet are changed into another thing:³³ or that which Gelasius saith, The substance of the bread, or the nature of the wine, ceaseth not so to be:³⁴ or that which Theodoret saith, After the consecration, the mystical signs do not cast off their own proper nature; for they remain still in their former substance, form, and kind.³⁵ Or that which Augustine saith, That which ye see is the bread and Cup, for so our eyes tell us, but that which your faith requireth to be taught is this, the bread is the body of Christ, and the Cup is his blood.³⁶ Or that which Origen saith: Bread which is sanctified by the Word of God, as touching the

---

³² **Marg.** Johan. cap. vi. [Theophylact of Ohrid (*c.* 1050–1107), Byzantine biblical scholar and exegete, *In Enarratio in evangelium Joannis*, 6. Although Harding charged that the statements of Theophylact, 'an abridger of Chrysostom,' about the Eucharist were occasionally inconsistent, Jewel allowed that 'in this place we alleged his words to good purpose.' Echoing Theophylact, Jewel insisted: 'the substance of the bread remaineth still.' *Works*, III, 491.]

³³ **Marg.** De Sacram. Lib. iv. cap. iv. [Ambrose, *De sacramentis*, IV. 4: '*Panis et vinum sunt quæ errant et in aliud commutantur.*' Bacon translates Ambrose with succinct accuracy.]

³⁴ In his *Sermon Preached at Paul's Cross*, Jewel cited Pope Gelasius (492–496), *Adversus Eutychetem et Nestorium*: '*et tamen esse non desinit substantia vel natura panis et vini [...] permanente tamen.*' *Works*, I, 11, n. 11. In the *Apologia* he connects debates about the nature of God and man, espoused by heretics Eutyches and Nestorius, to the nature of bread and wine. Eutyches (*c.* 380–455), Byzantine monk who preached the doctrine of Monophysitism, that Christ had only one divine nature, was declared a heretic at the Council of Chalcedon, 451. Nestorius, fifth-century Bishop of Constantinople, opposed the Arian stress on Christ's creatureliness by insisting that Christ's human and divine natures were distinct. Refusing to believe that the divine nature could be born of a woman, he was stripped of his position at the Council of Ephesus, 431.

³⁵ **Marg.** In Dialog. 1 & 2. [Theodoret (*c.* 393–458), Bishop of Cyrus and theologian, *Inconfus. dialogis*, II: '*Signa mystica post sanctificationem non recedunt a natura sua; manent enim in priori substantia, et figura, et forma.*' Harding extended Theodoret's proposition: '"Now," saith Theodoretus, "the mystical tokens be understood to be the things which they be made, and are believed and adored as being the things which they are believed to be." [...] so after the mind of Theodoret, they be the body and blood indeed, not bread and wine as before consecration.' *Works*, III, 509, 506.]

³⁶ **Marg.** In Serm. ad Infant. [Augustine, Sermo 272, *Ad infantes, de sacramento*]; De Consecr. Dist. 2. cap. Qui manducat. [*Corpus juris canonici*, Decretum Gratiani, Dist. II. '*Cælestis panis , qui [...] caro Christi est, suo modo vocatur corpus Christi; cum revera sit sacramentum corporis Christi.*' *Works*, III, 508.]

330 material substance thereof, goeth into the belly and is cast out into the privy.³⁷ Or that which Christ himself said, not only after the blessing of the cup, but after he had ministered the communion: I will drink no more of this fruit of the vine.³⁸ It is well known that the fruit of the vine is wine, and not blood.

And in speaking thus, we mean not to abase the Lord's supper, or to teach that it is but a cold ceremony only, and nothing to be wrought therein (as many falsely slander us we teach). For we affirm that Christ doth truly and presently give his own self in his Sacraments; in Baptism, that we may put him on; and in his 340 supper, that we may eat him by faith and spirit, and may have everlasting life by his cross and blood. And we say not this is done slightly and coldly, but effectually and truly. For although we do not touch the body of Christ with teeth and mouth, yet we hold him fast, and eat him by faith, by understanding, and by the spirit. And this is no vain faith which doth comprehend Christ: and that is not received with cold devotion, which is received with understanding, with faith, and with spirit. For Christ himself altogether is so offered and given us in these mysteries, that we may certainly know we be flesh of his flesh, and bone of his bones; 350 and that Christ continueth in us, and we in him. And therefore in celebrating these mysteries, the people are to good purpose exhorted before they come to receive the holy communion, to lift up their hearts, and to direct their minds to heavenward, because he is there, by whom we must be full fed and live.³⁹ Cyril saith,

---

³⁷ **Marg.** Orig. in Matt. Hom. 15. [Origen, *Commentaria in Evangelium Matthaeum* (Commentary on Matthew), 15.17, Book XI, hom. XIV. Harding accused Jewel of 'falsifying' Origen's words: *Ille cibus qui sanctificatur per verbum Dei*. As with this later translation, '*cibus*' is 'meat' and not 'bread'. 'Even the meat which has been sanctified through the Word of God and prayer, in accordance with the fact that it is material, passes into the belly, and going out from it is cast into the draught.' *The Ante-Nicene Fathers*, ed. by Allan Menzies, IX (1896), 443. As for the difference between *cibus* and *panis*, Jewel declared 'we stand only upon the substance of matter, and seek no such wanton advantages by shift of words.' *Works*, III, 515.]

³⁸ **Marg.** Luc. xxii. [Luke 22:18: 'For I say unto you, I will not drinke of the fruit of the vine, untill the kingdom of God be come.'] **L**

³⁹ **Marg.** De consecr. Dist. 1. Quando. [Cf. *Corpus juris canonici*, Decretum Gratiani, Dist. I. Reference here is to the prayer or preface before the consecration, what Jewel calls 'the holy ministration,' when (*quando*) the priest exhorts the people, Harding explains, 'to dispose themselves accordingly, and as it becometh them to pray; for to that end be these words *Sursum corda*, "up

when we come to receive these mysteries, all gross imaginations must quite be banished.⁴⁰ The Council of Nice, as is alleged by some in Greek, plainly forbiddeth us to be basely affectioned, or bent toward the bread and wine which are set before us.⁴¹ And, as Chrysostom very aptly writeth: We say that the body of Christ is the dead carcass, and we ourselves must be the eagles, meaning thereby, that we must fly high if we will come unto the body of Christ. For this table as Chrysostom saith, is a table of Eagles and not of Jays.⁴² Cyprian also, This bread saith he, is the food of the

---

with your hearts" pronounced by the priest.' Harding insists that 'Christ is in heaven, and also here.' Jewel rejoins: 'Where is this ecclesiastical tradition now become? [...] Where doth your people answer the priest at the common prayer? Or where doth the people understand either the meaning of the sacraments, or anything that is pronounced by the priest?' *Works*, III, 533–34. Bacon clearly understands lifting up one's heart and the importance of heaven-directed sight.]

⁴⁰ **Marg.** Ad Object. Theodor. [This reference to the source of the statement on Cyril (Patriarch of Alexandria, 412–444) was abandoned later. Jewel acknowledged the error in the marginal citation 'escaped in the print.' Harding explains Cyril's position on the heretic Nestorius, who maintained that 'in the sacrament we eat flesh and not Godhead. [...] Cyril saith that we eat not a common body, though the nature of Godhead properly be not eaten, but that body which is *proprium Verbi*, the proper body of the Word, which quickeneth all things, by receiving whereof we receive whole Christ, God and man.' *Works*, III, 536–37.]

⁴¹ Cf. Gelasius of Cyzicus (*c.* 475), church historian, *Historia concilii Nicaeni*, II. 30, 7. In his initial answer (1563) to the *Apologia*, Harding quoted the decree in Greek of the Council of Nice referred to here: 'lifting up our mind and spirit, we behold by faith on that holy table and laid (so for the better signification of the real presence their term soundeth) the Lamb of God that taketh away the sins of the world. And here, say they, we receive his precious body and blood αληθως, that is to say, verily and indeed.' Jewel rejoined both in the *Controversy with M. Harding* and later in *The Defence* that 'we may receive the body of Christ indeed and verily, without either transubstantiation or real presence.' *Works*, I, 464; III, 542.

⁴² **Marg.** Chrysost. in 1 Cor. x. [Chrysostom, *In epistolam primam ad Corinthios*, hom. XXIV. Jewel cited Chrysostom: '*Aquilas appellat, ut ostendat ad alta eum oportere contendere, qui ad hoc corpus accredit*. He calleth us eagles, to show that he must mount on high and fly aloft whoso will approach near to that body. [...] Thus are the faithful made eagles. Thus is the earth become heaven: not for that Christ's body is pulled down, as M. Harding imagineth, but for that our minds and affections be lifted up.' Harding did not mention pulling down, but rather quoted Chrysostom to the effect that eagles 'must have nothing to do with the earth, neither be drawn downward to base things and creep, but always fly upward and behold the Sun of Righteousness.' Harding commented, 'This spiritual flying up requireth Chrysostom, and yet in that homily, he declareth the body of Christ to be present here in earth (meaning in this holy sacrament).' *Works*, III, 543, 546.]

soul, and not the meat of the belly.⁴³ And Augustine, How shall I hold him, saith he, which is absent? How shall I reach my hand up to heaven, to lay hold upon him that sitteth there? He answereth, Reach hither thy faith, and then thou hast laid hold on him.⁴⁴

370 We cannot also away in our churches with the shows and sales, and buying and selling of Masses, nor the carrying about and worshipping of bread, nor such other idolatrous and blasphemous fondness, which none of them can prove that Christ or His Apostles did ever ordain, or left unto us. And we justly blame the Bishops of Rome, who without the word of God, without the authority of the holy fathers, without any example of antiquity, after a new guise do not only set before the people the sacramental bread to be worshipped as God, but do also carry the same about upon an ambling horse, whithersoever themselves journey,⁴⁵ as in old times the Persians' fire and the relics of the goddess Isis

---

⁴³ **Marg.** De Cœna Domini. [In the *Controversy with M. Harding* Jewel glossed this passage from Cyprian's *On the Lord's Banquet*: '*non dentes ad mordendum acuimus, sed fide sincera panem frangimus.*' We do not sharpen our teeth to bruise, but we break the bread with genuine faith. Editor Ayre comments that 'the exact words are not found in the treatise referred to.' *Works*, I, 141, n. 11.]

⁴⁴ **Marg.** In Johan. Tractat. 50. [Augustine, *In Johannis evangelium tractatus*, 11. 50. 4. Jewel cites Augustine on the Gospel of John: '*Dominus consolatur nos, qui ipsum jam in coelo sedentem manu contrectare non possumus; sed fide contingere (possumus)*. The Lord comforteth us, that cannot now touch him with hand, sitting in heaven; but by faith we may touch him.' Harding noted that Augustine was speaking not of 'receiving Christ in the sacrament but by faith only.' *Works*, III, 547–48.]

⁴⁵ **Marg.** In Lib. de Cærem. Roman. Eccl. [Translator of *An Apology*, Stephen Isaacson draws attention to Jewel's explanation in *The Defence*: 'Al this strange solemne festival guise Pope Urbanus the fourth learned, not of Christe, or Paule, but only by the Revelation of Dame Eva the Anchoresse: and by her good advise founded the newe Feaste of *corpus christi*, and caused the Sacramente to be borne about in Procession.' *An Apology for the Church of England*, trans. by Stephen Isaacson (London: John Hearne, 1825), p. 47. Harding defended the procession 'to the great comfort and help of sundry persons being in distress' by quoting and translating the passage from the *Book of the Ceremonies of the Church*: '*ducitur post hoc equus albus phaleratus, mansuetus et pulcher, cum tininnabulo ad collum bene sonante, qui capsulam vehit cum sacratissimo Christi corpore, supra quod cives nobiles portabunt baldachinum*. Then a white palfrey, trapped, gentle and fair, with a clear sounding bell hanging at his neck, is led, which carrieth the monstrance or pix, with the most holy body of Christ, over the which noble citizens shall bear a canopy.' *Works*, III, 551.]

380 were solemnly carried about in procession, and have brought the sacraments of Christ to be used now as a stage play, and a solemn sight, to the end that men's eyes should be fed with nothing else but with mad gazings and foolish gauds, in the self same matter wherein the death of Christ ought diligently to be beaten into our hearts, and wherein also the mysteries of our redemption ought with all holiness and reverence to be executed.

Besides, where they say and sometime do persuade fools, that they are able by their Masses to distribute and apply unto men's commodity all the merits of Christ's death, yea although many 390 times the parties think nothing of the matter, and understand full little what is done, this is a mockery, a heathenish fancy, and a very toy. For it is our faith that applieth the death and cross of Christ to our benefit, and not the Act of the Massing priest. Faith had in the Sacraments (saith Augustine) doth justify, and not the sacraments.[46] And Origen saith: Christ is the priest, the propitiation, and sacrifice, which propitiation cometh to everyone by means of faith.[47] So that by this reckoning we say, that the sacraments of Christ without faith, do not once profit these that be alive, a great deal less do they profit those that be dead.

400 And as for their brags they are wont to make of their Purgatory, though we know it is not a thing so very late risen amongst them, yet is it no better than a blockish and an old wives' device. Augustine indeed sometime saith, there is such a certain place: sometime he denieth not but there may be such a one; sometime he doubteth; sometime again he utterly denieth it to be, and thinketh that men are therein deceived by a certain natural good will they bear their friends departed.[48] But yet of this one

---

[46] Jewel cites Augustine, *In Joannis evangelium tractatus*, 15. 80. 3: '*Unde est ista tanta virtus aquæ, ut corpus tangat, et cor abluat, nisi faciente verbo? Non quia dicitur, sed quia creditur*. From whence hath the water this great power, that it toucheth the body and washeth the heart, saving by the working of the word. Not for that it is pronounced, but for that it is believed.' *Works*, III, 558–59.

[47] **Marg.** Orig. ad Rom. i. cap. iii. [Origen, *In epistolam ad Romanos*, III. 8. Jewel cites Origen's text: '*ipsum et propitiatorium, et pontificem, et hostiam quæ offertur pro populo, quæ tamen propitiatio ad unumquemque credentiam per viam fidei venit*.' Harding's response dealt with prayers, while Jewel stressed sacraments. *Works*, III, 556.]

[48] **Marg.** August. in Psal. Lxxxv. In Enchir. cap. lxvii. De Civ. Dei xxi. cap. xxvi. Hypog. [Augustine, *In Psalmum LXXXV*, enarr. 17. Jewel cites Augustine's text about the place whence God wishes our souls to be torn out: '*unde voluit Deus*

error hath there grown up such a harvest of these Mass mongers, the Masses being sold abroad commonly in every corner, the Temples of God became shops to get money, and silly souls were persuaded that nothing was more necessary to be bought. Indeed there was nothing more gainful for these men to sell.

As touching the multitude of vain and superfluous ceremonies, we know that Augustine did grievously complain of them in his own time: and therefore have we cut off a great number of them, because we know that men's consciences were cumbered about them, and the Churches of God overladen with them.[49] Nevertheless we keep still and esteem not only those ceremonies which we are sure were delivered us from the Apostles, but some others too besides, which we thought might be suffered without hurt to the church of God, because that we had a desire that all things in the holy congregation might (as Paul commandeth) be done with comeliness and in good order;[50] but as for all those things which we saw were either very superstitious or wholly unprofitable, or noisome, or mockeries, or contrary to the holy Scriptures, or else unseemly for honest or discreet folks, as there be an infinite number nowadays where Papistry is used, these I say we have utterly refused without all manner exception, because we would not have the right worshipping of God any longer defiled with such follies.

We make our prayers in that tongue which all our people, as

---

eruere animas nostras.' Harding declares that 'Augustine affirmeth purgatory, and that it cannot be shewed where he doubteth of it, much less where he utterly denieth any such to be.' Railing at Harding for making 'the house of God a cave of thieves,' Jewel responds by quoting Augustine's *Enchiridion* (ch. 59) about the fire of purgatory as not incredible but 'whether it be so or no, it may be a question, *incredibile non est, et utrum ita sit quæri potest.*' The marginal citation to *Libri Hypognosticon*, a work falsely attributed to Augustine, was deleted from *The Defence. Works*, III, 563–65.]

[49] **Marg.** Ad Jan. Epist. 119. [Augustine, *Ad inquisitiones Januarii*, II. 55 (alias 119). In responding to Harding's statement that Augustine 'speaketh only of the cutting away of such manners and rites as be crept into some one particular country,' Jewel quotes Augustine's concern: '*Hoc nimis doleo, quia multa quæ in divinis libris saluberrime præcepta sunt, minus curantur; et tam multis præsumptionibus sic plena sunt omnia.* This thing grieveth me, that so many things wholesomely commanded in the holy scriptures are not regarded; and all things are full of so many presumptions.' *Works*, III, 569–70.]

[50] 1 Corinthians 14.40: 'Let all things be done honestly, and by order.'

meet is, may understand, to the end they may (as Paul counselleth us)⁵¹ take common commodity by common prayer: even as all the holy fathers and catholic Bishops both in the old and new Testament did use to pray themselves, and taught the people to pray too, lest as Augustine saith, like parrots and ousels° we should seem to speak that we understand not.⁵²

440 Neither have we any other Mediator and Intercessor, by whom we may have access to God the Father, than Jesu Christ, in whose only name all things are obtained at his Father's hand. But it is a shameful part and full of infidelity that we see everywhere used in the Churches of our adversaries, not only in that they will have innumerable sorts of mediators, and that utterly without the authority of God's word. So that, as Jeremy saith, the Saints be now as many in number, or rather above the number of the Cities;⁵³ and poor men cannot tell to which Saint it were best to turn them first. And though there be so many as they cannot be told, yet every one of them hath his peculiar duty and office
450 assigned unto him of these folks, what thing they ought to ask, what to give, and what to bring to pass: but besides this also, in that they do not only wickedly, but also shamelessly call upon the blessed virgin Christ's mother, to have her remember that she is a mother, and to command her son, and to use a mother's authority over him.⁵⁴

---

⁵¹ I Corinthians 14.2: 'For he that speaketh a *strange* tongue, speaketh not unto men, but unto God: for no man heareth *him*: howbeit in the spirit he speaketh secret things.'

⁵² Augustine, *In Psalumum XVIII*, enarr. 2. sec. 1. In his *Reply to M. Harding's Answer*, Jewel quotes Augustine's commentary on Psalm 18: '*Quod hoc sit, intelligere debemus, ut humana ratione, non quasi avium voce, cantemus. Nam et merulæ, et psittaci, et corvi, et picæ, et hujuscemodi volucres, sæpe ab hominibus docentur sonare, quod nesciunt*. We ought to understand what this is, that we may sing with man's reason, not with voice, as birds do. For ousels, popinjays, ravens, pies, and such like birds ofttimes be taught of men to sound they know not what.' *Works*, I, 282–83.

⁵³ **Marg.** Jer. ii. & xi. [Jeremiah 2.28: 'But where are thy gods, that thou hast made thee? let them arise, if they can help thee in the time of thy trouble: for according to the number of thy cities, are thy gods, O Judah'; Jeremiah 11.13: 'For according to the number of thy cities were thy gods, O Judah, and *according* to the number of the streetes of Jerusalem have ye set up altars of confusion, *even* altars to burn incense unto Baal.'

⁵⁴ **Marg.** Bernardus. [In *The Defence* Jewel cites Bonaventure, *Corona Beatae Mariae Virg.* to inveigh against seeing Mary as a 'mediator of salvation.' In *An*

AN APOLOGY OR ANSWER IN DEFENCE OF THE CHURCH

460 We say also, that every person is born in sin, and leadeth his life in sin: that nobody is able truly to say his heart is clean. That the most righteous person is but an unprofitable servant: That the law of God is perfect, and requireth of us perfect and full obedience: That we are able by no means to fulfil that law in this worldly life: That there is no one mortal creature which can be justified by his own deserts in God's sight, and therefore that our only succour and refuge is to fly to the mercy of our Father by Jesu Christ, and assuredly to persuade our minds, that he is the obtainer of forgiveness for our sins. And that by his blood all our spots of sin be washed clean: That He hath pacified and set at one all things by the blood of his Cross: That He by the same one only Sacrifice, which he once offered upon the Cross, hath brought to effect and fulfilled all things, and that for that cause he said when
470 he gave up the Ghost, It is finished, as though he would signify that the price and ransom was now full paid for the sin of all mankind. If there be any, then, that think this Sacrifice not sufficient, let them go in God's name and seek another that is better. We verily, because we know this to be the only sacrifice, are well content with it alone, and look for none other: and forasmuch as it was to be offered but once, we command it not to be renewed again. And because it was full and perfect in all points and parts, we do not ordain in place thereof any continual succession of offerings.
480 Besides, though we say we have no meed° at all by our own works and deeds, but appoint all the means of our salvation to be in Christ alone, yet say we not that for this cause men ought to live loosely and dissolutely: nor that it is enough for a Christian to be Baptised only and to believe, as though there were nothing else required at his hand, for true faith is lively, and can in no wise be idle. Thus therefore teach we the people, that God hath called us not to follow riot and wantonness, but as Paul saith, unto good works, to walk in them.[55] That God hath plucked us out from the

---

Exposition upon the Two Epistles of St Paul to the Thessalonians Jewel quotes from the Bonaventure text 'full of horrible blasphemy': '*In te, virgo Maria, confidimus, in te speramus, nos defendas in æternum.* Our trust and hope we put in thee O virgin Mary, defend us everlastingly.' *Works*, III, 573; II, 899.]

[55] **Marg.** Eph. ii. [Ephesians 2.10: 'For we are his workmanship created in Christ Jesus unto good works, which God hath ordained, that we should walk in them.'] L

power of darkness, to the end that we should serve the living God,⁵⁶, to cut away all the remnants of sin, and to work our salvation in fear and trembling: that it may appear how that the Spirit of sanctification is in our bodies, and that Christ Himself doth dwell in our hearts.⁵⁷

To conclude, we believe, that this our self same flesh wherein we live, although it die and come to dust, yet at the last day it shall return again to life by the means of Christ's spirit which dwelleth in us, and that then verily, whatsoever we suffer here in the mean while for his sake, Christ will wipe away from our eyes all tears and lamentation, and that we through him shall enjoy everlasting life, and shall for ever be with him in glory. So be it.⁵⁸

---

⁵⁶ **Marg.** Col. i. [I Colossians 1.13: 'Who hath delivered us from the power of darkness, and hath translated us into the kingdom of his dear Son.'] **L**

⁵⁷ **Marg.** Eph. iii. [Ephesians 3.17: 'That Christ may dwell in your hearts by faith.'] **L**

⁵⁸ **Marg.** Apoc. vii. xii. [Revelation 7.12: 'Saying, Amen, Praise and glory, and wisdom, and thanks, and honor, and power, and might, *be* unto our God for evermore, Amen.'] **L**

PART III

Behold these are the horrible heresies for the which a good part of the world is at this day condemned by the Bishop of Rome, and yet were never heard to plead their cause. He should have commenced his suit rather against Christ, against the Apostles, and against the holy fathers. For these things did not only proceed from them, but were also appointed by them: except perhaps these men will say (as I think they will indeed) that Christ hath not instituted the holy Communion to be divided amongst the faithful: Or that Christ's Apostles and the ancient fathers said Private masses in every corner of the Temples, now ten, now twenty together in one day: Or that Christ and his Apostles banished all the common people from the Sacrament of his blood: Or that the thing which themselves do at this day everywhere, and do it so as they condemn him for a heretic which doth otherwise, is not called of Gelasius their own doctor plain sacrilege: Or that these be not the very words of Ambrose, Augustine, Gelasius, Theodoret, Chrysostom, and Origen, The bread and wine in the Sacraments remain still the same they were before, The thing which is seen upon the holy table is bread, There ceaseth not to be still the substance of bread and nature of wine, The substance and nature of bread are not changed, The self same bread as touching the material substance, goeth into the belly, and is cast out into the privy:[1] Or that Christ, the Apostles, and holy fathers prayed not in that tongue which the people might understand: Or that Christ hath not performed all things by that one offering which He once offered: or that the same sacrifice was imperfect, and so now we have need of another. All these things must they of necessity say, unless perchance they had rather say thus, that all law and right is locked up in the treasury of the Pope's breast, and that as once one of his soothing pages and clawbacks° did not stick to say, the Pope is able to dispense against the Apostles, against a council, and against the canons and rules of the Apostles, and that he is not bound to stand neither to the examples, nor to the ordinances, nor to the laws of Christ.[2] We

---

[1] See notes 35, 40, and 41 in Part II.

[2] **Marg.** Dist. 36. Lector, in Gloss; Dist. 82. ca. Presbyter. [As Jewel clarifies in *The Defence of The Apology*, 'the pope may dispense against the law of God

for our part have learned these things of Christ, of the Apostles, of the devout fathers, and do sincerely and with good faith teach the people of God the same. Which thing is the only cause why we at this day are called heretics of the chief prelates (no doubt) of Religion. O immortal God, hath Christ himself then, the Apostles and so many fathers, all at once gone astray? Were then Origen, Ambrose, Augustine, Chrysostom, Gelasius, Theodoret, forsakers of the catholic faith? Was so notable a consent of so many ancient Bishops and learned men nothing else, but a conspiracy of heretics? Or is that now condemned in us, which was then commended in them? Or is the thing now by alteration only of men's affection suddenly become schismatic, which in them was counted catholic? Or shall that which in times past was true, now by and by, because it liketh not these men, be judged false? Let them then bring forth another Gospel, and let them show the causes why these things which so long have openly been observed, and well allowed in the Church of God, ought now in the end be called in again. We know well enough, that the same word which was opened by Christ, and spread abroad by the Apostles is sufficient, both our salvation and all truth to uphold and maintain; and also to confound all manner of heresy. By that Word only do we condemn all sorts of the old heretics, whom these men say we have called out of hell again. As for the Arians, the Eutychians, the Marcionites, the Ebionites, the Valentinians, the Carpocratians, the Tatians, the Novatians,³ and shortly all them which have a wicked opinion either of God the Father, or of Christ, or of the holy Ghost, or of any other point of Christian Religion, forsomuch as they be confuted by the Gospel of Christ, we plainly pronounce them for detestable and castaway persons, and defy them even unto the Devil. Neither do we leave them so, but we also severely and straitly hold them in by lawful and politic punishments, if they fortune to break out anywhere, and bewray° themselves.

(*Papa potest dispensare contra jus divinum*)' and 'the pope may dispense against the apostles (*Papa potest dispensare contra apostolorum*).' Decret. Gratian. Decr. Sec. Pars, Quæst. i and Decret. Prim. Pars, Dist. xxxiv. *Works*, III, 218.]
³ Although these early heretics recognized the four gospels, they added their own dualist or peculiar tenets.

Indeed we grant that certain new and very strange sects, as the Anabaptists,[4] Libertines,[5] Menonians,[6] and Zwenckfeldians[7] have been stirring in the world ever since the Gospel did first spring. But the world seeth now right well, thanks be given to our God, that we neither have bred, nor taught, nor kept up these Monsters. In good fellowship I pray thee whosoever thou be, read our books, they are to be sold in every place. What hath there ever been written by any of our company, which might plainly bear with the madness of any of those heretics? Nay I say unto you, there is no country at this day so free from their pestilent infections, as they be wherein the gospel is freely and commonly taught. So that if they weigh the very matter with earnest and upright advisement, this thing is a great argument, that this same is the very truth of the Gospel which we do teach. For lightly neither is cockle° wont to grow without the wheat, nor yet the chaff without the corn. For from the very Apostles' times, who knoweth not how many heresies did rise up even together, so soon as the Gospel was first spread abroad? Who ever had heard tell of Simon, Menander, Saturninus, Basilides, Carpocrates, Cherinthus, Ebion, Valentinus, Secundus, Marcosius, Colorbasius, Heracleo, Lucianus, and Severus,[8] before the Apostles were sent abroad? But why stand we reckoning up these? Epiphanius rehearseth up fourscore sundry heresies, and Augustine many more, which sprang up even together with the Gospel. What then? Was the Gospel therefore not the Gospel, because heresies sprang up withal? Or was Christ therefore not Christ? And yet as we said, doth not this great crop and heap of heresies grow up amongst us, which do openly abroad and frankly teach the Gospel? These poisons take their beginnings, their increasings, and strength amongst our Adversaries, in blindness and in darkness, amongst

---

[4] Anabaptists, radical and persecuted reformers of the sixteenth century, rejected infant in favour of adult baptism and demanded a strictly holy life.
[5] Libertines, a sixteenth-century Flemish sect of Antinomians, also known as Spirituals, maintained that no action is evil and that by uniting with God through contemplation, one is free to act according to pleasure.
[6] Menonians (Mennonites) were a pacifist Anabaptist denomination following Menno Simons (1496–1561).
[7] Schwenckfeldians, followers of Caspar Schwenckfeld von Ossig (1489–1561), concentrated on an inner religion, depreciated external worship, and denied the presence of Christ in the Eucharist.
[8] This is a catalogue of heretics in the early church.

whom truth is with tyranny and cruelty kept under, and cannot be heard but in corners and secret meetings. But let them make a proof, let them give the Gospel free passage, let the truth of Jesu Christ give his clear light and stretch forth his bright beams into all parts, and then shall they forthwith see how all these shadows straight will vanish and pass away at the light of the Gospel, even as the thick mist of the night consumeth at the sight of the sun. For whilst these men sit still and make merry, and do nothing, we continually repress and put back all those heresies which they falsely charge us to nourish and maintain.

Where they say, that we have fallen into sundry sects, and would be called some of us Lutherans, some of us Zwinglians, and cannot yet well agree among ourselves touching the whole substance of doctrine, what would these men have said, if they had been in the first times of the Apostles and holy fathers, when one said: I hold of Paul, another I hold of Cephas, another I hold of Apollo,[9] when Paul did so sharply rebuke Peter;[10] when upon a falling out Barnabas departed from Paul;[11] when as Origen mentioneth, the Christians were divided into so many factions, as that they kept no more but the name of Christians in common among them, being in no manner of thing else like unto Christians, when as Socrates saith, for their dissensions and sundry sects they were laughed and jested at openly of the people in the common gameplays;[12] when, as Constantine the Emperor affirmeth, there were such a number of variances and brawlings in the church, that it might justly seem a misery far passing all the former miseries? When also Theophilus,[13]

---

[9] I Corinthians 1.12: 'Now this I say, that every one of you saith, I am Pauls, and I am Apollos, and I am Cephas, and I am Christs.'
[10] Galatians 2.11: 'And when Peter was come to Antiochia, I withstood him to his face: for he was to be condemned.'
[11] Acts 15.39: 'Then came they, and prayed them, and brought them out, and desired them to depart out of the citie.'
[12] Socrates (*c.* 380–439) 'Scholasticus', a contemporary of Sozomen and Theodoret and church historian, *Ecclesiastical History*, I. 6: 'To so disgraceful an extent was this affair carried, that Christianity became a subject of popular ridicule, even in the very theatres.' Game-play is a stage-play. *Nicene and Post-Nicene Fathers*, Series II, II (1890), 5.
[13] Both patriarchs, Theophilus of Antioch (*c.* 169–183) and Theophilus of Alexandria (d. 412) were defenders of Christianity. Theophilus of Alexandria destroyed the Serapeum, the Ptolemaic temple devoted to the Egyptian god Serapis.

AN APOLOGY OR ANSWER IN DEFENCE OF THE CHURCH

Epiphanius,[14] Chrysostom, Augustine, Ruffine, Hierom, being all Christians, being all fathers, being all catholics, did strive one against another, with most bitter and remediless contentions without end? When, as saith Nazianzen, the parts of one body were consumed and wasted one of another? When the East part was divided from the West, only for leavened bread and only for keeping of Easter day, which were indeed no great matters to be strived for? And when in all Councils new Creeds and new decrees continually were devised? What would these men (trow ye) have said in those days? Which side would they specially then have taken, and which would they then have forsaken? Which Gospel would they have believed? Whom would they have accounted for heretics, and whom for Catholics? And yet what a stir and revel keep they at this time upon two poor names only of Luther and Zwinglius, because these two men do not yet fully agree upon some one point, therefore would they needs have us think that both of them were deceived, that neither of them had the Gospel, and that neither of them taught the truth aright. But good God, what manner of fellows be these, which blame us for disagreeing, and do all they themselves, ween° you, agree well together? Is every one of them fully resolved what to follow? Hath there been no strifes, no debates, no quarrels amongst them at no time? Why then do the Scotists and Thomists[15] about that they call MERITUM CONGRUI and MERITUM CONDIGNI,[16]

---

[14] Epiphanius (*c*. 310–403), Bishop of Salamis, Church Father, and strong defender of orthodoxy.

[15] Franciscan John Duns Scotus (*c*. 1266–1308) and Domincan Thomas Aquinas (1225–1274) were the foremost Scholastic theologians of the Middle Ages. Scotus defended the absolute freedom of the will as independent of understanding, rejected Aquinas's ontological proof of God's existence, and defended the Immaculate Conception (the view that Mary was conceived without original sin). Aquinas distinguished reason and revelation and upheld the position that words applied to God and to creatures have different meanings. See Alexander W. Hall, *Thomas Aquinas and John Duns Scotus: Natural Theology in the High Middle Ages* (London: Continuum, 2009).

[16] Luther rejected any notion of merit as the basis of man's relation to God, seeing both concepts as potentially heretical. 'What a sinful man did for himself, insofar as he was able, was defined as merit of fitness or congruity (*meritum congrui* or *meritum de congruo*); what a just man, enabled by divine grace, did for himself or others, was defined as merit of worthiness or condignity (*meritum condigni* or *meritum de condigno*).' Jaroslav Pelikan, *The Christian Tradition: Reformation of Church and Dogma*, 5 vols (Chicago: University of Chicago Press, 1971–1989), IV (1983), 146.

no better agree together? Why agree they no better among themselves concerning original sin in the blessed virgin: concerning a solemn vow, and a single vow? Why say the Canonists that auricular confession is appointed by the positive law of man, and the Schoolmen contrariwise, that it is appointed by the law of God? Why doth Albertus Pius dissent from Cajetanus?[17] Why doth Thomas dissent from Lombardus,[18] Scotus from Thomas, Occamus[19] from Scotus, Alliacensis[20] from Occamus: And why do the Nominalists disagree from the Realists?[21] And yet say I

---

[17] Albert Pighius (c. 1490–1542), Dutch theologian and mathematician, and Thomas Cajetan (1469–1534), Italian theologian and cardinal, differed somewhat on the matter of infallibility. Opponent of Luther and Calvin, Pighius maintained that although councils without the authority of the Pope have frequently erred, the Pope himself has never erred (*De hierarchi*, Book 6). Cajetan championed the papal superiority of the see of Rome and the infallibility of the Pope's decrees in matters of faith (*Tractatus de comparatione auctoritatis Papae et Consilii*).

[18] Peter Lombard (c. 1095–1160), French scholastic theologian, whose *Four Books of Sentences* was a standard digest of evidence for the existence of God, the doctrine of angels, Christology, and the sacraments. Aquinas's *Commentary on the Sentences* (1252–1256) was a platform for his later *Summa Theologica*.

[19] William of Occam (c. 1287–1347), English Franciscan, who held that through faith alone can one understand theological truth; as a nominalist he believed that only individuals exist rather than universals. Instead of defining what he believed, it was enough for him that probability stood in all cases on the side of faith and revelation. Through his nullification of the efforts of classical scholasticism, little of the rational understanding of faith attempted by Aquinas was left after Occam. Etienne Gilson, *History of Christian Philosophy in the Middle Ages* (New York: Random House, 1955), p. 498. Alister McGrath questions the usefulness of the term 'nominalism', preferring instead 'realistic conceptualism'. Occam did not regard universals as 'figments of an overactive human imagination', but he did not recognize their '*independent* reality'. Alister McGrath, *The Intellectual Origins of the European Reformation* (Oxford: Basil Blackwell, 1987), p. 71.

[20] Aliacensis, Pierre d'Ailly (1351–1420), French theologian, cardinal, and proponent of Conciliarism, a view that the General Council is superior to the Pope. He was influential in healing the Western Schism (1378–1417), during which rival popes claimed authority, through his actions at the Council of Pisa (1409) and the Council of Constantinople (1414–1418), at which the rival popes abdicated.

[21] Building on Plato's theory of forms, Realists held that all entities are either particular or universal; there was a parallelism between being in nature and being in thought. Nominalists, by contrast, rejected Platonic realism and held that general ideas were only names; they believed only in physical particulars in space

nothing of so many diversities of friars and monks, how some of them put a great holiness in eating of fish, and some in eating of herbs; some in wearing of Shoes, and some in wearing of Sandals; some in going in a linen garment, and some in a woollen; some of them called white, some black; some being shaven broad, and some narrow; some stalking abroad upon pattens,° some barefooted; some girt, and some ungirt. They ought, I wiss,° to remember how there be some of their own company which say, that the body of Christ is in his supper naturally: Contrary other some of the self same company deny it to be so: Again that there be other of them which say, the body of Christ in the holy communion is rent and torn with our teeth, and some again that deny the same.[22] Some also of them there be, which write that the body of Christ is QUANTUM IN EUCHARISTIA, that is to say, hath his perfect quantity in the Sacrament; some other again say nay. That there be others of them which say, Christ did consecrate with a certain divine power, some that he did the same with his blessing, some again that say he did it with uttering five solemn chosen words, and some with rehearsing the same words afterward

---

and time. Disciples of Occam were nominalists or moderns, while Thomists and Scotists were realists, partisans of the ancient way. Gilson, p. 499.

[22] **Marg.** Steph. Gardiner in Diab. Soph. [Stephen Gardiner (*c.* 1483–1555), Bishop of Winchester, was Archbishop Cranmer's assistant. Gardiner defended the corporal presence in the Eucharist, against Cranmer's view of the spiritual presence. In the 1542 clerical debate about retaining the Great Bible in English, Gardiner argued for retaining a list of Latin words for their 'germane and native meaning'; among the words he catalogued were *sacrificium* and *communio*. David Norton, *A History of the Bible as Literature* (Cambridge: Cambridge University Press, 2000), p. 35. Although he worked to secure Henry's primacy as Head of the Church of England, Gardiner remained a strong champion of the Eucharist; his opposition to Edwardian policies landed him in the Tower for five years, but with Mary's accession he was restored to his bishopric and named Lord Chancellor. In *A Detection of the devils sophistrie* (1546), he defended 'the presence of Christes natural bodie and bloud in the most blessed sacrament of the aulter, in consecration of this most holy Sacrament by the common minister of the church. *This is my body.* But againste this truth the devyll striveth, and fyghteth by his ministers, and lewde apostels with sophistical devyses, wherewith he troubleth the grosse imaginacions of the simple people. [...] The devyll easely entangleth and byndeth fast to him with carnall reasons, deceitfull expositions, and counterfet contradictions, and therby leadeth them away, captive and thralde, from the true catholique byleefe in this moost holye sacramente.' (*A Detection of the devils sophistrie* (London: [n. pub.], 1546) fol. 5^{r-v}).]

again.²³ Some will have it that when Christ did speak those five words, the material wheaten bread was pointed by this demonstrative Pronoun HOC: Some had rather have that a certain VAGUM INDIVIDUUM, as they term it, was meant thereby.²⁴ Again, others there be that say, dogs and mice may truly and in very deed eat the body of Christ; and others again there be that steadfastly deny it.²⁵ There be others which say, that the very accidents of bread and wine may nourish: others again there be which say, how that the substance of bread doth return again. What need I say more? It were overlong and tedious to reckon up all things, so very uncertain and full of controversies is yet the whole form of these men's religion and doctrine, even amongst themselves, from whence it did first spring and begin. For hardly at any time do they well agree between themselves, except it be peradventure as in times past the Pharisees and Sadducees; or as Herod and Pilate did accord against Christ. They were best therefore to go and set peace at home rather among their own selves. Of a truth, unity and concord doth best become Religion, yet is not unity the sure and certain mark whereby to know the Church of God. For there was the greatest consent that might be amongst them that worshipped the Golden calf, and among them which with one voice jointly cried against our Saviour Jesus Christ, Crucify him. Neither because the Corinthians were unquieted with

---

²³ **Marg.** Thom. Aquinas. [The five solemn words of the Eucharistic consecration are *Hoc est enim corpus meum*: for this is my body. About the presence of the body of Christ in the sacrament, Thomas Aquinas wrote: 'the presence of Christ's true body and blood in this sacrament cannot be detected by the senses or by reason, but by faith alone, which rests upon Divine authority.' *Summa Theologica*, 5 vols (New York: Cosimo Classics, 2007), V, Part 3.57, 2440.]

²⁴ **Marg.** Steph. Gardiner. [Glossing this reference, Jewel quoted Gardiner's *A Detection of the devils sophistrie*: 'Christ spake plainly, "this is my body," making demonstration of the bread' (fol. 24ᵛ). Jewel insisted that afterward Gardiner 'utterly changed his whole mind, and thought it better to say that Christ by the same pronoun *hoc* pointed not the bread that he held in his hand, but only *individuum vagum*,' which Jewel glossed as 'what one certain thing it is, I cannot tell; but sure I am, bread it is not.' *Works*, II, 789.]

²⁵ **Marg.** De Consecr. Dist. Spe. Glos. Magist. Sent. et Schola. [In *The Reply to Harding's Answer*, Jewel quoted *Corpus juris canonici*: '[*Corpus Christi*] potest evomi*: The very body of Christ may be vomited up again.' (Corp. Jur. R, Dist ii, Not. In can. 28. Col. 1924). He declared he would not 'have used this unpleasant rehearsal, were it not that it behoveth each man to know how deeply the people hath been deceived, and to what villainy they have been brought.' *Works*, II, 784.]

private dissensions, or because Paul did square° with Peter, or Barnabas with Paul: or because the Christians upon the very beginning of the Gospel, were at mutual discord, touching some one matter, may we therefore think there was no Church of God amongst them. And as for those persons whom they upon spite call Zwinglians and Lutherians, in very deed they of both sides be Christians, good friends and brethren. They vary not betwixt themselves upon the principles and foundations of our religion, nor as touching God nor Christ nor the holy Ghost, nor of the means to justification, nor yet everlasting life, but upon one only question, which is neither weighty nor great: neither mistrust we or make doubt at all, but they will shortly be agreed. And if there be any of them which have other opinion than is meet, we doubt not but ere it be long, they will put apart all affections and names of parties, and that God will reveal it unto them: so that by better considering and searching out of the matter, as once it came to pass in the Council of Chalcedon, all causes and seeds of dissension shall be thoroughly plucked up by the root, and be buried, and quite forgotten forever. Which God grant.

But this is the most grievous and heavy case that they call us wicked and ungodly men, and say we have thrown away all care of religion. Though this ought not to trouble us much, whilst they themselves that thus have charged us, know full well how spiteful and false a saying it is: for Justin the martyr is a witness[26] how that all Christians were called αθεοι, that is Godless, as soon as the Gospel first began to be published, and the name of Christ to be openly declared. And when Polycarpus stood to be judged, the people stirred up the President to slay and murder all them which professed the Gospel, with these words, Αἴρε τούς ἀθέους, that is to say, Rid out of the way these wicked and godless creatures.[27]

---

[26] Justin Martyr (c. 100–165), early Christian apologist, *First Apology*, 6: 'Hence are we called atheists. And we confess that we are atheists, so far as gods of this sort are concerned, but not with respect to the most true God, the Father of righteousness and temperance and the other virtues, who is free from all impurity.' *The Ante-Nicene Fathers*, I (1885), 164.

[27] **Marg.** Euseb. Lib. iv. [Eusebius, *Church History*, IV. 15: Once Polycarp declared himself a Christian, 'and when this was proclaimed by the herald, the whole multitude, both of Gentiles and of Jews, who dwelt in Smyrna, cried out with ungovernable wrath and with a great shout, "This is the teacher of Asia, the father of the Christians, the overthrower of our gods, who teacheth many not to sacrifice nor to worship."' *Nicene and Post-Nicene Fathers*, Series II, I (1890), 190.]

And this was not because it was true that the Christians were Godless, but because they would not worship stones and stocks, which were then honoured as God. The whole world seeth plainly enough already, what we and ours have endured at these men's hands for religion and our only God's cause. They have thrown us into prison, into water, into fire, and imbrued° themselves in our blood, not because we were either adulterers or robbers, or murderers, but only for that we confessed the Gospel of Jesu Christ, and put our confidence in the living God. And for that we complained too justly and truly (Lord thou knowest) that they did break the law of God for their own most vain traditions: And that our Adversaries were the very foes to the Gospel, and enemies to Christ's cross, who so wittingly and willingly did obstinately despise God's commandments. Wherefore when these men saw they could not rightly find fault with our doctrine, they would needs pick a quarrel, and inveigh and rail against our manners, surmising how that we do condemn all welldoings, how we set open the door to all licentiousness and lust, and lead away the people from all love of virtue. And in very deed the life of all men, even of the devoutest and most Christian, both is and evermore hath been such, as one may always find some lack, even in the very best and purest conversation. And such is the inclination of all creatures unto evil, and the readiness of all men to suspect, that the things which neither have been done, nor once meant to be done, yet may be easily both heard and credited for true. And like as a small spot is soon spied in the neatest and whitest garment, even so the least stain of dishonesty is easily found out in the purest and sincerest life. Neither take we all them which have at this day embraced the doctrine of the Gospel to be Angels, and to live clearly without any mote or wrinkle; nor yet think we these men either so blind, that if anything may be noted in us, they are not able to perceive the same even through the least crevice, nor so friendly that they will construe aught to the best: nor yet so honest of nature nor courteous, that they will look back upon themselves, and weigh our fashions by their own. If so be we list to search this matter from the bottom, we know in the very Apostles' times there were Christians, through whom the name of the Lord was blasphemed and evil spoken of among the Gentiles. Constantius the Emperor bewaileth, as it is written in Sozomenus, how many waxed worse after they had fallen to the religion of Christ. And Cyprian in a lamentable Oration setteth out the corrupt manners in his time: The wholesome discipline, saith he, which the Apostles left unto us, hath idleness and long rest now utterly marred, everyone studied to increase his livelihood, and clean forgetting either what they had done before, whilst they were under the Apostles, or what they ought continually to do having received the faith: they earnestly laboured to make great their own wealth with an unsatiable desire of covetousness. There is no devout religion, saith he, in Priests, no sound faith in ministers, no charity showed in good works, no form of Godliness in their conditions, men are become effeminate, and women's beauty is counterfeited.[28] And before his days, said Tertullian, O how wretched be we, which are called Christians at this time: for we live as Heathens, under the name of Christ.[29] And without reciting of many more writers, Gregory Nazianzen speaketh this of the pitiful state of his own time: We saith he, are in hatred among the Heathen for our own vices' sake, we are also become now a wonder not alone to Angels and men, but even to all the ungodly.[30] In this case was the Church of God, when the Gospel first began to shine, and when the fury of Tyrants was not as yet cooled, nor the sword taken off from the Christians' necks. Surely it is no new thing that men be but men, although they be called by the name of Christians.

---

[28] **Marg.** Cypr. de Laps. [Cyprian, *De lapsis*: 'Each one was desirous of increasing his estate; and forgetful of what believers had either done before in the times of the apostles, or always ought to do, they, with the insatiable ardour of covetousness, devoted themselves to the increase of their property. Among the priests there was no devotedness of religion; among the ministers there was no sound faith: in their works there was no mercy; in their manners there was no discipline' (par. 6). *The Ante-Nicene Fathers*, v (1886), 438.]

[29] Tertullian, *Of Idolatry*, 14: 'the majority of Christians have by this time induced the belief in their mind that it is pardonable if at any time they do what the heathen do.' *The Ante-Nicene Fathers*, III (1887), 69.

[30] Nazianzen, Oration 2, section 84: 'Sinners are planning upon our backs; and what we devise against each other, they turn against us all: and we have become a new spectacle, not to angels and men [...] but to almost all wicked men.' *Nicene and Post-Nicene Fathers*, Second Series, VII (1893), 222.

PART IV

But will these men, I pray you, think nothing at all of themselves, while they accuse us so maliciously? And while they have leisure to behold so far off, and see both what is done in Germany and in England? Have they either forgotten, or can they not see what is done at Rome? Or be they our accusers, whose life is such as no man is able to make mention thereof but with shame and uncomeliness? Our purpose here is not to take in hand at this present to bring to light and open to the world those things which were meet rather to be hid and buried with the workers of them. It beseemeth neither our Religion, nor our modesty, nor our shamefastness.° But yet he, which giveth commandment that he should be called the vicar of Christ and the head of the Church, who also heareth that such things be done at Rome, who seeth them, who suffereth them (for we will go no further) he can easily consider with himself what manner of things they be. Let him on God's name call to mind, let him remember that they be of his own Canonists, which have taught the people that fornication between single folk is not sin[1] (as though they had fet° that doctrine from Micio in Terence) whose words be: It is no sin (believe me) for a young man to haunt harlots.[2] Let him remember they be of his own which have decreed, that a priest ought not to be put out of his cure for fornication.[3] Let him

---

[1] **Marg.** Johan. de Magist. de Temperantia. [Harding notes that Jewel should have cited *Martinus* de Magistris, 'a doctor of divinity, well learned for his time' and not Johannes. Harding quotes Martinus's *De Temperantia et de Luxuria*: 'Simple fornication excludeth from the kingdom of God; ergo, it is mortal sin.' In *The Defence* Jewel rebutted by quoting Alphonsus de Castro, *Adversus contra hæreses* (1543), and de Castro's citation of Martinus, *Conf. Mart. Magist. De Temp.Lib.* Par. 1511. *De Lux. Quaest.* III. fol. 50.2: '*sed quia idem sacri doctores, qui dicunt fornicationem simplicem esse peccatum mortale, non asserunt quod dicere oppositum sit haereticum*', to the effect that 'simple fornication is deadly sin, and yet it is no heresy to believe the contrary, for that, as he saith, the testimonies of the scriptures are not plain.' *Works*, IV, 626, 635–36.]

[2] 'There is nothing shameful in a young man loving women and drink, nothing at all.' Act I, Scene 2, *The Adelphi of Terence*, trans. by A. F. Burnet and J. H. Haydon (London: W.B. Clive, 1891).

[3] **Marg.** 3 Quest 7. Lat. Extr. de Bigam. Quia circa. [In *The Defence* Jewel quoted *Concil. Tolet.* 1. Cap. 17: '*Is qui non habet uxorem, et pro uxore concubinam habet, a communione non repellatur.* He that hath no wife and instead of a wife hath a

AN APOLOGY OR ANSWER IN DEFENCE OF THE CHURCH

remember also how Cardinal Campegius,⁴ Albertus Pighius and others many more of his own, have taught that the priest which keepeth a concubine doth live more holily and chastely, than he which hath a wife in matrimony. I trust he hath not yet forgotten, that there be many thousands of common harlots in Rome; and that himself doth gather yearly of the same harlots upon a thirty thousand Ducats, by the way of an annual pension. Neither can
30 he forget how himself doth maintain openly brothel houses, and by a most filthy lucre doth filthily and lewdly serve his own lust. Were all things then pure and holy in Rome, when Joan a woman rather of perfect age than of perfect life, was Pope there, and bare herself as the head of the Church. And after that for two whole years in that holy See, she had played the naughty Pack,° at last going in procession about the City, in the sight of all the Cardinals and Bishops, fell in travail openly in the streets?⁵

But what need one rehearse Concubines and Bawds, as for that is now an ordinary and a gainful sin at Rome? For harlots sit there
40 nowadays, not as they did in times past, without the City walls, and with their faces hid and covered,⁶ but they dwell in palaces

---

concubine, let him not be removed from the communion.' Harding accused Jewel of perverting and misconstruing the text and insisted that the 'concubine' was a wife privately taken without or before public solemnization. *Works*, IV, 631.]

⁴ Cardinal Lorenzo Campeggio (1474–1539), canonist and diplomat, was appointed cardinal protector of England in 1523; he supported the validity of Henry's marriage to Catharine of Aragon and was dismissed as legate in 1531. Campeggio's ecclesiatical career began after the death of his wife, in 1509, with whom he had five children.

⁵ **Marg.** This image of this woman pope, being in travail, is yet to be seen at Rome. [Editor Whittingham related the 'marvellous' story which 'remains of dubious authority. In the ninth century, a woman, having disguised herself in male attire, for convenience of intercourse with her paramour, a monk, eloped with him; studied philosophy at Athens; taught it at Rome, and attained such eminence as to be chosen successor to Pope Leo IV, who died in 855. She continued her former lewd habits and died in childbirth in the streets of Rome, during a public procession.' Harding called the story of Pope Joan 'a fond and vain fable.' After citing several examples of figures removed from the calendar, Jewel responded, 'therefore was pope Joan's name left out of the calendar of the bishops of Rome, not for that there never was any such pope there, but only for shame lest is should appear in record.' *Works*, IV, 648, 650. Whittingham, pp. 90–91.]

⁶ **Marg.** Gen. xxxviii. [Genesis 38.14–15: 'Then she put her widdowes garments off from her, and covered *her* with a vaile, and wrapped her selfe, and sate downe

and fair houses: they stray about in Court and market, and that with bare and open face: as who say they, may not only lawfully do it, but ought also to be praised for so doing. What should we say any more of this? Their vicious and abominable life is now thoroughly known to the whole world. Bernard writeth roundly and truly of the Bishop of Rome's house, yea and of the Bishop of Rome himself. Thy palace, saith he, taketh in good men, but it maketh none; naughty persons thrive there, and the good appaire° and decay.⁷ And whosoever he were which wrote the Tripartite work, annexed to the Council LATERANENSE, saith thus: So excessive at this day is the riot, as well in the Prelates and Bishops as in the Clerks and Priests, that it is horrible to be told.⁸ But these things be not only grown in ure,° and so by custom and continual time well allowed, as all the rest of their doings in manner be, but they are now waxen old and rotten ripe. For who hath not heard what a heinous act Peter Aloisius, Pope Paul the third's son,

---

in Pethah-enam which is by the way to Timnah, because she saw that Shelah was growen, and she was not given unto him to wife. When Judah saw her, hee judged her an whore: for she had covered her face.' This is an ironic allusion since Tamar was exposing the hypocrisy of her father-in-law Judah.]

⁷ **Marg.** De Consid. ad Eugen. [Bernard of Clairvaux (1090–1153), Cistercian reformer, addressed the advice in *On Consideration* to the fellow monk who had been elected Pope Eugenius III. 'Honour claims all, holiness nothing or but little. [...] Thus all humility is reckoned a disgrace among the inmates of the palace. [...] The fear of the Lord is counted simplicity, not to say folly. They revile a prudent man, who is on good terms with his own conscience, as a hypocrite.' *On Consideration*, trans. by George Lewis (Oxford: Clarendon, 1908), IV, 2, par. 5, 102.]

⁸ The Fourth Lateran Council (1215) addressed clerical incontinence in constitution 14: 'We decree that those who are caught giving way to the vice of incontinence are to be punished according to canonical sanctions, in proportion to the seriousness of their sins. We order such sanctions to be effectively and strictly observed, in order that those whom the fear of God does not hold back from evil may at least be restrained from sin by temporal punishment. Therefore, anyone who has been suspended for this reason and presumes to celebrate divine services, shall not only be deprived of his ecclesiastical benefices but shall also, on account of his twofold fault, be deposed in perpetuity.' It also addressed dissolute prelates in constitution 17: 'We regretfully relate that not only certain lesser clerics but also some prelates of churches pass almost half the night in unnecessary feasting and forbidden conversation, not to mention other things, and leaving what is left of the night for sleep, they are barely roused at the dawn chorus of the birds and pass away the entire morning in a continuous state of stupor.' *Decrees of the Ecumenical Councils*, I, 242, 243.

committed against Cosmus Cherius the Bishop of Fanum; what John Casus Archbishop of Beneventum the Pope's legate at Venice wrote in the commendation of a most abominable filthiness, and how he set forth, with most loathsome words and wicked eloquence, the matter which ought not once to proceed out of anybody's mouth? To whose ears hath it not come, that N. Diasius, a Spaniard, being purposely sent from Rome into Germany, did shamefully and devilishly murder his own brother John Diasius, a most innocent and a most godly man, only because he had embraced the Gospel of Jesu Christ, and would not return again to Rome?[9]

But it may chance to this they will say: These things may sometime happen in the best governed commonwealths, yea and against the magistrates' wills: and besides, there be good laws made to punish such. I grant it be so: but by what good laws (I would know) have these great mischiefs been punished amongst them? Petrus Aloisius after he had done that notorious Act that I spake of, was always cherished in his father's bosom Pope Paul the Third, and made his very darling. Diasius after he had murdered his own brother, was delivered by the Pope's means, to the end he might not be punished by good laws. John Casus, the Archibishop of Beneventum, is yet alive, yea and liveth at Rome, even in the eyes and sight of the most holy Father. They have put to death infinite numbers of our brethren, only because they believed truly and sincerely in Jesu Christ. But of that great and foul number of harlots, fornicators, Adulterers, what one have they at any time (I say not killed) but either excommunicated, or once attached?° Why voluptuousness, adultery, ribaldry, whoredom, murdering of kin, incest, and others more abominable parts, are not these counted sin at Rome? Or if they be sin, ought Christ's vicar, Peter's successor, the most holy Father, so lightly

---

[9] Jewel relied on Johannes Sleidanus's *Commentarium statu religionis et reipublicae Carolo V, Caesare* (1555) for this account of the murder committed by the Pope's son Petrus Aloisius. He added: 'Pope Paul nevertheless favoured his son above measure, and bestowed all his care to increase him in honour. And, whereas he heard sometime of his shameful acts, the report is that he was not much offended therewith, but used only thus to say, "Well ye wis, he never learned these vices by my example." So cruel and terrible is the pope in repressing of sin.' *Works*, IV, 658.

and slightly to bear them as though they were no sin, and that in the City of Rome, and in that principal tower of all holiness?

O holy Scribes and Pharisees, which knew not this kind of holiness. O what holiness, what a Catholic faith is this? Peter did not thus teach at Rome, Paul did not so live at Rome: they did not practise brothelry, which these do openly: they made not a yearly revenue and profit of harlots: they suffered no common Adulterers and wicked Murderers to go unpunished. They did not receive them into their entire familiarity, into their Council, into their household, nor yet into the company of Christian men. These men ought not therefore so unreasonably to triumph against our living. It had been more wisdom for them either first to have proved good their own life before the world, or at least to have cloaked it a little more cunningly. For we do use still the old and ancient laws, (and as much as men may do in the manners used at these days, when all things are so wholly corrupt) we diligently and earnestly put in execution the ecclesiastical discipline: we have not common brothel houses of strumpets, nor yet flocks of Concubines, nor herds of harlot hunters. Neither do we prefer adultery before matrimony, neither do we exercise beastly sensuality. Neither do we gather ordinary rents and stipends of stews, nor do we suffer to escape unpunished incest and abominable naughtiness, nor yet such manquellers° as the Aloisians, Casians, and Diazians were. For if these things would have pleased us, we needed not to have departed from these men's fellowship, amongst whom such enormities be in their chief pride and price. Neither needed we, for leaving them to run into the hatred of men, and into most wilful dangers. Paul the fourth not many months since, had at Rome in prison certain Augustine friars, many Bishops, and a great number of other devout men, for Religion's sake. He racked them and tormented them: to make them confess, he left no means unassayed. But in the end how many brothels, how many whoremongers, how many adulterers, how many incestuous persons could he find of all those? Our God be thanked, although we be not the men we ought and profess to be, yet whosoever we be, compare us with these men, and even our own life and innocency will soon prove untrue and condemn their malicious surmises. For we exhort the people to all virtue and well doing, not only by books and preachings, but also with our examples and behaviour. We also teach that the Gospel is not a boasting or bragging of knowledge, but that it is the law of life, and that a Christian man (as Tertullian saith) ought not to speak honourably, but ought to live honourably; nor that they be the hearers of the law, but the doers of the law, which are justified before God.[10]

Besides all these matters wherewith they charge us, they are wont also to add this one thing, which they enlarge with all kind of spitefulness: that is, that we be men of trouble, that we pluck the sword and Sceptre out of Kings' hands: that we arm the people: that we overthrow judgment places, destroy the laws, make havoc of possessions, seek to make the people Princes, turn all things upside down: and, to be short, that we would have nothing in good frame in a commonwealth. Good Lord, how often have they set on fire Princes' hearts with these words, to the end they might quench the light of the Gospel in the very first appearing of it, and might begin to hate the same ere ever they were able to know it, and to the end that every magistrate might think he saw his deadly enemy as often as he saw any of us.[11] Surely it should exceedingly grieve us to be so maliciously accused of most heinous treason, unless we knew that Christ himself, the Apostles, and a number of good and Christian men, were in time past blamed and envied in manner for the same faults. For although Christ taught they should give unto Caesar that which was Caesar's, yet was he charged with sedition, in that he was accused to devise some conspiracy and covet the kingdom. And hereupon they cried out with open mouth against him in the place

---

[10] **Marg.** In Apolog. cap. xlv. [Tertullian, *Apologia*, 45: 'You know that these very laws also of yours, which seem to lead to virtue, have been borrowed from the law of God as the ancient model.' *The Ante-Nicene Fathers*, III (1887), 50.]; Rom. ii. [Romans 2.13: 'For the hearers of the Law *are* not righteous before God: but the doers of the Law shall be justified.']

[11] **Marg.** Tertull. in Apolog. cap. i. ii. iii. [Tertullian, *Apologia*, 2: 'You look upon a Christian as the sum total of iniquity, a despiser of the gods, emperors, laws, morality, and, in one word, an enemy of human nature; and yet this is the man you rack, that you may absolve, because without racking him into a denial of his name you cannot absolve him. This, or nothing, is prevaricating with the laws; you would have him plead not guilty, for you to pronounce him innocent, and discharge him from all past crimes, whether he will or no. But how can men be so perverse as to imagine that he who confesses a thing freely is not more to be credited than he who denies it by compulsion?' *The Apologia of Tertullian*, trans. by William Reeves (London: Griffith, Farran, Okeden & Welsh, 1889), p. 10.]

of judgment, saying: If thou let this man escape, thou art not Caesar's friend.

And though the Apostles did likewise evermore and steadfastly teach, that magistrates ought to be obeyed, that every soul ought to be subject to the higher powers, not only for fear of wrath and punishment, but even for conscience sake[12] yet bear they the name to disquiet the people, and to stir up the multitude to rebel. After this sort did Haman specially bring the nation of the Jews into the hatred of the king Assuerus, because, said he, they were a rebellious and stubborn people, and despised the ordinances and commandments of princes.[13] Wicked King Ahab said to Elijah the Prophet of God, It is thou that troublest Israel.[14] Amasias, the priest at Bethel laid a conspiracy to the prophet Amos' charge before King Jeroboam saying, See, Amos hath made a conspiracy against thee in the midst of the house of Israel.[15] To be brief, Tertullian saith, this was the general accusation of all Christians while he lived, that they were traitors, they were rebels, and the enemies of mankind.[16] Wherefore, if nowadays the truth be likewise evil spoken of, and being the same truth it was then, if it be now like despitefully used as it was in times past, though it be a grievous and unkind dealing, yet can it not seem unto us a new or an unwonted matter. Forty years ago and upward, was it an easy thing for them to devise against us these accursed speeches, and other too sorer than these when, in the midst of the darkness of that age first began to spring and to give shine, some one glimmering beam of truth unknown at that time and unheard of

---

[12] **Marg.** Rom. xiii. [Romans 13.5: 'Wherefore we must be subject, not because of wrath onely, but also for conscience sake.'] **L**

[13] **Marg.** In the book of Hester. [Esther 3.8: 'Then Haman said unto king Ahashuerosh, There is a people scattered, and dispersed among the people in all the provinces of thy kingdome, and their lawes *are* divers from all people, and they doe not observe the King's lawes: therefore it is not the kings profit to suffer them.']

[14] **Marg.** 1 Kings xviii. [I Kings 18.17: 'And when Ahab saw Elijah, Ahab said unto him, Art thou he that troubleth Israel?']

[15] **Marg.** Amos vii. [Amos 7.10: 'Then Amaziah the Priest of Beth-el sent to Jeroboam king of Israel, saying, Amos hath conspired against thee in the midst of the house of Israel: the land is not able to beare all his wordes.']

[16] **Marg.** In Apolog. cap. xxxvii. [Tertullian, *Apologia*, 37: 'you declare a sect of men, which are not only not burdensome, but necessary, to be public enemies; as we are indeed, but not in your sense, enemies not of human kind but of human errors only.' *The Ante-Nicene Fathers*, III (1887), 45.]

when also Martin Luther and Hulderic Zwinglius, being most excellent men, even sent of God to give light to the whole world, first came unto the knowledge and preaching of the Gospel whereas yet the thing was but new, and the success thereof uncertain; and when men's minds stood doubtful and amazed, and their ears open to all slanderous tales; and when there could be imagined against us no fact so detestable, but the people then would soon believe it for the novelty and strangeness of the matter. For so did Symmachus, so did Celsus, so did Julianus, so did Porphyrius[17] the old foes to the Gospel attempt in times past to accuse all Christians of sedition and treason, before that either Prince or People were able to know who those Christians were, what they professed, what they believed, or what was their meaning.

But now sithence° our very enemies do see and cannot deny, but we ever in all our words and writings have diligently put the people in mind of their duty, to obey their Princes and Magistrates, yea though they be wicked: for this doth very trial and experience sufficiently teach, and all men's eyes, whosoever and wheresoever they be, do well enough see and witness for us, it was a foul part of them to charge us with these things: and seeing they could find no new and late faults, therefore to seek to procure us envy° only with stale and out worn lies. We give our lord God thanks, whose only cause this is, there hath yet at no time been any such example in all the Realms, Dominions and commonweals which have received the Gospel. For we have overthrown no kingdom, we have decayed no man's power or right, we have disordered no commonwealth. There continue in their own accustomed state and ancient dignity, the Kings of our country of England, the Kings of Denmark, the Kings of Sweden, the Dukes of Saxony, the Counts Palatine, the Marquesses of Brandenburg, the Landgraves of Hesse, the commonwealths of the Helvetians and Rhaetians, and the free cities, as Argentine, Basil, Frankfort, Ulm, Augusta,[18] and Nuremberg do all I say

---

[17] A group of anti-Christian adversaries: Symmacchus (340–402), wealthy Roman statesman who supported preserving traditional religions against Christianity; Celsus, second-century Greek philosopher who opposed Origen; Julianus (133–193), wealthy Roman senator who paid to become emperor for less than three months before his execution; Porphyrius (c. 234–305), Neoplatonic philosopher who wrote against Christianity.

[18] Argentine represents Strasbourg, and August Augsburg.

abide in the same authority and estate wherein they have been heretofore, or rather in a much better, for that by means of the Gospel they have their people more obedient unto them. Let them go I pray you into those places where at this present through God's goodness the Gospel is taught. Where is there more majesty? Where is there less arrogancy and tyranny? Where is the prince more honoured? Where is the people less unruly? Where hath there at any time the commonwealth or the Church been in more quiet? Perhaps ye will say, from the first beginning of this doctrine the common sort everywhere began to rage and to rise throughout Germany. Allow it were so, yet Martin Luther the publisher and setter forward of this doctrine, did write marvellously vehemently and sharply against them, and reclaimed them, home to peace and obedience.

But whereas it is wont sometime to be objected by persons wanting skill touching the Helvetians' change of state and killing of Leopoldus the duke of Austria, and restoring by force their Country to liberty, that was done, as appeareth plainly by all stories, for two hundred and threescore years past or above, under Boniface the eighth, when the authority of the Bishop of Rome was in greatest jollity about two hundred years before Hulderic Zwinglius either began to teach the Gospel, or yet was born. And ever since that time they have had all things still and quiet, not only from foreign enemies, but also from civil dissension. And if it were a sin in the Helvetians to deliver their own country from foreign government, specially when they were so proudly and tyrannously oppressed, yet to burden us with other men's faults, or them with the faults of their forefathers, is against all right and reason.

But O immortal God, and will the Bishop of Rome accuse us of treason? Will he teach the people to obey and follow their Magistrates? Or hath he any regard at all of the Majesty of Princes? Why doth he then as none of the old Bishops of Rome heretofore ever did, suffer himself to be called of his flatterers Lord of Lords,[19] as though he would have all Kings and Princes,

---

[19] **Marg.** August. Steuch. [Agostino Steuco, Steuchus (1497–1548), Italian humanist, Old Testament scholar, and Vatican librarian, upheld the papal prerogative. In *De fals. Donat. Constantini* Steuchus recorded: 'Constantine called the Pope God, and that he acknowledged him to be so. [...] He adored him as God, as the successor of Christ and of Peter.' As quoted by Monsieur

250 who and whatsoever they are, to be his underlings? Why doth he vaunt himself to be king of kings, and to have kingly Royalty over his Subjects?[20] Why compelleth he all emperors and princes to swear to him fealty and true obedience? Why doth he boast that the Emperor's majesty is a thousandfold inferior to him? And for this reason specially, because God hath made two lights in the heaven,[21] and because heaven and earth were created not at two beginnings, but at one?[22] Why hath he and his complices (like Anabaptists and Libertines, to the end they might run on more licentiously and carelessly) shaken off the yoke, and exempted

---

Jean Claude, *A Defence of the Reformation*, trans. by T. B. (London: Hatchard, 1815), p. 20.]

[20] **Marg.** Anton. de Rosel. [In *Monarchia sive Tractatus de potestate imperatoris et papae* (*c.* 1435), Antonio Roselli of Arezzo (1380–1463), a consistorial advocate at the Curia, defended papal absolutism with some reservations about papal plenitude; he maintained that councils could depose manifest heretics and schismatics. 'Even though he is concerned with vindicating princely authority as well as papal, [...] there is no doubt that he places the Papacy firmly at the head. [...] It was necessary for a man's salvation for him to be within the hierarchical Church as well as within the Imperium. *Deus constituit divinam et humanam monarchiam, et extra istam Ecclesiam et sanctam monarchiam, in qua consistit Ecclesia tota militans, non est salus.* The power of the monarch was seen as subordinate to that of the pope, who possessed the power of both swords.' His treatise was finally condemned as an anti-papal tract and became the first book to be prohibited by the Church in 1491. Citations are from the most recent edition by Melchior Goldast (Hanover, 1611) quoted by J. A. F. Thomson in 'Papalism and Conciliarism in Antonio Roselli's *Monarchia*', *Mediaeval Studies*, 37 (1975), pp. 449, 447. From Goldast, pp. 312, 525.]

[21] **Marg.** De Major. et Obed. Solitæ. [John Foxe quoted writing from the papacy of Pope Innocent III (1198–1216), *De major. et obed. solitae* (in Decretal. Greg. IX. Lib. I. tit. 33. c 6): 'for, as I said, look what difference there is betwixt the sun and the moon, so great is the power of the pope ruling over the day, that is, over the spirituality, above emperors and kings, ruling over the night; that is, over the laity.' *The Church Historians of England, Reformation Period: The Acts and Monuments of John Foxe*, 8 vols (London: Seeleys, 1853–1868), IV (1857), 146.]

[22] **Marg.** De Major. et Obed. Unam sanctam. [Boniface VIII's Bull *Unam Sanctam* asserted the doctrine of papal primacy against King Philip the Fair of France. 'Therefore whoever resists this power thus ordained by God, resists the ordinance of God [Rom 13.2], unless he invent like Manicheus two beginnings, which is false and judged by us heretical, since according to the testimony of Moses, it is not in the beginnings but in the beginning that God created heaven and earth [Gen 1.1].' 'Unam Sanctam', in Johann Peter Kirsch, *The Catholic Encyclopedia*, 15 vols (New York: Robert Appleton Company, 1907–1912), XV (1912).]

themselves from being under a civil power? Why hath he his Legates (as much to say as most subtle spies) lying in wait in all kings' Courts, Councils, and privy chambers? Why doth he, when he list, set Christian princes one against another, and at his own pleasure trouble the whole world with debate and discord? Why doth he excommunicate, and command to be taken as a heathen and a Pagan any Christian prince that renounceth his authority? And why promiseth he his Indulgences and his pardons so largely to any that will (what way soever it be) kill any of his enemies? Doth he maintain Empires and kingdoms? Or doth he once desire that common quiet should be provided for? You must pardon us, good Reader, though we seem to utter these things more bitterly and bitingly than it becometh Divines to do. For both the shamefulness of the matter, and the desire of rule in the Bishop of Rome is so exceeding and outrageous, that it could not well be uttered with other words, or more mildly. For he is not ashamed to say in open assembly, that all jurisdiction of all kings doth depend upon himself.[23] And to feed his ambition and greediness of rule, hath he pulled in pieces the Empire of Rome, and vexed and rent whole Christendom asunder: falsely and traitorously also did he release the Romans, the Italians, and himself too, of the oath whereby they and he were straitly bound to be true to the Emperor of Greece, and stirred up the Emperor's subjects to forsake him and calling Carolus Martellus out of France into Italy, made him Emperor, such a thing as never was seen before.[24] He put Chilpericus the French king, being no evil prince, beside his realm, only because he fancied him not, and wrongfully placed Pipin in his room.[25] Again, after he had cast out king Philip, if he

---

[23] **Marg.** Clem. v. in Cone. Vien. [Pope Clement V (*c.* 1264–1314) was the first of the Avignon popes. In *The Church Historians of England* Foxe quotes Clement V: 'And as I feared not to write this boldly unto Constantine, so now I say to all other emperors, that they, receiving of me their approbation, unction, consecration, and crown imperial, must not disdain to submit their heads under me, and swear unto me their allegiance' (Clementin. lib. II. Tit. IX. *de jure jurando*). Foxe, IV, 147.]

[24] **Marg.** Leo papa. [In 800, Pope Leo III (750–816) crowned Charlemagne, the grandson of Charles Martel, the first Holy Roman Emperor. Jewel corrected the reference to 'Carolus Magnus' in *Works*, IV, 672.]

[25] **Marg.** Zach. papa. [In 751, Pope Zachary (679–752) deposed Childeric III, the last Merovingian king, and installed Pepin the Short (father of Charlemagne) as king. Pepin subsequently rescued Rome from potential Lombard invasion.]

could have brought it to pass, he had determined and appointed the kingdom of France to Albertus king of Romans.²⁶ He utterly destroyed the state of the most nourishing city and commonweal of Florence, his own native country, and brought it out of a free and peaceable state, to be governed at the pleasure of one man:²⁷ he brought to pass by his procurement that whole Savoy on the one side was miserably spoiled by the Emperor Charles the fifth, and on the other side by the French king, so as the unfortunate duke had scant one City left him to hide his head in.²⁸ We are cloyed° with examples in this behalf, and it should be very tedious to reckon up all the notorious deeds of the Bishops of Rome. Of which side were they, I beseech you, which poisoned Henry the Emperor even in the receiving of the sacrament?²⁹ Which poisoned Victor the Pope even in the receiving of the Chalice? Which poisoned our king John, king of England, in a drinking cup?³⁰ Whosoever at least they were and of what sect soever, I am

---

²⁶ It was Pope Boniface VIII (*c.* 1235–1303) who in 1300 declared Albert of Habsburg Emperor. Although Boniface initially judged King Albert's electoral process illegal and found Albert 'totally unsuitable since he had rebelled against his predecessor and killed him,' in his controversy with Philip IV (le Bel) of France over papal and monarchical authority and consequent revenues, the Pope had 'urgent need of Albert as an ally.' Boniface maintained that 'the French are and have to be subject to the Roman emperor and him. [...] In a *promissio* Albert became the pope's subject.' In September 1303 Boniface was taken prisoner at Anagni by Philip's councillor and died a month later. Peter Herde, 'The Empire: From Adolph of Nassau to Lewis of Bavaria, 1292–1347', in *The New Cambridge Medieval History: Vol. 6 1300–c. 1415*, ed. by Michael Jones (Cambridge: Cambridge University Press, 2000), VI, 523–25.
²⁷ **Marg.** Clem. papa VII. [Clement VII (1478–1534), Medici Pope.]
²⁸ **Marg.** Idem Clem.
²⁹ Henry VII, German King (from 1308) and Holy Roman Emperor (from 1312), was at war with the King of Naples, against the injunction of Pope Clement V. In 1313 Henry died suddenly of fever at Bunoconvento. Editor Whittingham notes: 'A Dominican friar, Bernard of Montepulciano, was accused of poisoning him in the administration of the eucharist, and such height did these suspicions attain that the General of the Order found it necessary to obtain a justificatory document from the son of Henry thirty years after the death of the emperor. Jewel quotes several authorities of middling value in proof of the truth of the story [in] *The Defence*.' Whittingham, p. 105.
³⁰ In *The Defence* Jewel cited many sources about the poisoning deaths of Pope Victor III and King John, primarily Joannes Ravisius Textor's *Officina* (1520), 'a comprehensive compilation inspired by great contemporary Italian *farragines* [medleys], which contain many lists.' Olivier Pédeflous, 'Textor's School Drama and Its Links to Pedagogical School Drama in Early Modern France', in *The*

sure they were neither Lutherans nor Zwinglians. What is he at this day, which alloweth the mightiest Kings and Monarchs of the world to kiss his blessed feet? What is he that commandeth the Emperor to go by him at his horse bridle, and the French king to hold his stirrup? Who hurled under his table Francis Dandalus the duke of Venice, king of Crete and Cyprus, fast bound with chains, to feed of bones among his dogs?[31] Who set the Imperial

310 crown upon the Emperor Henry the sixth's head, not with his hand but with his foot and with the same foot again cast the same crown off, saying withal he had power to make Emperors, and to unmake them again at his pleasure?[32] Who put in arms Henry the son against the Emperor his father Henry the fourth, and wrought so that the father was taken prisoner of his own son, and being shorn and shamefully handled, was thrust into a monastery, where with hunger and sorrow he pined away to death?[33] Who so ill favouredly and monstrously put the Emperor Frederick's neck

---

Early Modern Cultures of Neo-Latin Drama, ed. by Philip Ford and Andrew Taylor (Leuven: Leuven University Press, 2013), p. 28. Ravisius wrote of Pope Victor, '*venemo in calice immixto dicitur extinctus*, it is said that he died of poison mixed in the chalice' (fol. 27). Victor III, whose papacy lasted one year (1086–1087), died during the Council at Benevento which excommunicated antipope Clement III. 'Touching the death of King John, whether he were poisoned by a monk, or no,' Jewel attested, 'I will not strive; referring myself therein to the credit of our Chronicles: the common report whereof, together with the general opinion of the people, is this, that he was destroyed with poison.' *Works*, IV, 687. BL Cotton MS Vitellius A XIII depicts John being offered a cup of poison: as the accompanying text relates, in Anglo-Norman French, 'e fuit enpoysone par une frere de la meson' (he was poisoned by a brother of the house). London, British Library, f. 5ᵛ.

[31] **Marg.** Sabellicus. [In *The Defence* Jewel quoted Marcantonio Sabellico of Vicovaro, born Cocci (1436–1506), historian of Venice. 'The Venetians had given aid to restore one Friscus, a banished man, unto the dukedom of Ferrara. Therefore Pope Clement V interdicted them and all that they had and signified that […] it should be lawful for any man, not only to take their bodies and to sell them for slaves, and to spoil their goods, but also to kill them whether it were by right or by wrong. For so Sabellicus writeth, *Ut eos fas esset unicuique jure, et injuria, interficere* (*Ennead.* IX, lib. 7). And this high indignation had never been slacked, had not so noble a person abased himself to be tied by the neck in a chain, and to creep under the Pope's table on all four like a dog. This disdainful fact Sabellicus the author reproveth vehemently […] as immoderate tyranny and intolerable pride.' *Works*, IV, 379.]

[32] **Marg.** Celest. papa. [Celestine III (*c.* 1106–1198), Pope from 1191 to 1198.]

[33] **Marg.** Hildeb. papa. [Gregory VII (*c.* 1020–1085), born Hildebrand of Sovana, Pope from 1073 to 1085.]

under his feet, and as though that were not sufficient, added further this text out of the Psalms, Thou shalt go upon the Adder and cockatrice, and shalt tread the Lion and Dragon under thy feet?[34] Such an example of scorning and contemning a Prince's majesty, as never before that was heard tell of in any remembrance except I ween either of Tamerlane's the king of Scythia a wild and barbarous creature, or else of Sapor king of the Persians. All these notwithstanding were Popes, all Peter's successors, all most holy fathers, whose several words we must take to be as good as several Gospels. If we be counted traitors which do honour our Princes, which give them all obedience, as much as is due to them by God's word, and which do pray for them, what kind of men then be these, which have not only done all the things before said, but also allow the same for specially well done? Do they then either this way instruct the people as we do to reverence their Magistrate? Or can they with honesty appeach° us as seditious persons, breakers of the common quiet, and despisers of princes' majesty?

Truly we neither put off the yoke of obedience from us, neither do we disorder realms, neither do we set up or pull down kings, nor translate governments, nor give our kings poison to drink, nor yet hold to them our feet to be kissed, nor, opprobriously triumphing over them, leap into their necks with our feet. This rather is our profession, this is our doctrine, that every soul, of what calling soever he be, be he Monk, be he preacher, be he prophet, be he Apostle, ought to be subject to kings and magistrates;[35] yea and that the Bishop of Rome himself, unless he will seem greater than Evangelists, than the Prophets, or the Apostles, ought both to acknowledge and to call the Emperor his Lord and master, which the old Bishops of Rome, who lived in times of more grace, ever did.[36] Our common teaching also is, that

---

[34] **Marg.** Innocent. papa III. [Jewel means Pope Alexander III (*c.* 1100–1181), who led the opposition to Emperor Frederick I (Barbarossa).]

[35] **Marg.** Chrysos. in xiii. cap. ad Rom. [Chrysostom, *In epist. ad Rom.*, hom. XXIII: 'And to show that these regulations are for all, even for priests, and monks, and not for men of secular occupations only, he hath made this plan at the outset, by saying as follows: "let every soul be subject unto the higher powers," if thou be an Apostle even, or an Evangelist, or a Prophet, or anything whatsoever, inasmuch as this subjection is not subversive of religion.' *Nicene and Post-Nicene Fathers*, XI (1889), 511.]

[36] **Marg.** Greg. papa sæpe in Epist. [Gregory the Great, *Registrum Epistolarum*,

350   we ought so to obey princes as men sent of God, and that whoso withstandeth them, withstandeth God's ordinance. This is our showing, and this is well to be seen both in our books and in our preachings, and also in the manners and modest behaviour of our people.

But where they say, we have gone away from the unity of the catholic Church, this is not only a matter of malice, but besides, though it be most untrue, yet hath it some show and appearance of truth. For the common people and ignorant multitude give not credit alone to things true and of certainty, but even to such things 360   also, if any chance, which may seem to have but a resemblance of truth. Therefore we see that subtle and crafty persons, when they had no truth on their side, have ever contended and hotly argued with things likely to be true, to the intent they which were not able to espy the very ground of the matter, might be carried away at least with some pretence and probability thereof. In times past where the first Christians, our forefathers, in making their prayers to God, did turn themselves towards the East, there were that said, they worshipped the sun, and reckoned it as God.[37] Again, where our forefathers said, that as touching immortal and 370   everlasting life, they lived by no other means but by the flesh and blood of that Lamb who was without spot that is to say, of our saviour Jesus Christ, the envious creatures and foes of Christ's Cross, whose only care was to bring Christian religion into slander by all manner of ways, made people believe that they were wicked persons, that they sacrificed men's flesh, and drunk men's

---

v, indict. XIII, *epistola xx as Mauricium Augustum*: 'Who is this that, against the evangelical ordinances, against the decrees of canons, presumes to usurp to himself a new name? Would indeed that one by himself he were, if he could be without any lessening of others — he that covets to be universal. He, then, is rather to be bent by the mandate of our most pious Lords, who scorns to render obedience to canonical injunctions. He is to be coerced, who does wrong to the holy Universal Church, who swells in heart, who covets rejoicing in a name of singularity, who also puts himself above the dignity of your Empire through a title peculiar to himself.' *Nicene and Post-Nicene Fathers*, Series II, XII (1895).]

[37] **Marg.** Tertull. in Apolog. cap. xvi. [Tertullian, *Apologia*, 16: 'Others, again, certainly with more information and greater verisimilitude, believe that the sun is our god. We shall be counted Persians perhaps, though we do not worship the orb of day painted on a piece of linen cloth, having himself everywhere in his own disk. The idea no doubt has originated from our being known to turn to the east in prayer.' *The Ante-Nicene Fathers*, III (1887), 31.]

AN APOLOGY OR ANSWER IN DEFENCE OF THE CHURCH

blood.³⁸ Also where our forefathers said, that before God there is neither man nor woman nor for attaining to the true righteousness there is no distinction at all of persons, and that they did call one another indifferently by the name of Sisters and Brothers: there wanted not men which forged false tales upon the same, saying that the Christians made no difference among themselves either of age or of kind, but like brute beasts without regard had to do one with another.³⁹ And where for to pray and hear the Gospel, they met often together in secret and by° places, because Rebels sometime were wont to do the like. Rumours were everywhere spread abroad how they made privy confederacies, and counselled together either to kill the magistrates, or to subvert the commonwealth. And where, in celebrating the holy mysteries, after Christ's institution, they took bread and wine, they were thought of many not to worship Christ, but Bacchus and Ceres;⁴⁰ forsomuch as those vain gods were worshipped of the Heathens in like sort, after a profane superstition, with bread and wine. These things were believed of many, not because they were true, indeed (for what could be more untrue?) but because they were like to be true, and through a certain shadow of truth might the more easily deceive the simple. On this fashion likewise do these men slander us as heretics, and say that we have left the Church and fellowship of Christ: not because they think it is true, for they do not much force° of that, but because to ignorant folk it might perhaps some way appear true. We have indeed put ourselves apart, not as heretics are wont, from the Church of Christ, but as

---

³⁸ **Marg.** Tertull. in Apolog. cap. vii. viii. ix. [Tertullian, *Apologia*, 7: 'Monsters of wickedness, we are accused of observing a holy rite in which we kill a little child and then eat it.' *The Ante-Nicene Fathers*, III (1887), 23.]

³⁹ **Marg.** Tertull. in Apolog. ix. [Tertullian, *Apologia*, 9: 'A persevering and stedfast chastity has protected us from anything like this: keeping as we do from adulteries and all post-matrimonial unfaithfulness, we are not exposed to incestuous mishaps. If now, therefore, you would turn your eyes inward, and see the guilt in yourselves, you would see innocence in us, for contraries are best seen together; but you labour under a twofold blindness, which is, not to see things that are, and to seem to see things which really are not.' *The Ante-Nicene Fathers*, III (1887), 26.]

⁴⁰ **Marg.** August. [Augustine, *Contra Faustum Manichaeum*, XX. 13: 'There is not the least resemblance between our reverence for the bread and wine, and your doctrines, which have no truth in them. To compare the two is even more foolish than to say, as some do, that in the bread and wine we worship Ceres and Bacchus.' *Nicene and Post-Nicene Fathers*, Series II, IV (1887), 259.]

all good men ought to do, from the infection of naughty persons and hypocrites.

Nevertheless, in this point they triumph marvellously that they be the Church, that their Church is Christ's spouse, the pillar of truth, the ark of Noah, and that without it there is no hope of salvation. Contrariwise, they say that we be renegades; that we have torn Christ's seat; that we are plucked quite off from the body of Christ, and have forsaken the catholic faith. And when they leave nothing unspoken that may never so falsely and maliciously be said against us, yet this one thing are they never able truly to say, that we have swerved either from the Word of God, or from the Apostles of Christ, or from the primitive Church. Surely we have ever judged the primitive Church of Christ's time, of the Apostles and of the holy fathers, to be the catholic Church: neither make we doubt to name it Noah's ark, Christ's spouse, the pillar and upholder of all truth: nor yet to fix therein the whole means of our salvation. It is doubtless an odious matter for one to leave the fellowship whereunto he hath been accustomed, and specially of those men, who though they be not, yet at least seem and be called Christians. And, to say truly, we do not despise the Church of these men (howsoever it be ordered by them nowadays), partly for the name sake itself, and partly for that the Gospel of Jesus Christ hath once been therein truly and purely set forth. Neither had we departed therefrom, but of very necessity, and much against our wills. But I put case, an idol be set up in the Church of God, and the same desolation which Christ prophesied to come, stood openly in the holy place?[41] What if some thief or pirate invade and possess Noah's ark? These folks as often as they tell us of the Church, mean thereby themselves alone, and attribute all these titles to their own selves, boasting as they did in times past which cried The temple of the Lord, the temple of the Lord;[42] or as the Pharisees and Scribes did, which craked° they were Abraham's children.[43] Thus with a gay and

---

[41] Matthew 24.15: 'When ye therefore shall see the abomination of desolation spoken of by Daniel the Prophet, set in the holy place (let him that readeth consider it).'

[42] Jeremiah 7.4: 'Trust not in lying words, saying, The Temple of the Lord, the Temple of the Lord; this is the Temple of the Lord.'

[43] **Marg.** Joh. viii. [John 8.39: 'They answered, and sayd unto him, Abraham is our father. Jesus sayd unto them, If ye were Abrahams children, ye would doe the workes of Abraham.'] L

AN APOLOGY OR ANSWER IN DEFENCE OF THE CHURCH

jolly show deceive they the simple, and seek to choke us with the very name of the church. Much like as if a thief, when he had gotten into another man's house, and by violence either hath thrust out or slain the owner, should afterward assign the same house to himself, casting forth of possession the right inheritor: or if Antichrist, after he hath once entered into the Temple of God should afterward say, This house is mine own, and Christ hath nothing to do withal. For these men now, after they have left nothing remaining in the church of God that hath any likeness of this Church, yet will they seem the Patrons and the valiant maintainers of the Church, very like as Gracchus amongst the Romans stood in defence of the treasury, notwithstanding with his prodigality and fond expenses he had utterly wasted the whole stock of the treasury. And yet was there never anything so wicked or so far out of reason, but lightly it might be covered and defended by the name of the Church. For the wasps also make honeycombs as well as Bees, and wicked men have companies like to the Church of God, yet for all that they be not straightway the people of God which are called the people of God: neither be they all Israelites as many as are come of Israel the father. The Arians, notwithstanding they were heretics, yet bragged they that they alone were Catholics, calling all the rest now Ambrosians, now Athanasians, now Johannites.44 And Nestorius, as saith Theodoret, for all that he was an heretic, yet covered he himself της ὀρθοδοξίας προσχήματι,45 that is to wit, with a certain cloak

---

44 **Marg.** August. in Epist. 48. ad Vinc. [Augustine, *Epistola*, 93, *ad Vincentio*, 7, sec. 23: 'In fact, however, this is the whole which you attempt to make us believe, that the Rogatists alone remain worthy of the name Catholics, on the ground of their observing all the Divine precepts and all the sacraments; and that you are the only persons in whom the Son of man when He comes shall find faith.']
45 Theodoret, *Compendium haereticarum fabularum*, IV. 17, *De Nestorio*. Theodoret, Bishop of Cyrrhus, near Antioch (*c.* 393–458), defended his friend Nestorius, Archbishop of Constantinople (386–451), in opposition to the anathemas pronounced against him by Cyril of Alexandria. Nestorius saw the human and divine nature of Godhead as two separate entities and refused to accept the term *theotokos* (God-bearer) for Mary. Cyril had insisted on the hypostatic union of God and man. Although Theodoret reluctantly agreed with the condemnation of Nestorius at the Council of Chalcedon in 451, his letter to Nestorius affirmed his loyalty to a friend. 'But to what has been done unjustly and illegally against your holiness, not even if one were to cut off both my hands would I ever assent, God's grace helping me and supporting my infirmity. This I have stated in writing to those who require it. I have sent to your holiness my

460 and colour of the true and right faith. Ebion though he agreed in opinion with the Samaritans, yet as saith Epiphanius, he would needs be called a Christian.⁴⁶ The Mahometists° at this day, for all that all histories make plain mention, and themselves also cannot deny, but they took their first beginning of Agar the bondwoman, yet for the very name and stock's sake, chose they rather to be called Saracens, as though they came of Sarah the free woman, and Abraham's wife.⁴⁷ So likewise the false prophets of all ages, which stood up against the Prophets of God, which resisted Isaiah, Jeremy, Christ, and the Apostles, at no time
470 craked° of anything so much, as they did of the name of the Church. And for no other cause did they so fiercely vex them, and call them Runaways and Apostates, than for that they forsook their fellowship, and kept not the ordinances of the elders. Wherefore if we would follow the judgments of those men only, who then governed the Church, and would respect nothing else neither God nor his Word, it must needs be confessed, that the Apostles were rightly and by just law condemned of them to death, because they fell from the Bishops and priests, that is you must think, from the Catholic Church: and because they made

---

reply to what you wrote to me, that you may know that, by God's grace, no time has changed me like the centipedes and chameleons who imitate by their colour the stones and leaves among which they live.' Letter CLXXII, *The Nicene and Post-Nicene Fathers*, Series II, III (1892), 345.

⁴⁶ Epiphanius, Bishop of Constantia / Salamis (*c.* 310–403), composed the three-volume *Panarion* (medicine chest), known as *Adversus Haereses* (374–377) detailing the arguments of heretics and ways to rebut them. In the Epistle against the Ebionites, he described Ebion: 'For he has the Samaritans' unpleasantness [...] And he wants to have just the Christians' title — most certainly not their behaviour, opinion and knowledge, and the consensus as to faith of the Gospels and Apostles.' From Part 30 of *The Panarion of Epiphanius of Salamis*, trans. by Frank Williams, 2 vols (Leiden: Brill, 1987–1994), I (1987).

⁴⁷ Salaminius Hermias Sozomenus (*c.* 400–450), Greek historian of the Christian church, wrote two major works on the subject of which only the second survives. Of the Saracens he wrote: 'This is the tribe which took its origin and had its name from Ishmael, the son of Abraham; and the ancients called them Ishmaelites after their progenitor. As their mother Hagar was a slave, they afterwards, to conceal the opprobrium of their origin, assumed the name of Saracens, as if they were descended from Sara, the wife of Abraham. Such being their origin, they practice circumcision like the Jews, refrain from the use of pork, and observe many other Jewish rites and customs.' *The Ecclesiastical History of Sozomen from 323 to 425*, Book VI, 38, in the *Nicene and Post-Nicene Fathers*, Series II, II (1891), 375.

480 many new alterations in Religion contrary to the Bishops' and priests' wills, yea and for all their spurning so earnestly against it. Wherefore like as it is written that Hercules in old time was forced in striving with Antaeus that huge giant, to lift him quite up from the earth that was his Mother ere he could conquer him, even so must our Adversaries be heaved from their Mother, that is from this vain colour and shadow of the church, wherewith they so disguise and defend themselves. Otherwise they cannot be brought to yield unto the word of God. And therefore, saith Jeremy the prophet, Make not such great boast that the Temple of the Lord

490 is with you, this is but a vain confidence, for these are lies. The Angel also saith in the Apocalypse, They say they be Jews; but they be the synagogue of Satan.[48] And Christ said to the Pharisees when they vaunted themselves of the kindred and blood of Abraham: Ye are of your father, the Devil,[49] for you resemble not your father Abraham. As much to say, ye are not the men ye would so fain be called, ye beguile the people with vain titles, and abuse the name of the Church to the overthrowing of the Church.

So that these men's part had been first to have clearly and truly proved that the Romish Church is the true and right instructed

500 Church of God, and that the same as they do order it at this day, doth agree with the primitive church of Christ, of the Apostles, and of the holy fathers, which we doubt not but was indeed the true catholic Church. For our parts if we could have judged ignorance, error, superstition, idolatry, men's Inventions, and the same commonly disagreeing with the holy Scriptures, either pleased God, or to be sufficient for the obtaining everlasting salvation, or if we could ascertain ourselves, that the word of God was written but for a time only, and afterward again ought to be abrogated and put away, or else that the sayings and

510 commandments of God ought to be subject to man's will, that whatsoever God saith and commandeth, except the Bishop of Rome willeth and commandeth the same, it must be taken as void

---

[48] Revelation 2.9: 'I know thy workes and tribulation, and povertie (but thou art riche) and *I knowe* the blasphemie of them, which say they are Jewes, and are not, but *are* the Synagogue of Satan.'

[49] **Marg.** John viii. [44: 'Ye are of your father the devill, and the lustes of your father yee will doe: he hath bene a murtherer from the beginning, and abode not in the trueth, because there is no trueth in him. When he speaketh a lie, then speaketh hee of his owne: for he is a liar, and the father thereof.']

and unspoken. If we could have brought ourselves to believe these things, we grant there had been no cause at all why we should have left these men's company. As touching that we have now done to depart from that Church, whose errors were proved and made manifest to the world, which Church also had already evidently departed from God's word, and yet not to depart so much from itself, as from the errors thereof, and not to do this disorderly or wickedly, but quietly and soberly, we have done nothing herein against the doctrine either of Christ or of His Apostles. For neither is the Church of God such as it may not be dusked° with some spot, or asketh not sometime reparation: else what needeth there so many assemblies and Councils, without the which, as saith Ægidius, the Christian faith is not able to stand? For look, saith he, how often Councils are discontinued, so often is the Church destitute of Christ.[50] Or if there be no peril that harm may come to the church, what need is there to retain to no purpose the names of Bishops, as is now commonly used among them? For if there be no sheep that may stray, why be they called shepherds? If there be no City that may be betrayed, why be they called watchmen? If there be nothing that may run to ruin, why be they called Pillars? Anon after the first creation of the world the church of God began to spread abroad, and the same was instructed with the heavenly word, which God Himself pronounced with his own mouth. It was also furnished with divine ceremonies. It was taught by the spirit of God, by the Patriarchs and Prophets, and continued so even till the time that Christ showed himself to us in the flesh. This notwithstanding, how often O good God, in the meanwhile, and how horribly was the same Church darkened and decayed! Where was that Church then, when all flesh upon earth had denied their own way?[51] Where was

---

[50] **Marg.** In Conc. Lat. sub Julio II. ['*Quoties concilia intermittuntur, toties Ecclesia a Christo derelinquitur.*' Ægidius Viterbensis, Giles of Viterbo, General of the Augustinian eremite monks, scholar, Christian cabalist, and cardinal at Rome, passed this comment on the fifth Lateran Council (1512–1517). Whittinghman comments: 'Jewel adopts his sentiment, doubtless, as an *argumentum ad homines* — a sufficient proof to men with the same creed with Ægidius, who admitted his authority, that the church *might* be in danger — There are no traces of a similar extravagant opinion of the necessity of councils in Jewel's own writings.' Whittingham, p. 120.]

[51] Genesis 6.12: 'Then God looked upon the earth, and behold, it was corrupt: for all flesh had corrupted his way upon the earth.'

AN APOLOGY OR ANSWER IN DEFENCE OF THE CHURCH

it when amongst the number of the whole world there were only eight persons (and they neither all chaste and good) whom God's will was should be saved alive from that universal destruction and mortality?[52] When Elijah the prophet so lamentably and bitterly made moan, that only himself was left of all the whole world which did truly and duly worship God?[53] And when Isaiah said, The silver of God's people (that is of the Church) was become Dross: and that the same City, which aforetime had been faithful, was now become a harlot, and that in the same was no part sound throughout the whole body from the head to the foot?[54] Or else, when Christ himself said, that the house of God was made by the Pharisees and Priests a Den of thieves?[55] Of a truth, the Church even as a cornfield, except it be eared,° manured, tilled, and trimmed, instead of wheat, it will bring forth thistles, darnel,° and nettles. For this cause did God send ever among both Prophets and Apostles, and last of all his own Son, who might bring home the people into the right way, and repair anew, the tottering Church after she had erred.

But lest some man should say that the aforesaid things happened in the time of the law only, of shadows, and of infancy, when truth lay hid under figures and ceremonies, when nothing as yet was brought to perfection, when the law was not graven in men's hearts, but in stone, and yet is that but a foolish saying, for even at those days was there the very same God that is now, the same spirit, the same Christ, the same faith, the same doctrine, the same hope, the same inheritance, the same league,° and the same efficacy and virtue of God's word. Eusebius also saith, all the faithful, even from Adam until Christ, were in very deed

---

[52] I Peter 3.20: 'Which were in time passed disobedient, when once the long suffering of God abode in the daies of Noe, while the arke was preparing, wherein fewe, that is, eight soules were saved in the water.'

[53] **Marg.** I Kings xix. [I Kings 19.10: 'And he answered, I have beene very jealous for the Lord God of hoastes: for the children of Israel have forsaken thy covenant, broken downe thine altars, and slaine thy Prophets with the sword, and I onely am left, and they seeke my life to take it away.']

[54] **Marg.** Isai. i. [Isaiah 1.21–22: 'How is the faithfull citie become an harlot? it was full of judgment, *and* justice lodged therein, but now *they are* murtherers. Thy silver is become drosse: thy wine is mixt with water.']

[55] **Marg.** Matt. xxi. [Matthew 21.13: 'And said to them, It is written, My house shall be called the house of prayer: but ye have made it a denne of theeves.']

Christians⁵⁶ though they were not so termed. But as I said, lest men should thus speak still, Paul the apostle found the like faults and falls even then in the prime and chief of the Gospel, in chief perfection, and in light, so that he was compelled to write in this sort to the Galatians, whom he had well before that instructed: I fear me (quod he) lest I have laboured among you in vain, and lest ye have heard the Gospel in vain.⁵⁷ O my little children, of whom I travail anew, till Christ be fashioned again in you.⁵⁸ And as for the Church of the Corinthians, how foully it was defiled, is nothing needful to rehearse. Now tell me, might the Churches of the Galatians and Corinthians go amiss, and the church of Rome alone may it not fail nor go amiss? Surely Christ prophesied long before of his Church, that the time should come when desolation should stand in the holy place.⁵⁹ And Paul saith, that Antichrist should once set up his own tabernacle and stately seat in the temple of God:⁶⁰ and that the time should be, when men should not away with wholesome doctrine, but be turned back unto fables and lies, and that within the very Church.⁶¹ Peter likewise telleth, how there should be teachers of lies in the church of Christ.⁶² Daniel

---

[56] **Marg.** Lib. i. cap. i. [Eusebius, *Church History*, I. 4: 'But although it is clear that we are new and that this new name of Christians has really but recently been known among all nations, nevertheless our life and our conduct, with our doctrines of religion, have not been lately invented by us, but from the first creation of man, so to speak, have been established by the natural understanding of divinely favored men of old.' *Nicene and Post-Nicene Fathers*, I (1890). 87.]

[57] Galatians 4.11: 'I am in feare of you, least I have bestowed on you labor in vaine.'

[58] Galatians 4.19: 'My little children, of whom I travaile in birth againe, untill Christ be formed in you.'

[59] **Marg.** Matt. xxiv. [Matthew 24.15: 'When ye therefore shall see the abomination of desolation spoken of by Daniel the Prophet, set in the holy place (let him that readeth consider it).'] L

[60] **Marg.** 2 Thess. ii. [II Thessalonians 2.4: 'Which is an adversary, and exalteth himselfe against all that is called God, or that is worshipped: so that he doeth sit as God in the Temple of God, showing himselfe that he is God.']

[61] **Marg.** 2 Tim. iv. [II Timothy 4.3–4: 'For the time will come when they will not suffer wholesome doctrine: but having their ears itching, shall after their own lusts get them an heap of teachers, And shall turn their ears from the truth, and shall be given unto fables.']

[62] **Marg.** 2 Pet. ii. [II Peter 2.1: 'But there were false prophets also among the people, even as there shallbe false teachers among you: which privily shall bring in damnable heresies, even denying the Lord that hath bought them, and bring upon themselves swift damnation.']

AN APOLOGY OR ANSWER IN DEFENCE OF THE CHURCH

610   the Prophet speaking of the latter times of Antichrist, Truth saith he, in that season shall be thrown under foot, and trodden upon in the world.[63] And Christ saith, how the calamity and confusion of things shall be so exceeding great, that even the chosen, if it were possible, shall be brought into error:[64] and how all these things shall come to pass, not amongst Gentiles and Turks, but that they should be in the holy place, in the Temple of God, in the church, and in the company and fellowship of those which profess the name of Christ.

      Albeit these same warnings alone may suffice a wise man to
620   take heed he do not suffer himself rashly to be deceived with the name of the Church, and not to stay to make further inquisition thereof by God's word, yet beside all this, many fathers also, many learned and godly men, have often and carefully complained how all these things have chanced in their lifetime. For even in the midst of that thick mist of darkness, God would yet there should be some, who though they gave not a clear and bright light, yet should they kindle, were it but some spark, which men might espy being in the darkness.

      Hilarius, when things as yet were almost uncorrupt, and in good
630   ease too, Ye are ill deceived, saith he, with the love of walls: ye do ill worship the Church, in that ye worship it in houses and buildings: ye do ill bring in the name of peace under roofs. Is there any doubt but Antichrist will have his seat under the same? I rather reckon hills, woods, pools, marshes, prisons, and quagmires, to be places of more safety: for in these the Prophets, either abiding of their accord, or drowned by violence, did prophesy by the spirit of God.[65]

---

[63] **Marg.** Dan. viii. [Daniel 8.12: 'And a time shall be given *him* over the dayly *sacrifice* for the iniquitie: and it shall cast downe the trueth to the ground, and thus shall it doe, and prosper.']

[64] **Marg.** Matt. xxiv. [Matthew 24.24: 'For there shall arise false Christs, & false prophets, & shall show great signes & wonders, so y^t if it were possible, they should deceive the very elect.']

[65] **Marg.** Contr. Aux. [Hilary of Poitiers (*c.* 300–368), bishop, Doctor of the Church, and opponent of Arianism, *Contra Arianos vel Auxentium Mediolanensum*, 17. Auxtentius became the Arian Bishop of Milan in 355. Jewel and Bacon present this passage in *Contra Auxentium* faithfully: '*Male vos parietum coepit: male Ecclesiam Dei in tectis, aedificiisque veneramini: male sub iis pacis nomen ingeritis. Anne ambiguum est, in iis Antichristum esse sussurum? Montes mihi, et sylvae, et lacus, et carceres, et voragines sunt tutiores; in illis enim prophetae, aut manentes, aut demersi, Dei Spiritu prophetabant.*' Hilary quoted in Whittingham, p. 124.]

Gregory, as one which perceived and foresaw in his mind the wrack of all things wrote thus to John Bishop of Constantinople, who was the first of all others that commanded himself to be called by this new name, the universal bishop of whole Christ's Church. If the Church saith he, shall depend upon one man, it will at once fall down to the ground.[66] Who is he that seeth not how this is come to pass long since? For long agone hath the Bishop of Rome willed to have the whole Church depend upon himself alone. Wherefore it is no marvel though it be clean fallen down long agone.

Bernard the Abbot above four hundred years past, writeth thus: Nothing is now of sincerity and pureness amongst the Clergy, wherefore it resteth that the man of sin should be revealed.[67] The same Bernard in his work of the conversion of Paul, It seemeth now saith he, that persecution hath ceased: no

---

[66] **Marg.** In Regist. Lib. iv. Epist. 32. ad Maurit. [The marginal gloss is incorrect. Pope Gregory the Great wrote to Emperor Mauritius: '*Si igitur illud nomen in ea Ecclesia sibi quisquam arripit, quod apud bonorum omnium judicium fecit; universa ergo Ecclesia, quod absit, a statu suo corruit, quando is qui appellatur universalis cadit.*' Harding, who maintained that Gregory was inveighing against John bishop of Constantinople 'for challenging that name of universal bishop,' translated: 'If any man hath caught unto himself that name (of universal bishop) in that church (of Constantinople), then the whole church (which God forbid) fell from his state, when he that is called universal fell.' Harding accused Jewel of using his own words, not Gregory's. Jewel insisted 'We neither lie ourselves, nor father lies upon the doctors,' and retorted with his translation of the second half of the statement: 'the whole universal church falleth from her state, when he falleth that is called the universal bishop.' *Ad Mauricium Augustum, Lib. v, Ep. xx, Registrum Epistolarum, Sancti Gregorii Papae Primi congnomen Magni Opera, Patrologia Latina*, LXXVII, col. 746. *Works*, IV, 731–32.]

[67] **Marg.** Sermone 33. [Bernard of Clairvaux, *In Psalmum XC, Qui Habitat*, sermo VI, sec. 7: '*Pro episcopatibus et archidiaconatibus impudenter hodie decertatur, ut ecclesiarum redditus in superfluitatis et vanitatis usus dissipentur. Superest jam ut reveletur homo peccati filius perditionis, daemonium non modo diurnum, sed et meridianum; quod non solum transfiguratur in angelum lucis, sed extollitur supra omne quod dicitur Deus, aut quod colitur.*' 'Today people scrap shamelessly to get archbishoprics and archdeaconries in order to dissipate church revenues in wanton waste and vain pursuits. Now it remains for us to disclose the man of sin, the son of perdition, who is no longer simply a day devil, but the noonday devil disguised as an angel of light and exalting himself above all that is called God or that is worshipped.' Bernard of Clairvaux, *Sermons on Conversion*, trans. by Marie-Bernard Saïd, OSB (Kalamazoo, Michigan: Cistercian Publications, 1981), p. 149.]

no, persecution seemeth but now to begin, even from them which have chief preeminence in the Church. Thy friends and neighbours have drawn near, and stood up against thee: from the sole of thy foot to the crown of thy head, there is no part whole. Iniquity is proceeded from the Elders, the judges and deputies which pretend to rule thy people. We cannot say now, Look how the people be, so is the priest. For the people, be not so ill as the priest is. Alas, alas, O Lord God, the selfsame persons be the chief in persecuting thee, which seem to love the highest place, and bear most rule in thy church.[68] The same Bernard again upon the Canticles writeth thus, All they are thy friends, yet are they all thy foes, all thy kinsfolk, yet are they all thy adversaries, being Christ's servants, they serve Antichrist. Behold, in my rest, my bitterness is most bitter.[69]

Roger Bacon, also a man of great fame, after he had in a vehement Oration touched to the quick the woeful state of his own time, These so many errors, saith he, require and look for Antichrist.[70] Gerson complaineth how in his days all the substance and efficacy of sacred divinity was brought unto a glorious contention and ostentation of wits, and to very

---

[68] *S. Pauli*, sermo I, sec. iii: '*Amici tui, Deus, et proximi adversum te appropinquaverunt et steterunt. Conjurasse videtur contra ae universitas populi Christiani a minimo usque ad maximum: a planta pedis usque ad verticem non est sanitas ulla: egressa est iniquitas a senioribus judicibus, vicariis tuis, qui videntur regere populum tuum. Non est jam dicere, Ut populus, sic sacerdos (Isai. XXIV, 2); quia nec si populus, ut sacerdos. Heu, heu! Domine Deus, quia ipsi sunt in persecutione tua primi, qui videntur in Ecclesia tua primatum diligere, gerere principatum!*' S. Bernardi Claraevallensis Opera Omnia, Patrologia Latina, CLXXXIII (1854). Bacon captures the sense of Bernard's observations including the exclamations (*heu, heu*) and the irony of highly placed persecutors.

[69] Bernard, *Sermones in Cantica Canticorum*: '*Omnes amici, et omnes inimici; omnes necessarii, et omnes adversarii; omnes domestici, et nulli pacifici; omnes proximi, et omnes quae sua sunt quaerunt. Ministri Christi sunt, et serviunt Antichristo.* [...] *Ecce in pace amaritudo mea amarissima (Isai. XXXVIII, 17).*' S. Bernardi Claraevallensis Opera Omnia, Patrologia Latina, CLXXXIII (1854), Sermo. XXXIII, secs. 15, 16.

[70] **Marg.** In Libello de idiomate linguarum. [Roger Bacon (*c.* 1214–1294), philosopher and Franciscan friar, whose skill, according to editor Whittingham, 'in natural philosophy and mechanics, far beyond that of his contemporaries, procured for him the reputation, and the punishment, of a magician.' Whittinghman, p. 126. Editor Ayre noted that 'the work of Bacon referred to was, as Harding rejoins, at this time unprinted. The passage here quoted does not appear in *De Utilitate Linguarum.*' Works, IV, 735–36.]

sophistry.⁷¹ The friars of Lyons, men as touching the manner of their life, not to be misliked, were wont boldly to affirm, that the Romish Church (from whence alone all counsel and order was then sought) was the very same harlot of Babylon and rout of Devils, whereof is prophesied so plainly in the Apocalypse. I know well enough the authority of these foresaid persons is but lightly regarded among these men. How then if I call forth those for witness whom they themselves have used to honour? What if I say that Adrian the Bishop of Rome did frankly confess that all these mischiefs brast° out first from the high throne of the Pope?⁷² Pighius acknowledgeth herein to be a fault, that many abuses are brought in, even into the very Mass, which Mass otherwise he would have seem to be a reverend matter.⁷³ Gerson saith, that through the number of most fond ceremonies, all the virtue of the holy Ghost, which ought to have operation in us, and all true Godliness is utterly quenched and dead.⁷⁴ Whole Greece and

680

---

⁷¹ Jean Charlier de Gerson (1363–1429), academic theologian and chancellor of the University of Paris, was a strong supporter of conciliarism, holding that general councils are superior to the papacy. Although the precise text for this complaint was not located, editor Ayre suggested the following: '*Fabulae, et non sanae doctrinae sunt, quae in persuasibilibus humanae sapientiae verbis, 1 Cor. ii. 4, vel in sublimitate sermonum, aut secundum zelum, et contentionem, aut inanem gloriam, non in revelatione Spiritus sancti, sed secundum traditionem hominum consistent.*' John Gerson, *Joannis Gersonii, Opera Omnia, Tomus secundus* (Antwerp: Sumptibus Societatis, 1706), *Serm. de Calam. Eccles. et de Sign. Fut. Jud.*, Tom III, Pars ii, col. 313. *Works*, IV, 736.

⁷² **Marg.** Platina. [Bartolomeo Sacchi, or Platina, was appointed Vatican librarian; his *Historia de vitis ac gestis Pontificum Romanorum* (1479) was extended after his death to include events to 1529. Pope Adrian VI (1522–1523) was a reformer whose initiatives were interrupted by his short papacy. Editor Whittingham quoted the message of Adrian's legate at Nuremburg from Sleidanus, *Commentarium*, IV, under ad 1523: 'that the iniquity of the people grew from the priests: and that now, for the space of many years, there have been great and grievous offences committed in Rome.' Whittingham, p. 127.]

⁷³ In *The Defence* Harding admitted that 'certain abuses be crept into that most holy and healthful thing,' citing Pighius: '*quod si qui abusus in rem sacratissimam et saluberrimam irrepserunt.*' Alb. Pigh. *Explic. Cathol. Controv. Par.* 1586 *Contr. VII. De Miss. Priv.* fol. 123.2. Jewel insisted that the emphasis in Pighius is not on abuses in the priests and the people, but 'plainly and simply he saith: "Errors have crept into the mass."' *Works*, IV, 738–739.

⁷⁴ The precise text in Gerson (1706) is elusive. Editor Booty suggested *Lib. De vit. spirit. Anim.*, lect. ii. Booty, p. 74. In *Sermo de Sancto Spiritu, Secunda consideratio*, Gerson perorated by reminding his hearers that one can be more suitably restored, as much as life, and more greatly fulfilled by the union and

AN APOLOGY OR ANSWER IN DEFENCE OF THE CHURCH

Asia, complain how the Bishops of Rome, with the marts° of their Purgatories and Pardons, have both tormented men's consciences, and picked their purses.

As touching the tyranny of the bishops of Rome, and their barbarous Persian-like pride, to leave out others whom perchance they reckon for enemies, because they freely and liberally find fault with their vices, the self same men which have led their life at Rome in the holy City, in the face of the most holy father, who also were able to see all their secrets, and at no time departed from the Catholic faith: As for example Laurentius Valla, Marsilius Patavinus, Francis Petrarch, Hierom Savonarola, Abbot Joachim, Baptist of Mantua,[75] and, before all these, Bernard the Abbot, have many a time and much complained of it, giving the world also sometime to understand that the Bishop of Rome himself (by your leave) is very Antichrist. Whether they spake it truly or falsely, let that go. Sure I am they spake it plainly. Neither can any man allege that those authors were Luther's or Zwinglius' scholars, for they were not only certain years, but also certain ages ere ever Luther's or Zwinglius' names were heard of. They well saw that even in their days errors had crept into the Church, and wished earnestly they might be amended.

And what marvel if the Church were then carried away with errors in that time, specially when neither the Bishop of Rome who then only ruled the roost, nor almost any other, either did his duty, or once understood what was his duty. For it is hard to be believed, while they were idle and fast asleep, that the Devil also all that while either fell asleep, or else continually lay idle. For how they were occupied in the meantime, and with what faithfulness they took care of God's house, though we hold our peace, yet I pray you, let them hear Bernard their own friend. The Bishops (saith he) who now have the charge of God's church, are not teachers but deceivers, they are not feeders, but beguilers, they

---

virtue of the Holy Spirit: *'magis idoneus redditus est tanquam vita, unione et virtute Sancti Spiritus magis adimpletus.'*

[75] Lorenzo Valla (*c.* 1407–1457), Italian philosopher, humanist, and literary critic; Marsilius of Padua (*c.* 1275–1342), Italian policital philosopher; Francesco Petrarch (AD 1304–1374), Italian classical scholar, humanist, and poet; Girolamo Savonarola (1452–1498), Dominican friar, reformer, and ultimately executed heretic; Joachim of Fiore (*c.* 1132–1202), Cistercian abbot and mystic; Baptista Spagnuoli Mantuanus, or Mantuan (1447–1516), Italian Carmelite, poet, and humanist.

720 are not Prelates but Pilates.⁷⁶ These words spake Bernard of that Bishop, who named himself the highest bishop of all, and of the other Bishops likewise which then had the place of government. Bernard was no Lutheran, Bernard was no heretic, he had not forsaken the Catholic church, yet nevertheless he did not let° to call the Bishops that then were, deceivers, beguilers, and Pilates. Now when the people was openly deceived, and Christian men's eyes were craftily bleared, and when Pilate sat in judgment place, and condemned Christ and Christ's members to sword and fire, O good Lord, in what case was Christ's church then? But yet tell
730 me, of so many and so gross errors, what one have these men at any time reformed, or what fault have they once acknowledged and confessed?

But, forsomuch as these men avouch the universal possession of the catholic Church to be their own, and call us Heretics, because we agree not in judgment with them, let us know I beseech you, what proper mark and badge hath that Church of theirs, whereby it may be known to be the Church of God. I wiss° it is not so hard a matter to find out God's Church, if a man will seek it earnestly and diligently. For the Church of God is set upon
740 a high and glittering place in the top of a hill,⁷⁷ and built upon the foundation of the Apostles and prophets:⁷⁸ There saith Augustine, let us seek the Church, there let us try our matter.⁷⁹ And as he saith again in another place, The Church must be

---

⁷⁶ **Marg.** Bernard. ad Eugen. [The pithy Latin phrasing, which Whittingham produces, '*Episcopi non doctores sunt, sed seductores; non pastores, sed impostores; non praelati sed Pilati,*' does not appear in Bernard's *De consideratione ad Eugenium*. Whittingham, p. 132. In *The Defence* Harding translates the proposed citation from *On Consideration*, II.8, about the pope's pastoral responsibility: 'Neither art thou only the pastor of all the sheep, but also the only pastor of all the pastors.' *Works*, IV, 746. Bernard was, however, genuinely critical of clerical laxity, especially at the Council of Reims (1148) and in *Sermo de Conversione ad Clericos, Patrologia Latina*, CLXXXII (1854), cols. 834–56.]

⁷⁷ Isaiah 2.2: 'It shalbe in the last dayes, that the mountaine of the House of the Lord shall be prepared in the top of the mountaines, and shall be exalted above the hilles, and all nations shall flow unto it.'

⁷⁸ Ephesians 2.20: 'And are built upon the foundation of the Apostles and Prophets, Jesus Christ himselfe being the chiefe corner stone.'

⁷⁹ **Marg.** August. de Unit. Eccles. cap. iii. ['*Ibi quaeramus Ecclesiam: ibi discutiamus causam nostram.*' *Contra Donatistas Vulgo de Unitate Ecclesiae, caput iii, sec. 5. Patrologia Latina*, XLIII (1847), col. 394.]

AN APOLOGY OR ANSWER IN DEFENCE OF THE CHURCH

showed out of the holy and canonical scriptures: and that which cannot be showed out of them is not the Church.[80] Yet, for all this I wot° not how, whether it be for fear or for conscience, or despairing of victory, these men alway abhor and fly the word of God, even as the thief flieth the gallows. And no wonder truly, for like as men say the cantharus[81] by and by perisheth and dieth, as soon as it is laid in balm, notwithstanding balm be otherwise a most sweet-smelling ointment, even so these men well see their own matter is damped and destroyed in the word of God, as if it were in poison. Therefore the holy scriptures which our Saviour Jesus Christ did not only use for authority in all his speech, but did also at last seal up the same with his own blood: these men to the intent they might with less business drive the people from the same, as from a thing dangerous and deadly, have used to call them a bare letter, uncertain, unprofitable, dumb, killing, and dead: which seemeth to us all one as if they should say, The scriptures are to no purpose, or as good as none. Hereunto they add a similitude not very agreeable, how the scriptures be like to a nose of wax, or a shipman's hose: how they may be fashioned and plied all manner of ways, and serve all men's turns.[82] Woteth° not the Bishop of Rome that these things are spoken by his own minions? Or understandeth he not he hath such champions to fight for him? Let him hearken then how holily and how godly one Hosius writeth of this matter, a bishop in Polonia as he testifieth of himself: a man doubtless well spoken and not

---

[80] **Marg.** Idem. Cap. iv. [Augustine, '*Quicumque de ipso capite, ab Scripturis sanctis dissentiunt, etiamsi in omnibus locis inveniantur in quibus Ecclesia designata est, non sunt in Ecclesia,*' *De Unitate Ecclesiae*, caput IV, sec. 7, *Patrologia Latina*, XLIII (1847), cols. 395–96. Bacon demonstrates a concise understanding of Augustine.]

[81] Cantharus: the pharmacopœial name of the dried beetle *cantharis vesicatoria* or Spanish Fly, used externally as a rubifacient and vesicant and internally as a diuretic; formerly considered an aphrodisiac. (OED).

[82] **Marg.** Albert. Pigh. in Hierarch. [Albertus Pighius did not claim that the Scriptures were worthless; rather, seeing that no place in Scripture was so clear and open that the adulteration and twisting of the heretics according to their depraved sense could not by force and injury straightforwardly appropriate, indeed these scriptures are just as a nose of wax, '*Sed quoniam nullus scripturae locus ita planus est aut apertus, qui ab haereticorumscripturas adulterantium, torquentium, & ad suum sensum depravantium, vi & iniuria se prorsus vindicet. Sunt enim illae velut nasus cereus.*' *Hierarchiae ecclesiasticae assertio. Coloniae Agrippinae* (Köln: *Apud Johannem Birckmannum*, 1558), III. 3, fol. CXXIIII.]

unlearned, and a very sharp and stout maintainer of that side. One will marvel, I suppose, how a good man could either conceive so wickedly or write so despitefully of those words which he knew proceeded from God's mouth, and specially in such sort, as he would not have it seem his own private opinion alone, but the common opinion of all that band. He dissembleth, I grant you indeed, and hideth what he is, and setteth forth the matter so, as though it were not he and his side, but the Zwenckfeldian heretics that so did speak. We, saith he, will bid away with the same scriptures, whereof we see brought not only diverse, but also contrary interpretations: and we will hear God speak, rather than we will resort to the naked elements, and appoint our salvation to rest in them. It behoveth not a man to be expert in the law and scripture, but to be taught of God. It is but lost labour that a man bestoweth in the scriptures, for the scripture is a creature, and a certain bare letter.[83] This is Hosius' saying, uttered altogether with the same spirit and the same mind wherewith in times past Montane and Marcion were moved, who as men report, used to say when with a contempt they rejected the holy scriptures, that themselves knew many more and better things than either Christ or the Apostles ever knew.

What then shall I say here, O ye principal posts of Religion, O ye Archgovernors of CHRIST's Church, is this that your reverence which ye give to God's word? The holy Scriptures, which St Paul saith came by the inspiration of God, which God did commend by so many miracles, wherein are the most perfect prints of Christ's own steps, which all the holy fathers, Apostles, and

---

[83] **Marg.** Hosius de Expr. Verb. Dei. [Stanislaus Hosius (1504–1579), Polish cardinal, quoted the views of Schwenckfeld, '*quod isti sui sensui scripturas attemperarent, nec pro scriptuarum, sed pro sua sententia dimicarent*,' who was adjusting the sense of scripture not on behalf of scripture but to fight on behalf of his own meaning. In their lengthy diatribe, Harding accused Jewel of resorting to 'patched note-books' and 'scattered authorities.' Harding insisted that Hosius was presenting the position of Schwenckfeld in this statement: '*Non oportet legis aut scripture esse peritum, sed a Deo doctum, vanus est labor, qui scripturae impenditu, scriptura enim creatura est, & egenum quoddam elementum*', captured in Bacon's translation. The main battle between these two contenders was the source of interpretative authority: the church or scripture. Harding maintained that 'whatsover is taught against the meaning and consent of the church, that is the express word of the devil.' Jewel rejoined with a *sola scriptura* position: 'all heretics are evermore reproved by the scriptures, as you be.' Hosius, p. 40. *Works*, IV, 753–761.]

Angels, which Christ himself the son of God, as often as was needful did allege for testimony and proof: will ye, as though they were unworthy for you to hear, bid them avaunt° away? That is, will ye enjoin God to keep silence, who speaketh to you most clearly by his own mouth in the Scriptures? Or that Word, whereby alone, as Paul saith, we are reconciled to God, and which the prophet David saith, is holy and pure, and shall last forever, will ye call that but a bare and dead letter?[84] Or will ye say that all our labour is lost, which is bestowed in that thing which Christ hath commanded us diligently to search and to have evermore before our eyes?[85] And will ye say that Christ and the Apostles meant with subtlety to deceive the people, when they exhorted them to read the holy Scriptures, that thereby they might flow in all wisdom and knowledge? No marvel at all, though these men despise us and all our doings, which set so little by God himself and his infallible sayings. Yet was it but want of wit in them, to the intent they might hurt us, to do so extreme injury to the Word of God.

But Hosius will here make exclamation saying we do him wrong, and that these be not his own words, but the words of the heretic Zwenckfeldius. But how then, if Zwenckfeldius make exclamation on the other side, and say that the same very words be not his but Hosius' own words? For tell me where hath Zwenckfeldius ever written them? Or if he have written them, and Hosius have judged the same to be wicked, why hath not Hosius spoken so much as one word to confute them? Howsoever the matter goeth, although Hosius peradventure will not allow of those words, yet he doth not disallow the meaning of the words. For well near in all controversies, and namely touching the use of the holy communion under both kinds, although the words of Christ be plain and evident, yet doth Hosius disdainfully reject them, as no better than cold and dead elements: and commandeth us to give faith to certain new lessons, appointed by the Church, and to I wot° not what revelations of the holy Ghost. And Pighius

---

[84] Psalm 19.8–9: 'The statutes of the Lord *are* right, and rejoyce the heart, the commandement of the Lord *is* pure, and giveth light unto the eyes. The feare of the Lord *is* cleane, and endureth forever: the judgments of the Lord *are* trueth: they are righteous altogether.'

[85] John 5.39: 'Search the Scriptures: for in them yee thinke to have eternall life, and they are they which testifie of me.'

830 saith, Men ought not to believe, no not the most clear and manifest words of the scriptures, unless the same be allowed for good by the interpretation and authority of the church.[86]

And yet, as though this were too little, they also burn the holy scriptures, as in times past wicked King Aza did, or as Antiochus, or Maximinus did, and are wont to name them Heretics' books. And out of doubt to see too, they would fain do as Herod in old time did in Jewry, that he might with more surety keep still his dominion. Who being an Idumaean born, and a stranger to the stock and kindred of the Jews, and yet coveting much to be taken
840 for a Jew, to the end he might establish to him and his posterity the kingdom of that country, which he had gotten of Augustus Caesar, he commanded all the genealogies and pedigrees to be burnt and made out of the way, so that there should remain no record, whereby he might be known to them that came after that he was an Alien in blood:[87] whereas even from Abraham's time these monuments had been safely kept amongst the Jews and laid up in their treasury because in them it might easily and most assuredly be found of what lineage everyone did descend. So (in good faith) do these men, when they would have all their own
850 doings in estimation, as though they had been delivered to us even from the Apostles, or from Christ himself, to the end there might

---

[86] In *Hierarchiae ecclesiaticae assertio*, Albert Pighius reinforced the doctrinal authority of the church. Turning and twisting to defend the authority of scripture were impossible without the authority of the church: '*Nunquam sane potuerunt, quoquo se veterint, quomodocumque se torserint servare ac defendere sacrarum scriptuarum autoritatem nisi ex autoritate traditionis ecclesiaticae*' (fol. VII). Therefore, the doctrine of Christ and the apostles reaches us more through the authority of church tradition than through scripture: '*Ex ecclesiaticae igitur traditionis autoritate magis, quam ex scripto ad nos pervenit Christi apostolorumque doctrina*' (fol. IX).

[87] **Marg.** Euseb. [Eusebius, *Church History*, I. 7: 'But as there had been kept in the archives up to that time the genealogies of the Hebrews as well as of those who traced their lineage back to proselytes, such as Achior the Ammonite and Ruth the Moabitess, and to those who were mingled with the Israelites and came out of Egypt with them, Herod, inasmuch as the lineage of the Israelites contributed nothing to his advantage, and since he was goaded with the consciousness of his own ignoble extraction, burned all the genealogical records, thinking that he might appear of noble origin if no one else were able, from the public registers, to trace back his lineage to the patriarchs or proselytes and to those mingled with them, who were called Georae.' *Nicene and Post-Nicene Fathers*, I (1890), 93.]

AN APOLOGY OR ANSWER IN DEFENCE OF THE CHURCH

be found nowhere anything able to convince such their dreams and lies, either they burn the holy Scriptures, or else they craftily convey them from the people surely.

Very rightly and aptly doth Chrysostom write against these men. Heretics, saith he, shut up the doors against the truth: for they know full well, if the door were open, the Church should be none of theirs.[88] Theophylact also: God's Word saith he, is the Candle whereby the thief is espied.[89] And Tertullian saith, the holy Scripture manifestly findeth out the fraud and theft of heretics.[90] For why do they hide, why do they keep under the Gospel, which Christ would have preached aloud from the housetop? Why whelm° they that light under a Bushel, which ought to stand on a Candlestick? Why trust they more to the blindness of the unskilful multitude and to ignorance, than to the goodness of their cause? Think they their sleights are not already perceived, and that they can walk now unespied, as though they had Gyges' ring,° to go invisibly by, upon their finger? No no: all men see now well and well again, what good stuff is in that Chest of the Bishop of Rome's bosom. This thing alone of itself may be an argument sufficient that they work not uprightly and truly. Worthily ought that matter seem suspicious which flieth trial, and is afraid of the light: for he that doeth evil, as Christ saith, seeketh darkness, and hateth the light.[91] A conscience that knoweth itself clear, cometh willingly into open show, that the works which proceed of God may be seen. Neither be they so very blind, but they see this well enough how their own kingdom straightway is at a point, if the scripture once have the upper hand: and that like as men say, the Idols of devils in times past, of whom men in doubtful matters were then wont to receive answers, were

---

[88] **Marg.** Chrysost. in Op. Imperf. [Chrysostom, *Opus imperfectum in Matthaeum*: 'sic et modo haeretici sacerdotes claudunt januam veritatis. Sciunt enim quoniam si manifestata fuerit veritas, eorum ecclesia est relinquenda.' Hom. XLIV, cap. XXIII. *Works*, IV, 767. This work has been wrongly attributed to Chrysostom.]

[89] Jewel quoted the Greek commentary on Luke 16.31 from Theophylact, *Ennaratio in Evangelium Lucae*, hom. XLIV, cap. XXIII, *Works*, IV, 767.

[90] Tertullian, *De Trinitate*: 'sed enim scriptura divina haereticorum et fraudes et furta facile convincit et detegit.' *Works*, IV, 767. This work is attributed to Novatian, third-century theologian and anti-pope.

[91] John 3.20: 'For every man that evill doeth, hateth the light, neither cometh to light, lest his deedes should be reproved.'

suddenly stricken dumb at the sight of Christ, when he was born and came into the world: even so they see that now all their subtle practices will soon fall down headlong upon the sight of the Gospel. For Antichrist is not overthrown but with the brightness of Christ's coming.[92]

As for us, we run not for succour to the fire, as these men's guise is, but we run to the scriptures: neither do we reason with the sword, but with the word of God: and therewith, as saith Tertullian, do we feed our faith; by it do we stir up our hope, and strengthen our confidence.[93] For we know that the Gospel of JESUS CHRIST is the power of God unto salvation;[94] and that therein consisteth eternal life. And as Paul warneth us, we do not hear, no, not an Angel of God coming from Heaven, if he go about to pull us from any part of this doctrine.[95] Yea more than this, as the holy martyr Justin speaketh of himself, we would give no credence to God himself, if He should teach us any other Gospel.[96]

For where these men bid the holy Scriptures away, as dumb and fruitless, and procure us to come to God himself rather, who speaketh in the Church and in Councils: which is to say, to believe their fancies and opinions. This way of finding out the truth is very uncertain and exceeding dangerous, and in manner a fantastical and mad way, and by no means allowed of the holy fathers. Chrysostom saith, there be many oftentimes which boast themselves of the holy Ghost: but truly whoso speak of their own head do falsely boast they have the spirit of God. For like as, saith he, Christ denied he spake of himself, when he spake out of the

---

[92] **Marg.** 2 Thess. ii. [II Thessalonians 2.8: 'And then shall that wicked man be revealed, whom the Lord shall consume with the Spirit of his mouth, and shall abolish with the brightnesse of his comming.'] **L**

[93] Tertullian, *Apologia*, 39: '*Certe fidem sanctis vocibus pascimus, spem erigimus, fiduciam figimus.* Therewith do we feed our faith; by it do we stir up our hope, and strengthen our confidence.' *Works*, IV, 769.

[94] **Marg.** Rom. i. [Romans 1.16: 'For I am not ashamed of the Gospell of Christ: for it is the power of God unto salvation to everyone that beleeveth, to the Jew first, and also to the Grecian.'] **L**

[95] **Marg.** Gal. i. [See note 26, Part II.] **L**

[96] Whittingham comments on this later omitted sentence from the translation of *The Fathers of the Church of England*: 'Although in the original Latin, it is not given in the text of the Apology printed by Jewel with his Defence. Probably his better judgment inclined him to omit an overstrained expression which it would have been difficult to defend' (p. 144).

910   law and Prophets, even so now, if anything be pressed upon us in the name of the holy Ghost, save the Gospel, we ought not to believe it. For as Christ is the fulfilling of the law and Prophets, so is the holy Ghost the fulfilling of the Gospel.[97] Thus far goeth Chrysostom.

---

[97] Quoting the Greek text of *Sermo de Sancto Spiritu, tom iii*, Jewel conceded that 'this homily is not considered genuine.' *Works*, IV, 774.

PART V

But here I look they will say, though they have not the Scriptures, yet may chance they have the Ancient Doctors and the holy fathers with them. For this is a high brag they have ever made, how that all antiquity and a continual consent of all ages doth make on their side; and that all our cases be but new, and yesterday's work, and until these few last years were never heard of. Questionless there can nothing be more spitefully spoken against the religion of God than to accuse it of novelty, as a new come up matter. For as there can be no change in God himself, no more ought there to be no change in his religion.

Yet nevertheless we wot° not by what means, but we have ever seen it come so to pass from the first beginning of all, that as often as God did give but some light, and did open his truth unto men, though the truth were not only of greatest antiquity, but also from everlasting, yet of wicked men and of the adversaries was it called Newfangled and of late devised. That ungracious and bloodthirsty Haman, when he sought to procure the king Assuerus' displeasure against the Jews, this was his accusation to him: Thou hast here (saith he) a kind of people that useth certain new laws of their own, but stiff-necked and rebellious against all thy laws.[1] When Paul also began first to preach and expound the Gospel at Athens, he was called a tidings bringer of new Gods: as much to say, as of a new religion: For (said the Athenians) may we not know of thee what new doctrine this is?[2] Celsus likewise when he of set purpose wrote against Christ, to the end he might more scornfully scoff out the Gospel by the name of novelty, What saith he, hath God after so many ages now at last, and so late bethought himself?[3] Eusebius

---

[1] **Marg.** Esth. iii. [Esther 3.8: 'Then Haman said unto king Ahashuerosh, There is a people scattered, and dispersed among the people in all the provinces of thy kingdome, and their laws *are* divers from all people, and they doe not observe the Kings lawes: therefore it is not the kings profit to suffer them.'] **L**

[2] **Marg.** Act. xvii. [Acts 17.18–19: 'Then certain Philosophers of the Epicures, and of the Stoicks, disputed with him, and some sayd, What will this babbler say? Others *sayd*, He seemeth to be a setter foorth of strange gods (because he preached unto them Jesus, and the resurrection.) And they tooke him, and brought him into Mars street, saying, May we not know, what this new doctrine, whereof thou speakest, is?'] **L**

[3] Celsus the Platonist was a second-century polemical writer against Christianity.

AN APOLOGY OR ANSWER IN DEFENCE OF THE CHURCH

also writeth, that Christian religion from the beginning for very spite was called νέος και ξένος, that is to say, New and Strange.[4] After like sort, these men condemn all our matters as strange and new; but they will have their own, whatsoever they are, to be praised as things of long continuance.[5] Doing much like to the enchanters and sorcerers nowadays, which working with devils use to say, they have their books and all their holy and hid mysteries from Athanasius, Cyprian, Moses, Abel, Adam, and from the archangel Raphael, because that their cunning coming from such patrons and founders, might be judged the more high and holy. After the same fashion these men, because they would have their own religion which they themselves, and that not long since, have brought forth into the world to be the easier and rather accepted of foolish persons, or of such as cast little whereabouts they or other do go, they are wont to say, they had it from Augustine, Hierom, Chrysostom, from the Apostles, and from Christ himself. Full well know they, that nothing is more in the people's favour, or better liketh the common sort than these names.

But how if the things, which these men are so desirous to have seem new, be found of greatest antiquity? Contrariwise, how if all the things well nigh, which they so greatly set out with the name of antiquity, having been well and thoroughly examined, be at length found to be but new, and devised of very late? Soothly to say, no man that hath a true and right consideration would think the Jews' laws and ceremonies to be new for all Haman's

---

Origen, *Contra Celsum*, IV. 7: Celsus 'raises a new objection, saying: After so long a period of time, then, did God now bethink himself of making men live righteous lives, but neglect to do so before?'

[4] Eusebius, *Church History*, I. 4: 'But that no one may suppose that his doctrine is new and strange, as if it were framed by a man of recent origin, differing in no respect from other men, let us now briefly consider this point also.' *Nicene & Post-Nicene Fathers*, VI (1890), 87. Bacon captures precisely the needed words from Eusebius.

[5] See 'The Abstract of Chronicles Written' added to the *Defence* (1567) and later elaborated in the 1570 edition of the *Defence* in evidence of the antiquity of the English church and its customs (Jewel, *Works*, IV, 780–82). Jewel made it clear that Augustine, the monk of Rome, did not bring the faith to England, but rather 'great heaps of novelties and superstitions, as candles, candlesticks, banners, and holy water.' Presenting Augustine as the 'inflamer of the war and so the causer of the slaughter' of those who opposed him, Jewel cited the 'true story of Bede translated by King Alfred.'

accusation: for they were graven in very ancient Tables of most antiquity. And although many did take Christ to have swerved from Abraham and the old fathers, and to have brought in a certain new religion in his own Name, yet answered he them directly: If ye believed Moses, ye would believe me also, for my doctrine is not so new as you make it. For Moses an author of greatest antiquity, and one to whom ye give all honour, hath spoken of me.[6] Paul likewise, though the Gospel of Jesus Christ be of many counted to be but new, yet hath it (saith he) the testimony most old, both of the law and prophets.[7] As for our doctrine which we may rightly call Christ's catholic doctrine, it is so far off from new, that God who is above all most ancient, and the father of our Lord Jesus Christ, hath left the same unto us in the Gospel, in the prophets' and Apostles' works, being monuments of greatest age. So that no man can now think our doctrine to be new, unless the same think either the prophets' faith, or the Gospel, or else Christ himself to be new.

And as for their religion, if it be of so long continuance as they would have men ween° it is, why do they not prove it so by the examples of the Primitive Church, and by the fathers and Councils of old times? Why lieth so ancient a cause thus long in the dust destitute of an Advocate? Fire and sword they have had always ready at hand, but as for the old Councils and the fathers, all Mum, not a word. They did surely against all reason to begin first with these so bloody and extreme means if they could have found other more easy and gentle ways. And if they trust so fully to antiquity, and use no dissimulation, why did John Clement[8] a countryman of ours, but few years past, in the presence of certain honest men and of good credit, tear and cast into the fire certain

---

[6] **Marg.** Joh. v. [John 5.46: 'For had ye beleeved Moses, ye would have beleeved me: for he wrote of me.'] L

[7] Romans 3.21: 'But now is the righteousness of God made manifest without the Law, having witness of the Law and of the Prophetes.'

[8] This is an act of recusant faith by John Clement (d. 1572), who had been a servant-pupil in the house of Thomas More, had married his ward, Margaret Giggs, and in 1528 been appointed physician to Henry VIII. President of the College of Physicians and Oxford professor, Clement left England to escape religious persecution during the reigns of Edward VI and Elizabeth I. Peter Bietenholz and Thomas Brian Deutscher, *Contemporaries of Erasmus: A Biographical Register of the Renaissance and Reformation*, 3 vols (Toronto: University of Toronto Press, 2003), I, 311–312.

leaves of Theodoret the most ancient father and a Greek Bishop, wherein he plainly and evidently taught, that the nature of bread in the Communion was not changed, abolished or brought to nothing? And this did he of purpose, because he thought there was no other copy thereof to be found. Why saith Albertus Pighius that the ancient father Augustine had a wrong opinion of original sin? And that he erred and lied, and used false logic as touching the case of matrimony, concluded after a vow made which Augustine affirmeth to be perfect matrimony indeed,[9] and cannot be undone again.[10] Also when they did of late put in print the ancient father Origen's work upon the Gospel of John, why left they quite out the whole sixth Chapter, wherein it is likely, yea rather, of very surety, that the said Origen had written many things concerning the sacrament of the holy Communion, contrary to these men's minds, and would put forth that book mangled rather than full and perfect, for fear it should reprove them and their partners of their error.[11] Call ye this trusting to antiquity, when ye rent in pieces, keep back, maim, and burn the ancient fathers' works?

---

[9] **Marg.** Dist. 27. Quidam. August. de Bono Viduit. cap. X. XXVII. 41. Nuptiar. bon. [Augustine, *De bono viduitatis*, 10. Cf. Jewel, *Works*, IV, 786. The controversy here is somewhat difficult to untangle. Augustine was referring to the marriage of those who had vowed chastity; in his letter 'On Good Widowhood' (*de bono viduitatis*), he addressed the matter of widows who marry again after consecration, as Jewel translated (IV, 788): 'they that say the marriage of such men or women is no marriage at all but rather advoutry, seem unto me not to consider discreetly or advisedly what they say.']

[10] Albertus Pighius, *Explic. Cathol. controv.*, Controv. I, f. c. Harding maintained that 'it is a great sin to break a simple vow of chastity made to God.' Jewel blended Harding's statement with Albert Pighius's opposition to Augustine's understanding of original sin. 'Thus methinketh I am able to prove,' Pighius wrote in *Controv. de Pecc. Orig.*, 'that St. Augustine's judgment herein is not only uncertain, but also certainly false.' *Works*, IV, 787.

[11] **Marg.** Liber hodie extat et circumfertur mutilus. [Editor Whittingham noted that the Latin translation of Origen was 'in many places mutilated, disconnected, and interpolated' (p. 149). In the discussion of Origen's views, Harding pointed out that although Origen wrote 39 volumes on John, 'the Latin translation printed in Venice hath but 32. Neither be all they whole and perfect.' While Harding upheld the doctrine of transubstantiation — 'when thou enjoyest that bread and cup of life, thou eatest and drinkest the body and blood of our Lord, then our Lord entreth under thy roof' — Jewel responded, 'The roof he meaneth is not material, but spiritual, that is to say, not the body of man but the soul.' *Works*, IV, 789–90.]

It is a world to see, how well favouredly and how towardly, touching Religion, these men agree with the fathers, of whom they use to vaunt that they be their own good. The old Council Eliberine made a decree, that nothing that is honoured of the people, should be painted in the Churches.[12] The old father Epiphanius saith, It is an horrible wickedness, and a sin not to be suffered for any man, to set up any picture in the Churches of the Christians, yea though it were the picture of Christ himself.[13] Yet these men store all their temples and each corner of them with painted and carved images, as though without them, religion were nothing worth.

The old fathers Origen[14] and Chrysostom[15] exhort the people to read the scriptures, to buy them books, to reason at home betwixt themselves of divine matters: wives with their husbands, and parents with their children. These men condemn the scriptures as dead elements and as much as ever they may, bar the

---

[12] As Jewel had noted in his Controversy with Henry Cole in 1560, the Council at Eliberine (Grenada, Spain), 'decreed that there should be no kind of image of anything that is worshipped painted in the church: *placuit, picturas in ecclesia esse non debere; ne quod colitur et adoratur in parietibus depingatur.*' Concil. Elib. In Concil. Stud. Labb. et Cossart. can. 36, Tom. I, col. 974. *Works*, I, 69–70. In *The Defence* Harding argued for 'the devout use of images' allowed by the Second Nicene Council, which Jewel characterized as 'peevish, wicked, blasphemous, and unworthy' since the bishops agreed that images in churches are 'devoutly and reverently to be honoured, and that with the same honour that is due to God himself.' *Works*, IV, 792.

[13] Epiphanius charged priests to command against the display of 'such veils as be contrary to our religion be no more hanged up in the church of Christ.' Jewel cites *Epist. cx, ad Joannis episcopum Hierosolymitanum, Tom. IV, pars 11, cols 828, 9*: '*Quæso ut jubeas presbyteros ejusdem loci præcipere in ecclesia Christi istiusimodi vela, quæ contra religionem nostrum veniunt, non appendi.*' *Works*, IV, 793–94.

[14] **Marg.** Orig. in Lev. cap. xvi. [Origen advised not only hearing the word of God in church but practicing it and meditating on it at home: '*non solum in ecclesia audire verba Dei, sed et in domibus vestris exerceri, et meditari in lege Domini die ac nocte.*' *In Leviticum*, hom. IX, ch. 5. *Works*, IV, 795. Bacon expands Origen's picture of the domestic scene.]

[15] **Marg.** Chrysost. in Matt. Hom. 2. [In *The Defence*, Harding offered this translation of Chrysostom, *In Matthaeum*, hom. II, who 'speaketh against them which contemned the scriptures and said, they were no monks, but had wives and children, and care of household, as though it pertained not to married men to read any part thereof, but to monks only.' *Works*, IV, 795.]; Idem in Johan. 31. [Chrysostom, *In Johannem*, hom. XXXII.]

AN APOLOGY OR ANSWER IN DEFENCE OF THE CHURCH

people from them. The Ancient fathers Cyprian,[16] Epiphanius,[17] and Hierom[18] say, it is better for one who perchance hath made a vow to lead a sole life, and afterwards liveth unchastely, and cannot quench the flames of lust, to marry a wife, and to live honestly in wedlock. And the old father Augustine judgeth the self same marriage to be good and perfect, and ought not to be broken again.[19] These men if a man have once bound himself by a vow, though afterward he burn, keep queans,° and defile himself with never so sinful and desperate a life, yet they suffer not that person to marry a wife: or if he chance to marry, they allow it not for marriage. And they commonly teach it is much better and more godly to keep a Concubine and harlot, than to live in that kind of marriage.

The old father Augustine complained of the multitude of ceremonies, wherewith he even then saw men's minds and consciences overcharged:[20] These men as though God regarded

---

[16] **Marg.** Cypr. Epist. 2. Lib. i. [Cyprian, Epist. IV, Lib. 1, *Ad Pomponio fratri* clarified that for those not willing or able to persevere, it was better to be married than fall in fire because of their desires: '*si autem perseverare nolunt vel non possunt, melius nubant quam in ignem delicitis suis cadant.*' *Corpus Scriptorum Ecclesiasticorum Latinorum*, III, Pars II, *S Thasci Caecili Cypriani, Opera Omnia*, ed. by W. Hartel (Vienna: C. Geroldi Filium Bibliopolam Academiae, 1871), p. 474.]

[17] **Marg.** Epiph. contr. Apost. Hær. 61. [Epiphanius, *Adversus Haereses*, Book II, *Haeresis* LXI, *Adversus Apostolicos*: 'And if God's holy church is composed only of those who have renounced marriage, marriage cannot be of God. And if it is not, the whole business of procreation is ungodly. And if the business of procreation is ungodly, so are they since they have been begotten by such behavior. But what becomes of scripture's "What God hath joined together, let no man put asunder"? To satisfy the necessities of nature is human, but voluntary continence displays, not the work of man but the work of God' (1.6–8). *The Panarion of Epiphanius of Salamis, A Treatise against Eighty Sects*, trans. by Frank Williams, 2 vols (Leiden: Brill, 1987–1994), I (1994), 116–17.]

[18] **Marg.** Hier. ad Demetr. [After lengthy praise of Demetrias who, on the eve of her wedding, embraced virginity, Jerome comments frankly on professed religious who, if they cannot contain themselves, should either marry or contain themselves if they do not wish to marry: '*quibus aperte dicendum est, ut aut nubant, si se non possunt continere, aut continent, si nolunt nubere.*' *Epistola* CXXX, *Ad Demetriadem de servanda Virginitate, Patrologia Latina*, XX.]

[19] See note 8 above and comments on the bridling of 'the priests' sensuality' in Part VI.

[20] **Marg.** Ad Jan. [Augustine, *Ad inquisitiones Januarii, liber II, epistola* LV: '*ipsam religionem servilibus oneribus premunt.*' Cited by Jewel, *Works*, IV, 797. Bacon's 'overcharged' neatly conveys the sense of burden.]

nothing else but their ceremonies, have so out of measure increased them, that there is now almost none other thing left in their Churches and places of prayer.

Again, that old father Augustine denieth it to be lawful for a Monk to spend his time slothfully and idly, and under a pretended and counterfeit holiness to live all upon others.[21] And whoso thus liveth, an old father Apollonius likeneth him to a thief.[22] These men have (I wot° not whether to name them) droves or herds of monks, who for all they do nothing, nor yet once intend to bear any show of holiness, yet live they not only upon others, but also riot lavishly of other folks' labours.

The old council of Rome decreed that no man should come to the service said by a Priest well known to keep a Concubine. These men let to farm Concubines to their priests, and yet constrain men by force against their will to hear their cursed paltry service.[23]

The old Canons of the Apostles command, that Bishop to be removed from his Office, which will both supply the place of a civil Magistrate, and also of an ecclesiastical person:[24] These men for all that, both do and will needs serve both places. Nay rather the one Office which they ought chiefly to execute, they once touch not, and yet nobody commandeth them to be displaced.

---

[21] **Marg.** Aug. de Op. Mon. [In *The Defence* Jewel cites Augustine, *De opera monachorum*, chapters 12–13, 22–25. '*Isti non Deo serviunt, sed suo ventri*: These monks serve not God, they serve their bellies. *Non apparent utrum ex proposito servitutis Dei venerint, an vitam inopem et laboriosam fugientes, vacui pasci et vestiri voluerunt*. We cannot tell whether they became monks for purpose to serve God, or else, being weary of their poor and painful life, were rather desirous to be fed and clothed doing nothing.' *Works*, IV, 798.]

[22] Jewel alludes to the depiction of monasteries as 'dens of thieves' in *Historia Ecclesiastica Tripartita*, a compilation by Epiphanius of the work of Socrates Scholasticus, Sozomen, and Theodoret, Lib. IV, chap. XI. *Works*, IV, 800.

[23] **Marg.** Conc. Rom. cap. 3. [Cf. Crabbe, *Concilia*, II, 765, Synod. Rom. under Nichol. I. Among the prohibitions issued by the Council of Rome (1059) during the papacy of Nicholas II (1059–1061) was the statement against assistance at the Mass of a priest living in notorious concubinage. Although he admitted finding 'no such canon', Harding did allow that 'popes have willed no man to hear the mass of that priest whom he knoweth undoubtedly to keep a concubine.' *Works*, IV, 801.]

[24] **Marg.** Can. 8. [The controversy here concerns marriage as an impediment or assistance. Harding maintained that marriage was 'unseemly for a bishop or a priest, as too base for his dignity and too much hinderance for his vocation.' Jewel responded that it was 'so little hinderance [...] that of his twelve apostles he chose eleven that were married.' *Works*, IV, 803.]

The old Council Gangrense commandeth, that none should make such difference between an unmarried Priest and a married Priest, as he ought to think the one more holy than the other for single life's sake.²⁵ These men put such a difference between them, that they straightway think all their holy service to be defiled, if it be done by a good and honest man that hath a wife.

The ancient emperor Justinian commanded, that in the holy administration all things should be pronounced with a clear, loud, and treatable voice, that the people might receive some fruit thereby.²⁶ These men lest the people should understand them, mumble up all their service, not only with a drowned and hollow voice, but also in a strange and barbarous tongue.

The old council at Carthage commanded that nothing should be read in Christ's congregation, but the canonical Scriptures. These men read such things in their Churches as themselves know of a truth to be stark lies, and fond fables.²⁷

But if there be any that think these above rehearsed authorities be but weak and slender, because they were decreed by Emperors, and certain petty Bishops, and not by so full and perfect Councils, taking pleasure rather in the authority and name of the Pope: let

---

[25] Cf. *Sacrosancta Concilia*, tom. II, col. 419, Concil. Gangr., canon 4. Korey D. Maas cites the views of Robert Barnes, Henrician reformer in the English evangelical movement, about clerical marriage: 'the fourth canon of the fourth-century Council of Gangra anathematized all who would condemn clerical marriage or abstain from the sacraments of married clergy.' Yet Barnes dispelled any rumours that he himself had married. *The Reformation and Robert Barnes: History, Theology and Polemic in Early Modern England*, p. 101.

[26] **Marg.** In Novell. Constit. 123. & 146. [*Corpus juris civilis* (2 vols; Amsterdam, 1663), II, 196–97, auth. coll. IX. tit. XX, novell. 137:6. The *Novellae* or Novels were Justinian's supplementary portion of the Digest or Pandects of Civil Law, collected in 566. In Novell. Constit. 123: 'We command all bishops and priests to minister the holy oblation, & not under silence, but with a loud voice.' Whittingham, ed., *Apology*, p. 157.]

[27] **Marg.** Conc. Carth. iii. cap. 47. [Cf. Crabbe, *Concilia*, I, 431, Concil. Carthag. III, 47. Harding and Jewel disagreed about the precise meaning of the forty-seventh chapter of the Third Council of Carthage. Harding quoted correctly: '*Placuit, ut præter Scripturas Canonicas nihil in Ecclesia legatur sub nomine divinarum scriptuarum*: It hath seemed good unto us, that besides the Canonical Scriptures nothing be read in church under the name of the divine Scriptures.' With chronology somewhat mangled in his justification, Jewel cited the abridgement of the Council of Hippo (cap. 38): 'The Scriptures Canonical which are to be read in the Church, and beside which nothing may be read.' Whittingham, ed., *Apology*, p. 158.]

such a one know, that Pope Julius doth evidently forbid, that a priest in ministering the Communion, should dip the bread in the Cup.²⁸ These men contrary to Pope Julius' decree, divide the bread, and dip it in the wine.

Pope Clement saith, it is not lawful for a Bishop to deal with both swords: for if thou wilt have both said he, thou shalt deceive both thyself, and those that obey thee.²⁹ Nowadays, the Pope challengeth to himself both swords, and useth both, wherefore, it ought to seem less marvel, if that have followed which Clement saith, that is, that he hath deceived both his own self, and those which have given ear unto him.

Pope Leo saith, upon one day it is lawful to say but one mass in one Church: These men say daily in one Church commonly ten Masses, twenty, thirty, yea oftentimes more. So that the poor gazer on, can scant tell which way he were best to turn him.

Pope Gelasius saith, it is a wicked deed and sibb° to sacrilege in any man to divide the Communion, and when he received one kind, to abstain from the other. These men contrary to God's word, and contrary to Pope Gelasius, command that one kind only of the holy Communion be given to the people, and by so doing, they make their priests guilty of sacrilege.

But if they will say that all these things are worn out of ure,° and nigh dead, and pertain nothing to these present times, yet to the end all folk may understand what faith is to be given to these men, and upon what hope they call together their general Councils, let us see in few words what good heed they take to the self same thing, which they themselves these very last years (and

---

²⁸ **Marg.** De Consecr. Dist. 2. Cum enim nemo. [Cf. *Corpus juris canonici*, Decret. Gratian., Decr. Tert. Pars, De Consecr., Dist II, canon 7, col. 1914. Julius I was Pope from 337 to 352. On the matter of Communion under both kinds, Jelf comments that Pope Julius declared: 'whereas for accomplishment of the communion, they dip the sacrament and deliver it unto the people, they have not received this witness of the gospel.' Although Harding maintained that the dipping signified Christ's rising from the dead, Julius called such practice 'a schismatical ambition, and a practice contrary to the apostles' doctrine.' Jelf, *Apology*, pp. 354, 424.]

²⁹ Cf. Crabbe, *Concilia*, I, 32, Clement ad. Jacob, Epist. 1. Harding pointed out that Saint Clement referred to 'worldly cares, *mundialibus curis*'; Jewel acknowledged the 'oversight' and corrected the reference to Saint Bernard, *de Consid. Lib.* II: '*apostolis interdici dominatum*: unto the apostles lordship or temporal princehood is forbidden.' *Works*, IV, 819.

AN APOLOGY OR ANSWER IN DEFENCE OF THE CHURCH

the remembrance thereof is yet new and fresh), in their own general council that they had by order called, decreed and commanded to be devoutly kept. In the last Council at Trident, scant fourteen years past, it was ordained by the common consent of all degrees, that one man should not have two benefices° at one time.³⁰ What is become now of that ordinance? Is the same so soon worn out of mind, and clean consumed? For these men ye see give to one man not two benefices only, but sundry Abbeys many times, sometime also two Bishoprics, sometime three, sometime four. And that not only to an unlearned man, but oftentimes also even to a man of war.

In the said Council a decree was made, that all Bishops should preach the Gospel.³¹ These men neither preach nor once go up into the Pulpit, neither think they it any part of their Office. What great pomp and crake° then is this they make of antiquity? Why brag they so of the names of the ancient fathers, and of the new and old Councils? Why will they seem to trust to their authority, whom when they list, they despise at their pleasure?

But I have a special fancy to commune a word or two rather with the Pope's good holiness, and to say these things to his own face. Tell us, I pray you, good holy father, seeing ye do crake° so much of all antiquity, and boast yourself that all men are bound to you alone, which of all the fathers have at any time called you by the name of the highest Prelate, the universal Bishop, or the head of the Church? Which of them ever said, that both the swords were committed to you?³² Which of them ever said that you have authority and right to call Councils? Which of them ever said the whole world is but your diocese? Which of them, that all

---

³⁰ Chapter 17 of the 24th session of the Council of Trent declares that such practice is a perversion of ecclesiastical order since no one should be enrolled in two churches: '*neminem oportere in duabus ecclesiis conscribi.*' *Sacrosancta Concilia ad Regiam Editionem Exacta*, ed. by Philippe Labbé and Gabriel Cossart, 23 vols (Venice: *Apud Jo. Baptistam Albrizzi Hieron. Fil. et Sebastianum Coleti*, 1728–1733) xx, col. 166.

³¹ Chapter 4 of the 24th session of the Council concerned the duty of bishops to preach the sacred scriptures and divine law: '*si ita oportere duxerint, sacras scripturas divinamque legem annuncient.*' col. 159.

³² **Marg.** De Major. et Obed. Unam. sanctam. [*Unam Sanctam*, Bull of Pope Boniface VIII, November 18, 1302: 'We are informed by the texts of the gospels that in this Church and in its power are two swords; namely, the spiritual and the temporal.' 'Unam Sanctam', in *The Catholic Encyclopedia*, xv (1912).]

230 Bishops have received of your fullness?³³ Which of them, that all power is given to you as well in heaven as in earth? Which of them, that neither kings nor the whole Clergy, nor yet all people together, are able to be judges over you?³⁴ Which of them, that kings and Emperors by Christ's commandment and will, do receive authority at your hand? Which of them with so precise and mathematical limitation hath surveyed and determined you to be seventy and seven times greater than the mightiest kings?³⁵ Which of them, that more ample authority is given to you, than to the residue of the Patriarchs? Which of them, that you are the
240 Lord God?³⁶ Or that you are not a mere natural man, but a certain substance made and grown together of God and man?³⁷

---

³³ **Marg.** Durandus. [William Durandus (*c.* 1237–1296), Canonist and liturgical writer, *Rationale divinorum officiorum*, II. 1, sec 17: '*praelatus Papa, id est pater patrum, vocatur & universalis: quia universae Ecclesiae principatur.*' The pope is called the universal prelate, the father of fathers because he is the ruler of the universal church. 2 vols (Lyon: Jacobus Myt, 1518), p. 87. In the diatribe of *The Defence* Harding cites Saint Bernard, *De consideratione ad Eugenium*, 'where he saith that he is called *plenitudinem potestatis*, into the fullness of power.' Jewel rejects 'all these vanities M. Harding thinketh may be well borne out by two bare words of St Bernard.' *Works*, IV, 829.]

³⁴ **Marg.** Conc. Lat. sub. Jul. II. [Concilium Lateranense. sub Jul. 2.]; Dist. 9. Innoc. [Distinct. 9, Innocentij. See *Sacrosancta Concilia*, tom. XIV, 5th Lateran Council. After citing many Councils, Jewel comments: 'Thus may the pope depose kings and princes, and trouble the whole state of the world, and do what he list, without controlment. Yet may no man dare say unto him, Sir, why do ye so?' *Works*, IV, 834. Also see Jewel, *Works*, IV, 833.]

³⁵ **Marg.** De Major. et Obed. Solitæ. [Whittingham remarks, 'this childish computation of absurd pretensions, Harding acknowledges to be made by Johannes Andreæ (a Canonist) in his comment on the Canon Law *De Major. et Obed. Solitæ*', p. 167. Harding had defended Andreas's claim as a 'pleasant allegorism referring the matter to the astronomers'. Jewel notes in *The Defence*, '*Joannes Andreas dicit: quod ratione non capio, astrologis relinquo.*' What I do not take in by reason, I leave to the astronomers. *Corp. Jur. Canon. Decretal. Gregor. IX. Lib. II, Tit. xxxiii, Gloss in cap. 6, col. 426. Works*, IV, 837.]

³⁶ **Marg.** Extrav. Johan. xxii. Cum inter, in Glos. in Edit. impress. Par. et Lugd. [In *The Defence* Jewel invokes Pope Nicolas the Great (858–867): '*Constat summum pontificem a pio principe Constantino* [...] *Deum appellatum*. It is well known that the pope of the godly prince Constantine was called God.' *Works*, IV, 843.]

³⁷ Harding attributed to the pope 'a certain divine power above the natural state of men.' Jewel rebutted: 'In the pope's own decretals it is noted thus in the margin, *Papa non est homo*. The pope is not a man. [...] And again: *Nec Deus est, nec homo: quasi neuter es inter utrunque*. Thou art neither God nor man, but

Which of them, that you are the only headspring of all law? Which of them, that you have power over purgatories? Which of them that you are able to command the Angels of God as you list yourself? Which of them that ever said that you are Lord of Lords and the King of Kings? We can also go further with you in like sort. What one amongst the whole number of the old Bishops and fathers, ever taught you either to say private Mass while the people stared on, or to lift up the sacrament over your head, in which point consisteth now all your religion. Or else to mangle Christ's sacraments, and to bereave the people of the one part, contrary to Christ's institution and plain expressed words? But that we may once come to an end: What one is there of all the fathers, which hath taught you to distribute Christ's blood and the holy martyrs' merits, and to sell openly as merchandises your pardons, and all the rooms and lodgings of purgatory?[38] These men are wont to speak much of a certain secret doctrine of theirs, and manifold and sundry readings. Then let them bring forth somewhat now if they can, that it may appear they have at least read or do know somewhat. They have often stoutly noised in all corners where they went how all the parts of their religion be very old, and have been approved not only by the multitude, but also by the consent and continual observation of all nations and times: let them therefore once in their life show this their antiquity: let them make appear at eye, that the things whereof they make such ado, have taken so long and large increase: let them declare that all Christian nations have agreed by consent to this their religion.

Nay nay, they turn their backs, as we have said already, and flee from their own decrees, and have cut off and abolished again within a short space, the same things which but a few years before themselves had established, for evermore forsooth to continue. How should one then trust them in the Fathers, in the old Councils, and in the words spoken by God? They have not good Lord they have not (I say) those things which they boast they have: they have not that antiquity, they have not that universality,

---

rather a mean between both. By the authority of this doctor it appeareth that the pope is neither God nor man. Angel, I trow, he is not.' Jewel quotes *Copr. Jur. Canon. Lugd. 1624. Sext. Decretal. Lib. I, Tit. VI, cap. 17, col. 132* and *Clement., Lib I, Proem., col. 4. Works,* IV, 844. Bacon's 'substance made and grown together' suggests scepticism about this unnatural hybrid or grafting.

[38] **Marg.** Anton. de Rosel. [Antonio Roselli; see note 20 in Part IV above.]

they have not that consent of all places, nor of all times. And though they have a desire rather to dissemble, yet they themselves are not ignorant hereof: yea and sometime also they let not to confess it openly. And for this cause they say, that the ordinances of the old Councils and fathers be such as may now and then be altered, and that sundry and divers Decrees serve for sundry and divers times of the church. Thus lurk they under the name of the Church, and beguile silly creatures with their vain glozing.° It is to be marvelled, that either men be so blind that they cannot see this, or if they see it, to be so patient, as they can so lightly and quietly bear it.

But whereas they have commanded that those Decrees should be void as things now waxen too old, and that have lost their grace, perhaps they have provided in their stead certain other better things, and more profitable for the people. For it is a common saying with them that, if Christ Himself or the Apostles were alive again, they could not better nor godlier govern God's Church, than it is at this present governed by them. They have put in their stead indeed: but it is chaff instead of wheat, as Jeremy saith,[39] and such things as, according to Isaiah's words, God never required at their hands. They have stopped up saith he all the veins of clear springing water, and have digged up for the people deceivable and puddle like pits full of mire and filth, which neither have nor are able to hold pure water.[40] They have plucked away from the people the holy Communion, the word of God, from whence all comfort should be taken, the true worshipping of God also, and the right use of sacraments and prayer, and have given us of their own to play withal in the meanwhile, salt, water, oil boxes, spittle, palms, bulls, jubilees, pardons, crosses, censings, and an endless rabble of ceremonies (and as a man might term with Plautus) pretty games to make sport withal. In these things have they set all their religion, teaching the people that by these God may be duly pacified, spirits be driven away, and men's consciences well quieted. For these lo, be the orient colours and

---

[39] Jeremiah 23.28: 'The prophet that hath a dreame, let him tell a dreame, and he that hath my word, let him speake my word faithfully: what is the chaffe to the wheat, saith the Lord?'

[40] Isaiah 1.13: 'Bring no more oblations, in vaine: incense is an abomination unto me: I cannot suffer *your* new moones, nor Sabbath, *nor* solemne dayes (*it is iniquitie*) nor solemne assemblies.' Cf. Isaiah 24.18.

AN APOLOGY OR ANSWER IN DEFENCE OF THE CHURCH

precious savours of Christian religion: these things doth God look upon and accepteth them thankfully: these must come in place to be honoured and put quite away, the institutions of Christ and of his Apostles. And like as in times past when wicked king Jeroboam had taken from the people the right serving of God, and brought them to worship the golden calves, lest perchance they might afterward change their mind and slip away, getting them again to Jerusalem to the Temple of God there, he exhorted them with a long tale to be steadfast, saying thus unto them: O Israel, these Calves be thy Gods.[41] In this sort commanded your God you should worship him. For it should be wearisome and troublous for you to take upon you a journey so far off, and yearly to go up to Jerusalem, there to serve and honour your God. Even after the same sort every whit,° when these men had once made the law of God of none effect through their own traditions, fearing that the people should afterward open their eyes and fall another way, and should somewhence else seek a surer mean of their salvation, Jesu, how often have they cried out: This is the same worshipping that pleaseth God, and which he straitly requireth of us, and wherewith he will be turned from his wrath, that by these things is conserved the unity of the Church by these all sins be cleansed and consciences quieted: and whoso departeth from these, hath left unto himself no hope of everlasting salvation. For it were wearisome and troublous (say they) for the people to resort to Christ, to the Apostles, and to the ancient fathers, and to observe continually what their will and commandment should be. This ye may see, is to withdraw the people of God from the weak elements of the world, from the leaven of the Scribes and Pharisees, and from the traditions of men. It were reason no doubt that Christ's commandments and the Apostles' were removed, that these their devices might come in place. O just cause I promise you, why that ancient and so long allowed doctrine should be now abolished, and a new form of religion be brought into the Church of God.

And yet whatsoever it be, these men cry still that nothing ought to be changed, that men's minds are well satisfied herewithal, that the Church of Rome, the Church which cannot err, hath decreed

---

[41] 1 Kings 12.28: 'Whereupon the king tooke counsell, and made two calves of golde, and sayd unto them, It is too much for you to goe up to Jerusalem: Behold, O Israel, thy gods which brought thee up out of the land of Egypt.'

these things. For Silvester Prierias saith that the Romish church is the squire and rule of truth, and that the holy scripture hath received from thence both authority and credit.[42] The doctrine saith he, of the Romish church is the rule of most infallible faith, from the which the holy scripture taketh his force. And Indulgences and pardons (saith he) are not made known to us by the authority of the scriptures, but they are made known to us by the authority of the Romish Church, and of the Bishops of Rome, which is greater. Pighius also letteth not to say, that without the license of the Romish Church, we ought not to believe the very plain scriptures:[43] much like as if any of those that cannot speak pure and clean Latin, and yet can babble out quickly and readily a little some such law Latin as serveth the Court, would needs hold that all others ought also to speak after the same way which Mammetrectus and Catholicon[44] spake many years ago, and which themselves do yet use in pleading in Court, for so may it be understood sufficiently what is said, and men's desires be satisfied: and that it is a fondness now in the latter end to trouble the world with a new kind of speaking, and to call again the old finesse and eloquence that Cicero and Caesar used in their days in the Latin tongue. So much are these men beholden to the folly and darkness of the former times. Many things as one writeth, are had in estimation oftentimes, because they have been once dedicate to the temples of the Heathen gods: even so we see at this day many things allowed and highly set by of these men, not because they judge them so much worth, but only because they have been received into a custom, and after a sort dedicate to the Temple of God.

Our Church say they, cannot err: they speak that (I think) as the Lacedæmonians long since used to say, that it was not possible

---

[42] Sylvester Prierus (Sylvester Mazzolini da Prierio, *c.* 1456–1523), Dominican theologian and opponent of Martin Luther, *Dialogus ad Martin Luther: una cum Lutheri Responsione* (Wittemberg, 1518), fund. 3.

[43] '*Ex ecclesiasticae igitur traditionis autoritate magis quam ex scripto ad nos venit Christi, apostolorumque doctrina.*' Therefore, the doctrine of Christ and the apostles comes to us more through the authority of church traditions than through scripture. Pighius, *Hierarchiae ecclesiasticae assertio. Coloniae Agrippinae*, I. 2.

[44] *Mammetrectus* was an elementary work by Marchesinus, printed in 1470, to teach the pronunciation and mearning of Latin words in the Bible; the *Catholicon* was a Latin vocabulary compiled by Joannes Januensis de Balbis, printed by Faust in 1460. *Works*, IV, 861.

AN APOLOGY OR ANSWER IN DEFENCE OF THE CHURCH

to find any Adulterer in all their commonwealth: whereas indeed they were rather all Adulterers, and had no certainty in their marriages, but had their wives common amongst them all. Or as the Canonists at this day, for their bellies' sake used to say of the Pope, that forsomuch as he is Lord of all benefices,° though he sell for money Bishoprics, monasteries, priesthood, spiritual promotions, and parteth with nothing freely, yet, because he counteth all his own he cannot commit Simony, though he would never so fain.[45] But how strongly and agreeably to reason these things be spoken, we are not as yet able to perceive, except perchance these men have plucked off the wings from the truth, as the Romans in old time did proin° and pinion° their goddess Victory,[46] after they had once gotten her home, to the end that with the same wings she should never more be able to flee away from them again. But what if Jeremy tell them, as is afore rehearsed, that these be lies? What if the same Prophet say in another place that the self same men, who ought to be keepers of the vineyard, have brought to nought and destroyed the Lord's vineyard? How if Christ say, that the same persons, who chiefly ought to have care over the Temple, have made of the Lord's Temple a den of Thieves?[47] If it be so that the Church of Rome cannot err, it must needs follow, that the good luck thereof is far greater than all these men's policy. For such is their life, their doctrine and their diligence, that for all them the Church may not

---

[45] **Marg.** Sum. Angel. Dict. Papa. [Angelo Carletti di Chiavasso (1411–1495), *Summa angelica de casibus conscientiae* (1476), 'Simonia,' no. 6, fol. 271.2. Trained in civil and canon law, moral theologian Carletti was Vicar-General of the Friars Minor. His *Summa*, a dictionary of moral theology, addressing divine, natural and canon law, went through 31 editions by 1520. Luther burned it publicly. Dietrich of Nieheim (c. 1340–1418), *De schismate inter Urban et Clement* (Basle, 1566), II. 32, p. 89. German historian and member of the papal Curia, Nieheim wrote of schisms occurring in his day. Jewel cites both sources, *Works*, IV, 866–68.]

[46] **Marg.** Plutarch. [Although the marginal gloss in the Latin text indicated Plutarch, Jewel's note in *The Defence* identifies the source in Pausanias (fl. 150–75), Greek traveller and writer: 'just as the Athenians have a notion about the Victory called Wingless, that she will always stay where she is because she has no wings.' *Pausanias's Description of Greece*, trans. by J. G. Frazer, 6 vols (London: Macmillan, 1898), I (1898), III.15, sec. 7, 157. Jewel, *Works*, IV. 865.]

[47] **Marg.** Matt. xxi. [Matthew 21.13: 'And said to them, It is written, My house shall be called the house of prayer: but ye have made it a denne of theeves.'] L

only err, but also utterly be spoiled and perish. No doubt, if that church may err which hath departed from God's word, from Christ's commandments, from the Apostles' ordinances, from the primitive Church's examples, from the old Fathers' and Councils' orders, and from their own Decrees, and which will be bound within the compass of none neither old nor new, nor their own, nor other folks', nor man's law, nor God's law, then it is out of all question, that the Romish Church hath not only had power to err, but also that it hath shamefully and most wickedly erred in very deed.

But say they, ye have been of our fellowship, but now ye are become forsakers of your profession, and have departed from us.[48] It is true we have departed from them, and for so doing we both give thanks to almighty God, and greatly rejoice on our own behalf. But yet for all this, from the primitive Church, from the Apostles, and from Christ we have not departed, true it is. We were brought up with these men in darkness, and in the lack of the knowledge of God, as Moses was taught up in the learning and in the bosom of the Egyptians. We have been of your company saith Tertullian, I confess it, and no marvel at all, for saith he, men be made and not born Christians.[49] But wherefore I pray you have they themselves, the citizens and dwellers of Rome removed and come down from those seven hills, whereupon Rome sometime stood, to dwell rather in the plain called Mars his field? They will say peradventure, because the conduits of water, wherewithout men cannot commodiously live, have now failed and are dried up in those hills. Well then, let them give us like leave in seeking the water of eternal life, that they give themselves in seeking the water of the well, for the water verily failed amongst them. The elders of the Jews saith Jeremy, sent their little ones to the waterings, and they finding no water, being in a miserable case and utterly marred for thirst, brought home

---

[48] I John 2.19: 'They went out from us, but they were not of us: for if they had bene of us, they wolde have continued with us. But *this cometh to passe*, that it might appeare, that they are not all of us.'

[49] Tertullian, *Apology*, 18: 'We are of your stock and nature: men are made, not born, Christians.' *The Ante-Nicene Fathers*, ed. by Alexander Roberts, James Donaldson, and A. Cleveland Coxe, trans. by Robert Ernest Wallis, 10 vols (Buffalo, NY: Christian Literature Publishing Company, 1885–1896) III (1887), 32.

again their vessels empty.[50] The needy and poor folk saith Isaiah, sought about for water, but nowhere found they any, their tongue was even withered for thirst. Even so these men have broken in pieces all the pipes and conduits, they have stopped up all the springs, and choked up the fountain of living water with dirt and mire. And as Caligula many years past locked fast up all the storehouses of corn in Rome, and thereby brought a general dearth and famine amongst the people, even so these men, by damming up all the fountains of God's word, have brought the people into a pitiful thirst. They have brought into the world, as saith the prophet Amos, a hunger and a thirst, not the hunger of bread, nor the thirst of water, but of hearing the word of God.[51] With great distress went they scattering about, seeking some spark of heavenly life to refresh their consciences withal, but that light was already thoroughly quenched out, so that they could find none. This was a rueful state. This was a lamentable form of God's Church. It was a misery to live therein without the Gospel, without light, and without all comfort.

Wherefore though our departing were a trouble to them, yet ought they to consider withal, how just cause we had of our departure. For if they will say, it is in nowise lawful for one to leave the fellowship wherein he hath been brought up, they may as well in our names, or upon our heads, condemn both the Prophets, the Apostles, and Christ himself. For why complain they not also of this, that Lot went quit his way out of Sodom, Abraham out of Chaldee, the Israelites out of Egypt, Christ from the Jews, and Paul from the Pharisees? For except it be possible there may be a lawful cause of departing, we see no reason why Lot, Abraham, the Israelites, Christ and Paul may not be accused of sects and sedition, as well as others. And if these men will needs condemn us for Heretics, because we do not all things at their commandment, whom (in God's name) or what kind of men ought they themselves to be taken for, which despise the commandment of Christ, and of the Apostles? If we be schismatics because

---

[50] Isaiah 41.17: '*When* the poor and the needy seek water, and there *is* none (their tongue faileth for thirst: I the Lord will hear them: I the God of Israel will not forsake them.'

[51] **Marg.** Amos. viii. [Amos 8.11: 'Behold, the dayes come, saith the Lord God, that I will send a famine in the Land, not a famine of bread, nor a thirst for water, but of hearing the word of the Lord.'] L

we have left them, by what name shall they be called themselves, which have forsaken the Greeks, from whom they first received their faith, forsaken the primitive Church, forsaken Christ himself and the Apostles, even as children should forsake their parents? For though those Greeks, who at this day profess religion, and Christ's name, have many things corrupted amongst them, yet hold they still a great number of those things which they received from the Apostles. They have neither private Masses, nor mangled Sacraments, nor Purgatories, nor Pardons. And as for the titles of high Bishops, and those glorious names, they esteem them so, as whosoever he were that would take upon him the same, and would be called either Universal bishop, or the Head of the universal church, they make no doubt to call such a one both a passing proud man, a man that worketh despite against all the other Bishops his brethren, and a plain Heretic.

Now then since it is manifest and out of all peradventure, that these men have fallen from the Greeks, of whom they received the Gospel, of whom they received the faith, the true Religion and the Church, what is the matter why they will not now be called home again to the same men, as it were to their originals and first founders? And why be they afraid to take a pattern of the Apostles' and old Fathers' times, as though they all had been void of understanding? Do these men, ween° ye, see more, or set more by the Church of God than they did who first delivered us these things?

We truly have renounced that church wherein we could neither have the word of God sincerely taught, nor the Sacraments rightly administered, nor the name of God duly called upon, which Church also themselves confess to be faulty in many points: And wherein was nothing able to stay any wise man, or one that hath consideration of his own safety. To conclude, we have forsaken the Church as it is now, not as it was in old time, and have so gone from it, as Daniel went out of the Lions' den, and the three Children out of the furnace: and to say the truth, we have been cast out by these men (being cursed of them, as they used to say, with book, bell, and candle), rather than have gone away from them of ourselves.

And we are come to that Church, wherein they themselves cannot deny (if they will say truly, and as they think in their own conscience) but all things be governed purely and reverently, and as much as we possibly could, very near to the order used in the old time.

AN APOLOGY OR ANSWER IN DEFENCE OF THE CHURCH

510 Let them compare our Churches and theirs together, and they shall see that themselves have most shamefully gone from the Apostles, and we most justly have gone from them. For we following the example of Christ, of the Apostles, and the holy fathers, give the people the holy Communion whole and perfect: But these men contrary to all the fathers, to all the Apostles, and contrary to Christ himself, do sever the sacraments, and pluck away the one part from the people, and that with most notorious sacrilege, as Gelasius termeth it.[52]

We have brought again the Lord's supper unto Christ's institution, and will have it to be a Communion in very deed, common and indifferent to a great number, according to the name. 520 But these men have changed all things contrary to Christ's institution, and have made a private Mass of the holy Communion: and so it cometh to pass, that we give the Lord's supper unto the people, and they give them a vain pageant to gaze upon.

We affirm together with the ancient fathers, that the body of Christ is not eaten but of the good and faithful, and of those that are endued with the spirit of Christ. Their doctrine is, that Christ's very body effectually, and as they speak, really and substantially, may not only be eaten of the wicked and unfaithful men, but also (which is monstrous to be spoken) of mice and dogs.

530 We use to pray in our churches after that fashion, as according to Paul's lesson,[53] the people may know what we pray, and may answer Amen, with a general consent. These men like sounding metal, yell out in the churches unknown and strange words without understanding, without knowledge, and without devotion, yea and do it of purpose, because the people should understand nothing at all.

---

[52] Jewel and Harding continued to battle about the understanding of the reception of communion under one or both species. Harding insisted that Gelasius was writing against the heretical Manichees who 'divided the mystery of the body and blood of Christ.' Jewel quoted Gelasius about the practice of 'certain superstitious priests': *'Erant quidam sacerdotes, qui ordine debito consecrabant corpus et sanguinem Christi: corpus sumebant, sed a sanguine abstinebant.* There were certain priests that consecrated the body and blood of Christ in due order, and received the body but abstained from the blood.' *Works*, III, 257–58. See note 27 above.

[53] **Marg.** I Cor. xiv. [I Corinthians 14.16: 'Else, when thou blessest with the spirit, how shall hee that occupieth the roume of the unlearned, say Amen, at thy giving of thankes, seeing he knowest not what thou sayest?']

But not to tarry about rehearsing all points wherein we and they differ, for they have well nigh no end, we turn the scriptures into all tongues, they scant suffer them to be had abroad in any tongue. We allure the people to read and to hear God's word, they drive the people from it. We desire to have our cause known to all the world, they flee to come to any trial. We lean unto knowledge, they unto ignorance: We trust unto light, they unto darkness: We reverence as it becometh us, the writings of the Apostles and Prophets, and they burn them. Finally, we in God's cause desire to stand to God's only judgment, they will stand only to their own. Wherefore if they will weigh all these things with a quiet mind, and fully bent to hear and to learn, they will not only allow this determination of ours who have forsaken errors, and followed Christ and his Apostles, but themselves also will forsake their own selves, and join of their own accord to our side.

PART VI

But peradventure they will say, it was treason to attempt these matters without a sacred general council: for in that consisteth the whole force of the Church: there CHRIST hath promised he will ever be a present assistant. Yet they themselves, without tarrying for any general council, have broken the commandments of God, and the decrees of the Apostles: and as we said a little above, they have spoiled and disannulled almost all, not only ordinances, but even the doctrine of the primitive Church. And where they say it is not lawful to make a change without a
10 Council, what was he that gave us these laws, or from whence had they this Injunction?

King Agesilaus truly did but fondly, who when he had a determinate answer made him of the opinion and will of mighty Jupiter, would afterward bring the whole matter before Apollo, to know whether he allowed thereof as his father Jupiter did or no.[1] But yet should we do much more fondly, when we hear God himself plainly speak to us in the most holy scriptures, and may understand by them his will and meaning, if we would afterward (as though this were of none effect) bring our whole cause to be
20 tried by a Council, which were nothing else but to ask whether men would allow as God did, and whether men would confirm God's commandment by their authority. Why I beseech you, except a Council will and command, shall not truth be truth, or God be God? If Christ had meant to do so from the beginning,

---

[1] **Marg.** Plutarchus. [Plutarchus. Plutarch, Greek historian and biographer (*c.* 46–122), included the life of the Spartan king Agesilaus (*c.* 444–360 BC) in his *Parallel Lives*; the Spartan's Roman counterpart was Pompey. Plutarch's *Moralia* recounts his answer to the ephors (overseers) about the agreement between Jupiter (or Zeus) and Apollo: 'Desiring to bring about the war against the Persian for the sake of setting free the Greeks living in Asia, he consulted the oracle of Zeus at Dodona, and when the god bade him to go on, he reported the answer to the Ephors. And they bade him go to Delphi and ask the same question. Accordingly he proceeded to the prophetic shrine and put his question in this form: "Apollo, are you of the same opinion as your father?" And Apollo concurring, Agesilaus was chosen, and began the campaign.' (191B) Apophthegmata Laconica, in *Moralia*, ed. by T.E. Page, E. Capps, and A. Post for the Loeb Classical Library 245, trans. by Frank Cole Babbitt, 15 vols (Cambridge, MA: Harvard University Press, 1927–1969), III (1931), 247.]

as that He would preach or teach nothing without the Bishop's consent, but refer all his doctrine over to Annas and Caiaphas, where should now have been the Christian faith? Or who at any time should have heard the Gospel taught? Peter verily, whom the Pope hath oftener in his mouth and more reverently useth to speak of, than he doth of Jesus Christ, did boldly stand against the holy Council, saying, It is better to obey God, than men.[2] And after Paul had once entirely embraced the Gospel, and had received it not from men, nor by man, but by the only will of God, he did not take advice therein of flesh and blood, nor brought the case before his kinsmen and brethren, but went forthwith into Arabia, to preach God's Divine mysteries by God's only authority.[3]

Yet truly we do not despise Councils, assemblies, and conference of Bishops and learned men: neither have we done that we have done altogether without Bishops or without a Council. The matter hath been treated in open Parliament with long consultation, and before a notable Synod and Convocation.[4]

But touching this Council which is now summoned by the Pope Pius, wherein men so lightly are condemned, which have been neither called, heard, nor seen, it is easy to guess what we may look for or hope of it. In times past, when Nazianzen saw in his days how men in such assemblies were so blind and wilful that they were carried with affections, and laboured more to get the victory than the truth, he pronounced openly that he never had seen any good end of any Council.[5] What would he say now if he

---

[2] Acts 4.19: 'But Peter and John answered unto them, and sayd, Whether it be right in the sight of God, to obey you rather than God, judge ye.'

[3] Galatians 1.12: 'For neither received I it of man, neither was I taught it, but by the revelation of Jesus Christ.'

[4] The first Parliament of Queen Elizabeth's reign was summoned in 1559 to establish religious uniformity, known as the Elizabethan Religious Settlement, which was consolidated further by the first Convocation of the English clergy in 1563.

[5] Gregory Nazianzen (*c.* 329–390), Bishop of Constantinople, withdrew from the Second Ecumenical Council at Constantinople (381) after the failure to unite Egyptian and Macedonian bishops with Constantinople and to eliminate Arianism; he expressed his exhaustion and refusal to return to the Council in a letter to Procopius, the prefect of the city: '*semper enim contentiones, et dominandi cupiditates*' (*Epistola* CXXX, *ad Procopio, S.P.N. Gregorii Operum Pars II Epistolae*). Thomas Cranmer, Archbishop of Canterbury, translated: 'For the lusts of strife and desire and of lordship reign there.' (*Works*, ed. by John

were alive at this day, and understood the heaving and shoving of these men? For at that time, though the matter were laboured on all sides, yet the controversies were well heard, and open errors were put clean away by the general voice of all parts. But these men will neither have the case to be freely disputed, nor yet how many errors soever there be, suffer they any to be changed. For it is a common custom of theirs, often and shamelessly to boast that their Church cannot err, that in it there is no fault, and that they must give place to us in nothing.[6] Or if there be any fault, yet must
60   it be tried by Bishops and Abbots, only because they be the directors and Rulers of matters, and they be the Church of God. Aristotle saith that a City cannot consist of Bastards: but whether the Church of God may consist of these men, let their own selves consider. For doubtless neither be the Abbots legitimate Abbots, nor the Bishops natural right Bishops. But grant they be the Church: let them be heard speak in Councils: let them alone have authority to give consent: yet in old time when the Church of God (if ye will compare it with their Church) was very well governed, both Elders and Deacons as saith Cyprian, and certain also of the
70   common people were called thereunto, and made acquainted with ecclesiastical matters.[7]

But I put case these Abbots and Bishops have no knowledge: what if they understand nothing what religion is, nor how we ought to think of God? I put case the pronouncing and ministering of the law be decayed in priests, and good counsel fail in the Elders, and as the prophet Micah saith, the night be unto them

---

Edmund Cox for the Parker Society, 2 vols (Cambridge: Cambridge University Press, 1844–1846), II (1846), 36.).
[6] **Marg.** Ecclesia non errat. [The Church does not err. *Theologiae Cursus Completus*, ed. by J-P Migne, 28 vols (Paris: [n. pub.], 1840–1845), *Tractatus Tertius: De Articulis Necessariis, Sectio 13 Ecclesiam Romanam esse veram*, I (1840), col. 849.] L
[7] Cyprian (*c.* 200–258), Bishop of Carthage and martyr, exerted a moderating influence in arguing for unity between the laxists and rigorists. In Letter 14, To the Presbyters and Deacons Assembled at Rome, he wrote to justify his going into hiding rather than face Roman execution for his refusal to sacrifice to pagan gods: 'when the Lord has given to us peace, and several bishops shall have begun to assemble into one place, we may be able to arrange and reform everything, having the advantage also of your counsel. I bid you, beloved brethren, ever heartily farewell.' *Ante-Nicene Fathers*, v (1886), 295.

instead of a vision, and darkness instead of prophesying.⁸ Or as Isaiah saith, what if all the watchmen of the city are become blind?⁹ What if the salt have lost his proper strength and savorines, and as Christ saith, be good for no use, scant worth the casting on the dunghill?¹⁰

Well yet then, they will bring all matters before the Pope, who cannot err. To this I say, first it is a madness to think that the holy Ghost taketh his flight from a general Council to run to Rome, to the end if he doubt or stick in any matter, and cannot expound it of himself, he may take counsel of some other spirit, I wot° not what, that is better learned than himself. For if this be true, what needed so many Bishops, with so great charges and so far journeys, have assembled their Convocation at this present at Trident? It had been more wisdom and better, at least it had been a much nearer way and handsomer to have brought all things rather before the Pope, and to have come straight forth, and have asked counsel at his divine breast. Secondly, it is also an unlawful dealing to toss our matter from so many Bishops and Abbots, and to bring it at last to the trial of one only man, specially of him who himself is appeached° by us of heinous and foul enormities, and hath not yet put in his answer: who hath also aforehand condemned us without judgment by order pronounced, and ere ever we were called to be judged.

How say ye, do we devise these tales? Is not this the course of the Councils in these days? Are not all things removed from the whole holy Council and brought before the Pope alone? That as though nothing had been done to purpose by the judgments and consents of such a number, he alone may add, alter, diminish, disannul, allow, remit, and qualify whatsoever he list? Whose words be these, then? And why have the Bishops and Abbots in the last council of Trident but of late concluded with saying thus in the end: Saving always the authority of the see Apostolic in all

---

⁸ **Marg.** Mic. iii. [Micah 3.6: 'Therefore night shall be unto you for a vision, and darknesse *shall be* unto you for a divination, and the Sunne shall go downe over the prophets, and the day shall be darke over them.'] **L**

⁹ Isaiah 56.10: 'Their watchmen are all blind: they have no knowledge: they are all dumbe dogs: they cannot barke: they lie and sleepe, and delight in sleeping.'

¹⁰ **Marg.** Matt. v. [Matthew 5.13: 'Ye are the salt of the earth: but if the salt have lost his savor, wherewith shall it be salted? It is thenceforth good for nothing, but to be cast out, and to be troden under foot of men.'] **L**

things? Or why doth Pope Paschal write so proudly of himself as though saith he, there were any general Council able to prescribe a law to the Church of Rome, whereas all Councils both have been made and have received their force and strength by the Church of Rome's authority? And in ordinances made by Councils, is ever plainly excepted the authority of the Bishop of Rome.[11] If they will have these things allowed for good, why be Councils called? But if they command them to be void, why are they left in their books as things allowable?

But be it so, let the Bishop of Rome alone be above all Councils, that is to say, let some one part be greater than the whole, let him be of greater power, let him be of more wisdom than all his, and in spite of Hierom's head, let the authority of one City be greater than the authority of the whole world.[12] How then if the Pope have seen none of these things, and have never read either the scriptures or the old Fathers, or yet his own Councils? How if he favour the Arians, as once Pope Liberius did? Or have a wicked and a detestable opinion of the life to come, and of the immortality of the soul, as Pope John had but few years since? Or to increase his own dignity, do corrupt other Councils, as Pope Zosimus corrupted the council holden at Nice in times past, and do say that those things were devised and appointed by the holy Fathers, which never once came into their thought, and to have the full sway of authority, do wrest the Scriptures, as Camotensis saith, is an usual custom with the Popes?[13] How if he have

---

[11] **Marg.** De Elect. et Elect. Potest. Significasti. [Paschal II was Pope from 1099 to 1118. The paragraph contains a series of allusions to the tenets of Canon Law, likely gleaned from Archbishop Cranmer's 'A Collection of Tenets extracted from Canon Law shewing the Extravagant Pretensions of the Church of Rome': 'The bishop of Rome hath authority to judge all men, and specially to discern the articles of the faith, and that without any council' (*De jurejando*, Decret. II, causa IX, quaest. 3); 'The emperor is the bishop of Rome's subject' (*De major. et obedient.*); 'It belongeth to the bishop of Rome to allow or disallow the emperor after he is elected' (*De elect. et electi potestate*, Greg IX, I.VI). *Miscellaneous Writings and Letters of Thomas Cranmer*, p. 69.]

[12] **Marg.** Hieron. ad. Evag. [Jerome, *Epistola Ad Euagrium*. As cited in note 8, Part II of this edition, Eugubium was a small bishopric.]

[13] During the papacy of Liberius (352–366), Antipope Felix II was expelled and moderate Arians were admitted to the Church. For most of his Avignon papacy, John XXII (1316–1334) maintained that the dead would not see the presence of God until the Last Judgement, although he moderated this view to concede that those who die in grace do see the Beatific Vision. Pope Zosimus (417–418) ignited

renounced the faith in Christ, and become an Apostate, as Lyranus saith many Popes have been?[14] And yet for all this, shall the holy Ghost, with turning of a hand, knock at his breast, and even whether he will or no, yea and wholly against his will, kindle him a light so as he may not err? Shall he straightway be the head spring of all right, and shall all treasure of wisdom and understanding be found in him, as it were laid up in store? Or if these things be not in him, can he give a right and apt judgment of so weighty matters? Or, if he be not able to judge, would he have that all those matters should be brought before him alone?

What will ye say, if the Pope's Advocates, Abbots and Bishops dissemble not the matter, but show themselves open enemies to the Gospel, and though they see, yet they will not see, but wry°

---

a dispute with the African bishops over the right of an appeal to Rome by an excommunicated priest; Zosimus accepted the appeal in accord with the canon of the First Council of Nicaea, which was not included in the African copy of the Nicene canons. On the identity of Camotensis, Jewel's later translator and editor William Rollinson Whittingham believed — despite Jewel's insistence that he meant 'Camotensis' — that it is a probable reference to the bishopric called Carotensis of John of Salisbury: 'a learned scholastic theologian of the twelfth century, who in his writings freely inveighed against the Papal tyranny.' (*Apology*, trans. Whittingham, p. 203.) In his Preface to the Reader, Jewel identified the quotation attributed to Camotensis by Cornelius Agrippa (*De Vanit. Scient.*): *In ecclesiam Romanam sedent scribae et Pharisaei. Ipse papa jam factus intolerabilis. papae pompam et fastum nullus tyrannorum unquam aequavit.* Scribes and Pharisees sit in the Roman church. The pope himself is now become intolerable. None of the tyrants has ever matched him in pomp and pride. *Works*, IV, 119.

[14] Nicholas of Lyra (1270–1349), Franciscan teacher and biblical exegete, whose commentary on the Bible, *Postilla litteralis super totam bibliam* (*c.* 1333) was the first such commentary to be printed. His Conventual order was compelled to accept two papal Bulls (1322, 1323) of Pope John XXII forcing the Franciscans to accept ownership of property and declaring it heresy to claim that Christ and the Apostles did not have the right of possession. Challenging reactions within the order and the eventual submission of Antipope Nicholas V could underlie Jewel's remark about apostasy. Additional influences are in Nicholas's commentary on *Revelation* 11, where he revisits sixth-century figures, Pope Silverius and Menas, Patriarch of Constantinople. Although Silverius was stripped of his pallium and deposed and Menas was excommunicated twice by Pope Vigilius, Nicholas presents them as resisting the designs of Justinian and Theodora and the heresy of Monophysitism, a denial of the historical Jesus. Philip Krey, 'The Apocalypse Commentary of 1329: Problems in Church History', *Nicholas of Lyra: The Senses of Scripture*, ed. by Philip Krey and Lesley Smith (Leiden: Brill, 2000), pp. 267–88.

AN APOLOGY OR ANSWER IN DEFENCE OF THE CHURCH

150 the Scriptures, and wittingly and knowingly corrupt and counterfeit the word of God, and foully and wickedly apply to the Pope all the same things which evidently and properly be spoken of the person of Christ only, nor by no means can be applied to any other? And what though they say, the Pope is all and above all?[15] Or, that he can do as much as Christ can: and that one judgment place and one Council house serve for the Pope and for Christ both together?[16] Or that the Pope is the same light which should come into the world? Which words Christ spake of himself alone:[17] and that whoso is an evil doer, hateth and flieth from that light?[18] Or that all the other Bishops have received of the Pope's fulness?[19] Shortly, what though they make decrees

---

[15] **Marg.** Host. cap. Quanto. [Henricus de Segusio (*c.* 1200–1271), cardinal and decretalist, known as Hostiensis because of his bishopric of Ostia, was the first to apply the label *potestas absoluta* to the Pope. For the Roman church the Pope is so much as the voice of God: '*Ecclesia Romana voce Domini tantum praelata est.*' In Primum Decretalium librum Commentaria Doctissimorum Virorum, De transl. Episc. Venetiis: Apud Iuntas, 1581., p. 81ᵛ, seq. 170. Kenneth Pennington, *The Prince and the Law, 1200–1600: Sovereignty and Rights in the Western Legal Tradition* (Berkeley: University of California Press, 1993), p. 64.]

[16] **Marg.** Abb. Pan. de Elect. cap. Venerabilis. [Niccolo de Tudeschi (1386–1445), Benedictine canonist and Archbishop of Palermo (Greek: Panormus), known as Panormitanus, wrote at great length on the unity of the Pope and Christ. The Pope controls all things which Christ controls through an unerring key. The emperor recognizes the Pope's rule: '*Papa potest omnia, quae potest Christus clave non errante. Imperator recogniscit imperium à Papa.*' Abbatis Panormitani Commentaria. Prima Partis in Primum Decretalium Librum, '*De Electione.c.Cum Iure,*' (Venice: Apud Iuntas, 1571), ch. 34, p. 183r.]

[17] **Marg.** Joh. i. [John 1.9: 'This was that true light, which lighteth every man that commeth into the world.'] **L**

[18] **Marg.** Joh. iii. [John 3.20: 'For every man that evill doeth, hateth the light, neither commeth to light, lest his deedes should be reproved.'] **L**; Corn. Episc. in Conc. Trid. [Previous Jewel translator Whittingham (1831) and editor Booty (1963) draw attention to the inaugural oration at the Council of Trent delivered by Dutch Conventual Franciscan Cornelius Masso (1511–1574), *Oratio ad Concil. Trident.*, in *Sacrosancta Concilia*, tom. XIV, col. 996, in which he cites the Johannine passage.]

[19] **Marg.** Durandus. [*Rationale divinorum officiorum* by Guillaume Durand (1230–1296), Bishop of Mende, France, is a treatise on the symbolism of Christian ritual, first published in 1459. He stressed the supreme position of the priest and the patriarchal dignity of the Pope which extends to Archbishops and Metropolitans: '*In templo errant summus sacerdos. [...] Dignitatis ut papa patriarcha: primas archiepiscop. sive metropolitan. quod idem est.*' Rationale divinorum officiorum, '*De mini. et ordi. eccle. et de eorum officiis,*' II, fol. 17.]

expressly against God's Word, and that not in hucker mucker° or covertly, but openly and in the face of the world: must it needs yet be Gospel straight whatsoever these men say? Shall these be God's holy army? Or will Christ be at hand among them there? Shall the holy Ghost flow in their tongues: or can they with truth say, We and the holy Ghost have thought so? Indeed Peter Asotus[20] and his companion Hosius stick not to affirm, that the same Council wherein our Saviour Jesus Christ was condemned to die, had both the spirit of prophesying, and the holy Ghost, and the spirit of truth in it: and that it was neither a false nor a trifling saying, when those Bishops said, We have a law, and by our law he ought to die:[21] and that they so saying did light upon the very truth of judgment: for so be Hosius' words, and that the same plainly was a just decree, whereby they pronounced that Christ was worthy to die.[22] This methinketh is strange, that these men are not able to speak for themselves and to defend their own

---

[20] In his voluminous controversy Thomas Harding (1516–1572), Jewel's exiled Catholic contemporary, 'rails at Lady Bacon for calling Peter a Soto, Peter Asotus' (meaning dissolute or debauched). Peter a (or de) Soto (1493–1563), Spanish Dominican theologian at the third convocation of the Council of Trent, had also participated in the persecution that led to the execution of the Oxford martyrs, bishops Hugh Latimer and Nicholas Ridley and Archbishop Thomas Cranmer in 1555–1556. In *The Defence of the Apology* Jewel elucidated: 'Sotus and Hosius say, whatsoever is determined in council must be taken as the undoubted judgment and word of God. Hereunto the godly learned father Johannes Brentius replieth thus "Councils sometimes have erred."' Harding called Jewel's depiction of Sotus and Hosius's treatment of the council in which Christ was condemned by Caiaphas 'false dealing and shameless lying': 'Where ye impute to Hosius, to have said that the same plainly was a just decree whereby they pronounced that Christ was worthy to die, that is your slanderous lie, not Hosius' saying. For he saith clean contrary, and that sundry times, that it was a wicked council, and most unjust decree.' *Works*, IV, 941–42.

[21] John 19.8: 'The Jewes answered him, We have a law, and by our law he ought to die, because he made himselfe the Sonne of God.'

[22] **Marg.** Hos. contr. Brent. Lib. ii. [Stanislaus Hosius (*c.* 1504–1579), Polish Cardinal and papal legate to the Council of Trent, rebutted Brentius's claim about councils erring by both upholding inerrancy and declaring the act of sentencing Christ to death wicked. Jewel editor and translator Stephen Isaacson (1829) and editor John Ayre (1849) identify the passage: '*Nulla esse potest tanta pontificum improbitas, quae impedire queat, quo minus vera sit illa Dei promisso, Qui indicabunt tibi judicii veritatem.* Be the wickedness of bishops never so great, it can never hinder but that this promise of God shall ever be true, the bishops shall shew thee the truth of judgment.' *Hosius contra Brentium*, II, 62–63. Quoted in Isaacson, p. 210; *Works*, IV, 942.]

AN APOLOGY OR ANSWER IN DEFENCE OF THE CHURCH

cause, but they must also take part with Annas and Caiaphas. For if they will call that a lawful and a good Council, wherein the Son of God was most shamefully condemned to die, what Council will they then allow for false and naught? And (yet as all their Councils, to say truth, commonly be) necessity compelled them to pronounce these things of the Council holden by Annas and Caiaphas.

But will these men (I say) reform us the Church, being themselves both the persons guilty and the Judges too? Will they abate their own ambition and pride? Will they overthrow their own matter, and give sentence against themselves, that they must leave off to be unlearned Bishops, slowbellies,° heapers together of benefices,° takers upon them as princes and men of war? Will the Abbots the Pope's dear darlings judge that monk for a thief, which laboureth not for his living? And that it is against all law, to suffer such a one to live and to be found either in city or in country, or yet of other men's charges? Or else that a monk ought to lie on the ground, to live hardly with herbs and peason,° to study earnestly, to argue, to pray, to work with hand, and fully to bend himself to come to the ministry of the church? In faith, as soon will the Pharisees and Scribes repair again the temple of God, and restore it unto us a house of prayer, instead of a thievish den.

There have been, I know, certain of their own selves which have found fault, with many errors in the church, as Pope Adrian, Æneas Sylvius, Cardinal Pole, Pighius and others, as is aforesaid, they held afterwards their Council at Trident in the selfsame place where it is now appointed. There assembled many Bishops and Abbots and others whom it behoved. For that matter they were alone by themselves, whatsoever they did nobody gainsaid it: for they had quite shut out and barred our side from all manner of assemblies, and there they sat six years feeding folks with a marvellous expectation of their doings. The first six months, as though it were greatly needful, they made many determinations of the holy Trinity, of the Father, of the Son, and of the holy Ghost, which were godly things indeed, but not so necessary for that time. Let us see in all that while of so many, so manifest, so often confessed by them and so evident errors, what one error have they amended? From what kind of idolatry have they reclaimed the people? What superstition have they taken away? What piece of their tyranny and pomp have they diminished? As though all the world may not now see, that this is a Conspiracy and not a Council, and that those Bishops whom the Pope hath now called together, be wholly sworn and become bound to bear him their faithful allegiance, and will do no manner of thing, but that they perceive pleaseth him, and helpeth to advance his power, and as he will have it: Or that they reckon not of the number of men's voices, rather than have weight and consideration of the same: Or that might doth not oftentimes overcome right.

And therefore we know that divers times many good men and Catholic Bishops did tarry at home, and would not come when such Councils were called, wherein men so apparently laboured to serve factions and to take parts, because they knew they should but lose their travail and do no good, seeing whereunto their enemies' minds were so wholly bent. Athanasius denied to come when he was called by the Emperor to his Council at Caesarea, perceiving plain he should but come among his enemies, which deadly hated him.[23] The same Athanasius, when he came afterward to the Council at Syrmium, and foresaw what would be the end by reason of the outrage and malice of his enemies, he packed up his carriage, and went away immediately. John Chrysostom, although the Emperor Constantius[24] commanded him by four sundry letters to come to the Arians' Council, yet kept he himself at home still.[25] When Maximus the Bishop of Jerusalem sat in the Council at Palestine, the old Father Paphnutius took him by the hand and led him out at the doors saying, It is not lawful for us to confer of these matters with

---

[23] **Marg.** Theod. Eccl. Hist. Lib. i. cap. xxviii. [Theodoret, *Historia ecclesiastica*, I. 28: 'After having accused Athanasius of crimes which they described as too shocking to be tolerated, or even listened to, his calumniators persuaded the emperor to convene a council at Cæsarea in Palestine, where Athanasius had many enemies, and to command that his cause should be there tried. The emperor, utterly ignorant of the plot that had been devised, was persuaded by them to give the required order. But the holy Athanasius, well aware of the malevolence of those who were to try him, refused to appear at the council. This served as a pretext to those who opposed the truth to criminate him still further; and they accused him before the emperor of contumacy and arrogance.' Theodoret, *Historia ecclesiastica*, I. 26, *Nicene and Post-Nicene Fathers*, III (1892), 61.]
[24] The Emperor Arcadio is meant here, as the Latin correctly indicates.
[25] **Marg.** Tripart. Hist. Lib. x. cap. xiii. [Cassiodorus (*c.* 490–583), *Tripartita historia* (Paris, [n.d.]), x. 13.] **L**

AN APOLOGY OR ANSWER IN DEFENCE OF THE CHURCH

wicked men.[26] The Bishops of the East would not come to the Syrmian Council, after they knew Athanasius had gotten himself thence again. Cyril called men back by letters from the Council of them which were named Patropassians.[27] Paulinus Bishop of Triers, and many others more, refused to come to the Council at Milan, when they understood what a stir and rule Auxentius kept there:[28] for they saw it was in vain to go thither, where not reason but faction should prevail, and where folk contended not for the truth and right judgment of the matter, but for partiality and favour.

250

And yet, for all those fathers had such malicious and stiff necked enemies, yet if they had come they should have had free speech at least in the Councils. But now sithence° none of us may

---

[26] **Marg.** Eus. Lib. i. cap. xvii. [Rufinus (*c*. 345–410), who translated Books 1–9 of Eusebius's *Church History* and added his own Books 10–11, described the plot of 'depraved priests' to entrap Athanasius: 'Their purpose was that the emperor might order Athanasius to be condemned at a council he would summon, and he did order one to convene at Tyre. [...] There Athanasius was brought, the case with the human arm [they claimed Athanasius had severed it from the body] was shown around, and an indignant horror invaded the souls of all, religious and ordinary folk alike. This Arsenius, whose arm was supposed to have been cut off, had once been a lector of Athanasius, but fearing rebuke for some fault, he had withdrawn from his company. [...]But while in hiding he heard of the crime they intended to commit in his name against Athanasius. Moved either by human feeling or by divine providence, he secretly escaped his confinement in the silence of the night, sailed to Tyre, presented himself to Athanasius on the day before the final day for pleading his case, and explained the affair from the beginning. [...]The confessor Paphnutius was there at the time and was aware of Athanasius's innocence. Now he saw Bishop Maximus of Jerusalem sitting with the others whom the shameful plot had united. [...] He went up to him fearlessly where he was sitting in their midst and said, "I will not let you sit in the council of evildoers and go in with the workers of malice." And taking hold of him he lifted him up from their midst, informed him in detail of what was taking place, and joined him thereafter in lasting communion to Athanasius.' *The Church History of Rufinus of Aquileia*, trans. by Philip R. Amidon, S. J. (New York: Oxford University Press, 1997) x, 17–18.]

[27] Heresy based on John 10.30, 14.9–10, that the Father was incarnate and suffered for us.

[28] **Marg.** Tripart. Soz. Liv. v. cap. xv. [In his *Ecclesiastical History*, Socrates Scholasticus described the refusal of some bishops to ratify the sentence against Athanasius, exclaiming that 'this proposition indicated a covert plot against the principles of Christian truth. For they insisted that the charges against Athanasius were unfounded, and merely invented by his accusers as a means of corrupting the faith.' *Nicene and Post-Nicene Fathers*, II (1890), 60.]

be suffered so much as to sit, or once to be seen in these men's meetings, much less suffered to speak freely our mind, and seeing the Pope's Legates, Patriarchs, Archbishops, Bishops, and Abbots, all being conspired together, all linked together, in one kind of fault, and all bound by one oath, sit alone by themselves, and have power alone to give their consent: and at last when they have all done, as though they had done nothing, bring all their opinions to be judged at the will and pleasure of the Pope, being but one man, to the end he may pronounce his own sentence of himself, who ought rather to have answered to his complaint, sithence° also the same ancient and Christian liberty, which of all right should specially be in Christian Councils, is now utterly taken away from the Council: for these causes I say wise and good men ought not to marvel at this day, though we do the like now, that they see was done in times past in like case of so many Fathers and Catholic Bishops, which as though we choose rather to sit at home and leave our whole cause to God, than to journey thither, whereas we neither shall have place nor be able to do any good: whereas we can obtain no audience, whereas Princes' Ambassadors be but used as mocking stocks, and whereas also we be condemned already before trial, as though the matter were aforehand despatched and agreed upon.

Nevertheless, we can bear patiently and quietly our own private wrongs: but wherefore do they shut out Christian Kings, and good Princes from their Convocation? Why do they so uncourteously, or with such spite leave them out, and as though they were not either Christian men, or else could not judge, will not have them made acquainted with the cause of Christian Religion, nor understand the state of their own Churches? Or if the said kings and princes happen to intermeddle in such matters, and take upon them to do that they may do, that they be commanded to do, and ought of duty to do, and the same things that we know both David and Solomon and other good princes have done, that is, if they, whilst the Pope and his Prelates slug° and sleep, or else mischievously withstand them, do bridle the Priests' sensuality, and drive them to do their duty, and keep them still to it: if they do overthrow Idols, if they take away superstition, and set up again the true worshipping of God, why do they by and by make an outcry upon them, that such Princes trouble all, and press by violence into another body's office, and do thereby wickedly and malapertly?° What scripture hath at any time forbidden a Christian prince to be made privy to such causes? Who but themselves alone made ever any such law?

They will say to this, I guess, Civil Princes have learned to govern a commonwealth, and to order matters of war, but they understand not the secret mysteries of Religion. If that be so, what is the Pope I pray you, at this day, other than a Monarch or a Prince? Or what be the Cardinals, who must be none other nowadays, but Princes and kings' sons? What else be the Patriarchs, and, for the most part the Archbishops, the Bishops, the Abbots? What be they else at this present in the Pope's kingdom, but worldly Princes, but Dukes and Earls, gorgeously accompanied with bands of men whithersoever they go? Oftentimes also gaily arrayed with chains and collars of gold. They have at times too, certain ornaments by themselves, as Crosses, pillars, hats, mitres, and Palls°, which pomp the ancient Bishops Chrysostom, Augustine and Ambrose never had. Setting these things aside, what teach they? What say they? What do they? How live they? I say not, as may become a Bishop, but as may become even a Christian man? Is it so great a matter to have a vain title, and by changing a garment only to have the name of a Bishop?

Surely to have the principal stay and effect of all matters committed wholly to these men's hands, who neither know nor will know these things, nor yet set a jot by any point of Religion, save that which concerneth their belly and Riot, and to have them alone sit as Judges, and to be set up as overseers in the watch tower being no better than blind spies: of the other side, to have a Christian Prince of good understanding and of a right judgment, to stand still like a block or a stake, not to be suffered: neither to give his voice, nor to show his judgment, but only to wait what these men shall will and command, as one which had neither ears nor eyes nor wit, nor heart, and whatsoever they give in charge, to allow it without exception, blindly fulfilling their commandments, be they never so blasphemous and wicked, yea although they command him quite to destroy all Religion, and to crucify again Christ himself. This surely, besides that it is proud and spiteful, is also beyond all right and reason and not to be endured of Christian and wise princes. Why, I pray you, may Caiaphas and Annas understand these matters, and may not David and Ezechias do the same? Is it lawful for a Cardinal being a man of war and delighting in blood, to have place in a Council?

And is it not lawful for a Christian Emperor or a king? We truly grant no further liberty to our Magistrates than that we know hath both been given them by the word of God, and also been confirmed by the examples of the very best governed commonwealths. For besides that a Christian Prince hath the charge of both Tables committed to him by God, to the end he may understand that not temporal matters only, but also Religious and ecclesiastical causes pertain to his office. Besides also that God by his Prophets often and earnestly commandeth the king to cut down the groves, to break down the Images and altars of Idols, and to write out the book of the law for himself: and besides that the prophet Isaiah saith, a king ought to be a patron and a nurse of the Church:[29] I say besides all these things, we see by histories and by examples of the best times, that good princes ever took the administration of ecclesiastical matters to pertain to their duty. Moses a Civil Magistrate and chief guide of the people, both received from God, and delivered to the people all the order for religion and Sacrifices, and gave Aaron the Bishop a vehement and sore rebuke for making the golden calf, and for suffering the corruption of Religion.[30] Joshua also, though he were none other than a Civil Magistrate, yet as soon as he was chosen by God, and set as a ruler over the people, he received commandments specially touching Religion and the service of God.[31] King David, when the whole religion was altogether brought out of frame by wicked king Saul, brought home again the Ark of God,[32] that is to say, he restored Religion again, and was not only amongst them himself as a counsellor and furtherer of the work, but he appointed also hymns and Psalms, put in order the companies, and was the only doer in setting forth that whole solemn show,

---

[29] Isaiah 49.23: 'And Kings shall be thy nursing fathers, and Queenes shall be thy nurses: they shall worship thee with *their* faces toward the earth, and licke up the dust of thy feete: and thou shalt know that I am the Lord: for they shall not be ashamed that waite for me.'

[30] **Marg.** Exod. xxxii. [Exodus 32.21: 'Also Moses said unto Aaron, What did this people unto thee, that thou hast brought so great a sinne upon them?']

[31] **Marg.** Jos. i. [Joshua 1.8: 'Let not this booke of the Law depart out of thy mouth, but meditate therein day and night, that thou mayest observe and doe according to all that is written therein: for then shalt thou make thy way prosperous, and then shalt thou have good successe.']

[32] **Marg.** 1 Chron. xiii. [I Chronicles 13.3: 'And we will bring againe the Arke of our God to us: for we sought not unto it in the dayes of Saul.']

AN APOLOGY OR ANSWER IN DEFENCE OF THE CHURCH

and in effect ruled the priests. King Solomon built unto the Lord the Temple, which his father David had but purposed in his mind to do:³³ and after the finishing thereof, he made a goodly oration to the people concerning Religion and the service of God,³⁴ he afterward displaced Abiathar the priest, and set Zadok in his place.³⁵ After this, when the Temple of God was in shameful wise polluted through the naughtiness and negligence of the priests, King Hezekiah commanded the same to be cleansed from the rubble and filth,³⁶ the priests to light up candles, to burn Incense, and to do their divine service, according to the old and allowed custom. The same king also commanded the brazen Serpent, which then the people wickedly worshipped, to be taken down and beaten to powder.³⁷ King Jehoshaphat overthrew and utterly made away the hill altars and Groves³⁸, whereby he saw God's honour hindered, and the people holden back with a private superstition from the ordinary Temple which was at Jerusalem, whereto they should by order have resorted yearly from every part of the Realm. King Josiah with great diligence put the Priests and Bishops in mind of their duty:³⁹ King Joash bridled the Riot

---

³³ **Marg.** 2 Chron. vi. [II Chronicles 6.9: 'Notwithstanding, thou shalt not build the house, but thy sonne, which shall come out of thy loynes, he shall build an house unto my Name.']

³⁴ **Marg.** 1 Kings viii. [I Kings 8.55–56: 'And stood and blessed all the Congregation of Israel, with a loud voyce, saying, Blessed be the Lord that hath given rest unto his people Israel, according to all that he promised: there hath not failed one word of all his good promise which he promised by the hand of Moses his servant.']

³⁵ I Kings 2:26: 'Then the King said unto Abiathar the Priest, Go to Anathoth unto thine own fields: for thou art worthy of death: but I will not this day kill thee, because thou barest the Ark of the Lord God before David my father, and because thou hast suffered in all, wherein my father hath been afflicted.'

³⁶ **Marg.** 2 Chron. xxix. [II Chronicles 29.5: 'And said unto them, Hear me, ye Levites: sanctify now yourselves, and sanctify the house of the Lord God of your fathers, and carry forth the filthiness out of the Sanctuary.']

³⁷ **Marg.** 2 Kings xviii. [II Kings 18.4: 'He tooke away the hie places, and brake the images, and cut downe the groves, and brake in pieces the brasen serpent that Moses had made: for unto those dayes the children of Israel did burne incense to it, and he called it Nehushtan.']

³⁸ **Marg.** 2 Chron. xvii. [II Chronicles 17.6: 'And he lifted up his heart unto the wayes of the Lord, and he tooke away moreover the high places and the groves out of Judah.']

³⁹ **Marg.** 2 Kings xxiii. [II Kings 23.2: 'And the king went up into the house of the Lord, with all the men of Judah, and all the inhabitants of Jerusalem with

and arrogancy of the priests:[40] Jehu put to death the wicked prophets.[41]

And to rehearse no more examples out of the old law, let us rather consider since the birth of Christ, how the Church hath been governed in the Gospel's time. The Christian Emperors in old time appointed the Councils of the Bishops. Constantine called the Council at Nice, Theodosius the first, called the Council at Constantinople. Theodosius the second, the Council at Ephesus, Martian, the Council at Chalcedon: and when Ruffine the heretic had alleged for authority, a Council which, as he thought, should make for him: Hierom his adversary to confute him, Tell us (quod he) what Emperor commanded that Council to be called?[42] The same Hierom again in his Epitaph upon Paula, maketh mention of the Emperor's letters, which gave commandment to call the Bishops of Italy and Greece to Rome to a Council.[43] Continually for the space of five hundred years, the Emperor alone appointed the ecclesiastical assemblies, and called the Councils of the Bishops together.

We now therefore marvel the more at the unreasonable dealing of the Bishop of Rome, who knowing what was the Emperor's right when the Church was well ordered, knowing also that it is now a common right to all princes, for so much as the kings are

---

him, and the Priests and Prophets, and all the people both small and great: and he read in their eares all the words of the booke of the covenant, which was found in the house of the Lord.']

[40] **Marg.** 2 Kings xii. [II Kings 12.7: 'Then King Jehoash called for Jehoiada the Priest, and the *other* Priests, and sayd unto them, Why repair yee not the ruines of the Temple? now therefore receive no more money of your acquaintance, except yee deliver it to *repaire* the ruines of the Temple.']

[41] **Marg.** 2 Kings x. [II Kings 10.25: 'And when hee had made an ende of the burnt-offering, Jehu sayd to the guard, and to the captaines, Goe in, slay them, let not a man come out. And they smote them with the edge of the sword. And the guard, and the captaines cast them out, and went unto the city, *where was* the temple of Baal.']

[42] Saint Jerome and Rufinus (cited above, Part I, note 16 and Part VI, note 26) engaged in a lengthy, vituperative pamphlet war. Jerome faulted Rufinus's translation of Origen and repudiated the sympathy for Origen which Rufinus had attributed to Jerome himself.

[43] In his letters to both Paula and Eustochium, Jerome expressed his deep admiration for Saint Paula, a widow who renounced her wealth to follow Jerome and, with her daughter Eustochium, to lead an ascetic life; Paula founded three convents in Bethlehem.

AN APOLOGY OR ANSWER IN DEFENCE OF THE CHURCH

now fully possessed in the several parts of the whole Empire, doth so without consideration assign that office alone to himself, and taketh it sufficient in summoning a general Council, to make a man that is prince of the whole world no otherwise partaker thereof than he would make his own servant.[44] And although the modesty and mildness of the Emperor Ferdinand be so great that he can bear this wrong, because peradventure he understandeth not well the Pope's packing,° yet ought not the Pope of his holiness to offer him that wrong, nor to claim as his own another man's right.

But hereto some will reply: the Emperor indeed called Councils at that time ye speak of, because the Bishop of Rome was not yet grown so great as he is now, but yet the Emperor did not then sit together with the Bishops in Council, or once bare any stroke with his authority in their consultation. I answer nay, that it is not so, for as witnesseth Theodoret, the Emperor Constantine sat not only together with them in the Council of Nice, but gave also advice to the Bishops how it was best to try out the matter by the Apostles' and Prophets' writings, as appeareth by these his own words. In disputation (saith he) of matters of divinity, we have set before us to follow the doctrine of the holy Ghost. For the Evangelists' and the Apostles' works, and the Prophets' sayings show us sufficiently what opinion we ought to have of the will of God.[45] The Emperor Theodosius (as saith Socrates) did not only

---

[44] **Marg.** Pius IV. in Bulla sua ad Imp. Ferdin. ['Despite the recalcitrance of the emperor Ferdinand and the objections of the French government, Pius IV declared the conciliar suspension of 28 April 1552, at an end, and by the Bull *Ad Ecclesiae regimen* of 29 November, 1560, he convoked the reassembly of the council [...] Certain words had therefore been used at the request of the Emperor Ferdinand, "lest they [Lutherans] should be deprived of all hope."' However, 'the second set of words are being employed to indicate the truth, since certainly this is a continuation of the council previously summoned under Paul III and suspended under Julius III, and it will always be the same council until such time as it shall have been closed and dissolved.' Kenneth M. Setton, *The Papacy and the Levant (1204–1571): The Sixteenth Century from Julius III to Pius V*, 4 vols (Philadelphia: American Philosophical Society, 1976–1984), IV (1984), 769. After long negotiations, Holy Roman Emperor Ferdinand, the Kings of Spain and Portugal, Catholic Switzerland, and Venice left the matter to the Pope. J.P. Kirsch, 'Council of Trent,' in *The Catholic Encyclopedia*, XV (1912).]

[45] **Marg.** Hist. Eccles. Lib. i. cap. vi. [Theodoret, *Historia ecclesiastica*, I. 6: 'For the gospels (continued he), the writings, and the oracles of the ancient prophets,

sit amongst the Bishops, but also ordered the whole arguing of the cause, and tare° in pieces the Heretics' books, and allowed for good the judgment of the Catholics.[46] In the Council at Chalcedon a civil Magistrate condemned for heretics by the sentence of his own mouth, the Bishops Dioscorus, Juvenalis, and Thalassius, and gave judgment to put them down from that promotion in the Church.[47] In the third Council at Constantinople, Constantine a civil Magistrate, did not only sit amongst the Bishops, but did also subscribe with them: for saith he, we have both read and subscribed.[48] In the second council

---

clearly teach us what we ought to believe concerning the divine nature. Let, then, all contentious disputation be discarded; and let us seek in the divinely-inspired word the solution of the questions at issue.']

[46] **Marg.** Socrat. Lib. v. cap.x. [Socrates, *Ecclesiastical History*, I. 10: 'So after a very short time he called together a general conference of the sects, thinking that by a discussion among their bishops, their mutual differences might be adjusted, and unanimity established.' *Nicene and Post-Nicene Fathers*, II (1890), 122.]

[47] **Marg.** Socrat. Lib. v. cap.x. [Socrates, *Ecclesiastical History*, I. 10.]; Act 1. [Commentary on the fourth Church Council (after Nicea [325], Constantinople [381], and Ephesus [431]), the Council of Chalcedon (451), where Christological debates focused on the two complete and inseparable natures of the Godhead and manhood in Jesus Christ, was another flashpoint between Jewel and Harding. In *The Defence of the Apology* Jewel cited Council documents to rebut Harding's charge that not all three bishops were condemned by a civil magistrate. '*Videtur nobis justum esse [...] eidem poenae Dioscorum reverendum episcopum Alexandriae, et Juvenalem reverendum episopum Hierosolymorum, et Thalassium reverendum episopum Caesariae Cappadociae, [...] subjacere; et a sancto concilio, secundum regulas, ab episcopali dignitate fieri alienos.* Unto us it seemeth right that Dioscorus the reverend bishop of Alexandria, and Juvenalis the reverend bishop of Hierusalem, and Thessalius the reverend bishop of Caesaria in Cappadocia should be put to the same punishment and by the holy council, according to the canons, should be removed from their episcopal dignities. *Gloriosissimi judices et amplissimus senatus dixerunt.* The most noble judges and most worthy senate said.' Jewel quotes *Concil. Chalced. Act I in Concil. Stud. Labb. et Cossart*, Tom. IV, col. 323, 322. However, Harding maintained that Pope Leo was also disciplining Dioscorus for presiding over the second council at Ephesus (449), called the 'Robber Synod' because it was conducted without the authorization of Rome. Describing the pope's 'universal authority' as 'at that time unknown,' Jewel insisted 'all that you imagine, of usurping the pope's authority, is but a fantasy.' Pope Leo did not ratify Canon 28 of the Council of Chalcedon, which declared Constantinople the new Rome with the same honour as the old Rome. The Canons of the Council of Chalcedon were not accepted by the Coptic and other ancient Eastern churches. *Works*, IV, 1022–24.]

[48] **Marg.** Conc. II. [Eruptions between Jewel and Harding continued. Jewel cited

called Arausicanum, the Prince's Ambassadors being noble men born, not only spake their mind touching Religion, but set to their hands also, as well as the Bishops. For thus it is written in the latter end of that Council: Petrus, Marcellinus, Felix and Liberius, being most noble men, and the famous Lieutenants and Captains of France, and also Peers of the Realm, have given their consent, and set to their hands. Further, Syagrius, Opilio, Pantagathus, Deodatus, Cariattho and Marcellus, men of very great honour have subscribed.[49] If it be so then, that Lieutenants, Captains and Peers have had authority to subscribe in Council, have not Emperors and Kings the like authority?

Truly there had been no need to handle so plain a matter as this is, with so many words, and so at length, if we had not to do with those men who for a desire they have to strive and to win the mastery, use of course to deny all things, be they never so clear, yea the very same which they presently see and behold with their own eyes. The Emperor Justinian made a law to correct the behaviour of the Clergy, and to cut short the insolency of the priests. And albeit he were a Christian and a Catholic prince, yet put he down from their Papal Throne, two Popes, Sylverius and Vigilius, notwithstanding they were Peter's successors and Christ's vicars.

Let us see then, such men as have authority over the Bishops, such men as receive from God commandments concerning Religion, such as bring home again the Ark of God, make holy hymns, oversee the priests, build the Temple, make Orations touching divine service, cleanse the Temples, destroy the hill Altars, burn the Idols' groves, teach the priests their duty, write them out precepts how they should live, kill the wicked Prophets, displace the high Priests, call together the Councils of Bishops, sit together with the Bishops, instructing them what they ought to do, condemn and punish an Heretical Bishop, be made acquainted with matters of Religion, which subscribe and give

---

Edict. Imp. Constant. In Concil. Constant. III in eod. [*Stud. Labb. et Cossart*], Tom. VI. Col. 1098 to affirm Constantine's signing *Consentiens subscripsi.* Giving consent hereto I have subscribed. Harding insisted that Constantine did not use the formula reserved for bishops: *Definiens subscripsi.* I have subscribed with giving definitive sentence. Jewel observed: 'Thus have you found out a knot in a rush and devised a diversity without a difference.' *Works*, IV, 1024–25.]
[49] Booty cites Crabbe, *Concilia*, I, 629; II, 1–3.

sentence, and do all these things, not by any other man's Commission, but in their own name, and that both uprightly and godly. Shall we say it pertaineth not to such men to have to do with Religion? Or shall we say, a Christian Magistrate which dealeth amongst others in these matters, doth either naughtily, or presumptuously, or wickedly? The most ancient and Christian Emperors and Kings that ever were, did busy themselves with these matters, and yet were they never for this cause noted either of wickedness or of presumption. And what is he that can find out either more catholic princes or more notable examples?

Wherefore, if it were lawful for them to do thus being but Civil Magistrates, and having the chief rule of commonweals, what offence have our princes at this day made, which may not have leave to do the like, being in the like degree? Or what especial gift of learning or of judgment, or of holiness, have these men now, that contrary to the custom of all the ancient and Catholic Bishops, who used to confer with princes and peers concerning religion, they do now thus reject and cast off Christian princes from knowing of the cause, and from their meetings?

Well thus doing, they wisely and warily provide for themselves and for their kingdom, which otherwise they see is like shortly to come to nought. For if so be they whom God hath placed in greatest dignity did see and perceive these men's practices, how Christ's commandments be despised by them, how the light of the Gospel is darkened and quenched out by them, and how themselves also be subtly beguiled and mocked, and unawares be deluded by them, and the way to the kingdom of heaven stopped up before them, no doubt they would never so quietly suffer themselves neither to be disdained after such a proud sort, nor so despitefully to be scorned and abused by them. But now through their own lack of understanding, and through their own blindness, these men have them fast yoked and in their danger.

We truly for our parts, as we have said, have done nothing in altering Religion, either upon rashness or arrogancy, nor nothing but with good leisure and great consideration. Neither had we ever intended to do it, except both the manifest and most assured will of God, opened to us in his holy scriptures, and the regard of our own salvation had even constrained us thereunto. For though we have departed from that Church which these men call Catholic, and by that means get us envy° amongst them that want skill to judge, yet is this enough for us, and it ought to be enough for every wise and good man, and one that maketh account of everlasting life, that we have gone from that Church which had power to err, which Christ, who cannot err, told so long before it should err, and which we ourselves did evidently see with our eyes to have gone both from the holy fathers and from the Apostles, and from Christ his own self, and from the primitive and catholic church: and we are come as near as we possibly could to the Church of the Apostles and of the old catholic Bishops and Fathers, which Church we know hath hereunto been sound and perfect, and as Tertullian termeth it, a pure virgin, spotted as yet with no Idolatry, nor with any foul or shameful fault: and have directed according to their customs and ordinances not only our doctrine, but also the Sacraments and the form of common prayer.

And as we know both Christ himself and all good men heretofore have done, we have called home again to the original and first foundation that Religion which hath been foully foreslowed,° and utterly corrupted by these men. For we thought it meet thence to take the pattern of reforming Religion, from whence the ground of Religion was first taken, because this one reason, as saith the most ancient father Tertullian, hath great force against all Heresies. Look whatsoever was first, that is true: and whatsoever is latter, that is corrupt.[50] Irenaeus oftentimes appealed to the oldest Churches, which had been nearest to Christ's time, and which it was hard to believe had erred.[51] But why at this day is not the same respect and consideration had? Why return we not to the pattern of the old Churches? Why may not we hear at this time amongst us the same saying, which was openly pronounced in times past in the Council at Nice by so many Bishops and Catholic fathers, and nobody once speaking

---

[50] Tertullian, *Adversus Praxeam* 2: 'In this principle also we must henceforth find a presumption of equal force against all heresies whatsoever — that whatever is first is true, whereas that is spurious which is later in date.' *Ante-Nicene Fathers*, III (1887), 598.

[51] Irenaeus (*c.* 130–202), *Contra haereses*, III. 3: 'From this document, whosoever chooses to do so, may learn that He, the Father of our Lord Jesus Christ, was preached by the Churches, and may also understand the tradition of the Church, since this Epistle is of older date than these men who are now propagating falsehood, and who conjure into existence another god beyond the Creator and the Maker of all existing things.' Irenaeus was an early Church Father and bishop of Lyons. *Ante-Nicene Fathers*, I (1885), 416.

against it ἔθη ἀρχαῖα κρατείτω: that is to say, hold still the old customs?⁵² When Esdras went about to repair the ruins of the Temple of God, he sent not to Ephesus, although the most beautiful and gorgeous temple of Diana was there, and when he purposed to restore the Sacrifices and ceremonies of God, he sent not to Rome, although peradventure he had heard in that place were the solemn Sacrifices called Hecatombae, and other called Solitaurilia, Lectisternia, and Supplicationes, and Numa Pompilius' ceremonial books, he thought it enough for him to set before his eyes, and follow the pattern of the old Temple which Solomon at the beginning builded, according as God had appointed him, and also those old customs and ceremonies which God himself had written out by special words for Moses.⁵³

The prophet Aggaeus, after the Temple was repaired again by Esdras, and the people might think they had a very just cause to rejoice on their own behalf, for so great a benefit received of almighty God, yet made he them all burst out in tears, because that they which were yet alive and had seen the former building of the Temple before the Babylonians destroyed it, called to mind how far off it was yet from that beauty and excellency which it had in the old times past before.⁵⁴ For then indeed would they have thought the Temple worthily repaired, if it had answered to the ancient pattern, and to the majesty of the first Temple. Paul because he would amend the abuse of the Lord's Supper which the Corinthians even then began to corrupt, he set before them Christ's institution to follow, saying: I have delivered unto you that which I first received of the Lord.⁵⁵ And when Christ did confute the error of the Pharisees, Ye must, saith he, return to the first beginning, for from the beginning it was not thus.⁵⁶ And

---

⁵² Booty cites *Sacrosancta Concilia*, tom II, col. 32, Concil. Nic., canon 6.
⁵³ Ezra 3.2: 'Then stood up Jeshua the sonne of Jozadak, and his brethren the Priests, and Zerubbabel the sonne of Shealtiel, and his brethren, and built the Altar of the God of Israel to offer burnt-offerings thereon, as it is written in the Law of Moses the man of God.'
⁵⁴ Haggai 2.4: 'Who is left among you that saw this House in her first glory, and how do you see it now? is it not in your eyes, in comparison of it as nothing?'
⁵⁵ **Marg.** 1 Cor. xi. [I Corinthians 11.23: 'For I have received of the Lord that which I also have delivered unto you, *to wit*, That the Lord Jesus in the night when he was betrayed, tooke bread.'] L
⁵⁶ Matthew 19.8: 'He sayd unto them, Moses, because of the hardnesse of your heart, suffered you to put away your wives: but from the beginning it was not so.'

when he found great fault with the priests for their uncleanness of life and covetousness, and would cleanse the Temple from all evil abuses, This house, saith he, at the first beginning it was a house of prayer, wherein all the people might devoutly and sincerely pray together, and so were your parts to use it now also at this day. For it was not builded to the end it should be a den of thieves. Likewise all the good and commendable Princes mentioned of in the Scriptures were praised, specially by these words that they had walked in the ways of their father David. That is because they had returned to the first and original foundation, and had restored Religion even to the perfection wherein David left it. And therefore when we likewise saw all things were quite trodden under foot of these men, and that nothing remained in the Temple of God but pitiful spoils and decays, we reckoned it the wisest and the safest way to set before our eyes those Churches which we knew for a surety that they never had erred, nor never had private Mass, nor prayers in a strange and barbarous language, nor this corrupting of Sacraments, and other toys.

And forsomuch as our desire was to have the Temple of the Lord restored anew, we would seek none other foundation than the same which we knew was long agone laid by the Apostles, that is to wit, our saviour, Jesus Christ.[57] And forasmuch as we heard God himself speaking unto us in his word, and saw also the notable Examples of the old and primitive Church: again how uncertain a matter it was to wait for a general Council, and that the success thereof would be much more uncertain, but specially forsomuch as we were most ascertained of God's will, and counted it a wickedness to be too careful and overcumbered about the judgments of mortal men, we could no longer stand taking advice with flesh and blood, but rather thought good to do the same thing that both might rightly be done, and hath also many a time been done as well of good men as of many catholic Bishops: that is, to remedy our own Churches by a Provincial Synod. For thus know we the old fathers used to put in experience before they came to the public universal Council. There remain yet at this day Canons written in Councils of free Cities, as of Carthage under Cyprian, as of Ancyra, Neocaesarea and of Gangra, also which is in Paphlagonia, as some think, before that the name of the general

---

[57] **Marg.** 1 Cor. iii. [1 Corinthians 3.11: 'For other foundation can no man lay, than that which is laid, which is Jesus Christ.'] **L**

Council at Nice was ever heard of. After this fashion in old time did they speedily meet with, and cut short those Heretics the Pelagians[58] and the Donatists[59] at home with private disputation, without any general Council. Thus also when the Emperor Constantine evidently and earnestly took part with Auxentius the Bishop of the Arians' faction, Ambrose the Bishop of the Christians appealed not unto a general Council, where he saw no good could be done, by reason of the Emperor's might and great labour, but appealed to his own Clergy and people, that is to say, to a Provincial Synod. And thus it was decreed in the Council at Nice, that the Bishops should assemble twice every year. And in the Council at Carthage it was decreed, that the Bishops should meet together in each of their provinces, at least once in the year, which was done, as saith the Council of Chalcedon, of purpose, that if any errors and abuses had happened to spring up anywhere, they might immediately at the first entry be destroyed where they first began. So likewise when Secundus and Palladius rejected the Council at Aquileia, because it was not a general and a common Council, Ambrose Bishop of Milan made answer that no man ought to take it for a new or strange matter that the Bishops of the west part of the world did call together Synods, and make private assemblies in their Provinces, for that it was a thing before then used by the west Bishops no few times, and by the Bishops of Greece used oftentimes and commonly to be done. And so Charles the great being Emperor, held a provincial Council in Germany for putting away Images, contrary to the second Council at Nice. Neither pardy° even amongst us is this so very a strange and new a trade: for we have had ere now in England provincial Synods, and governed our Churches by home made laws. What should one say more? Of a truth even those greatest Councils, and where most assembly of people ever was (whereof these men use to make such an exceeding reckoning) compare them with all the Churches which throughout the world acknowledge and profess the name of Christ, and what else I pray you can they seem to be, but certain private Councils of Bishops, and provincial Synods? For admit peradventure, Italy, France, Spain, England, Germany, Denmark, and Scotland: meet together, if there want Asia,

---

[58] Pelagianism, a heresy of the fifth century, held that original sin did not corrupt humanity and that moral perfection was possible without divine grace.
[59] See note 28 in Part I about the Donatists.

Greece, Armenia, Persia, Media, Mesopotamia, Egypt, Ethiopia, India, and Mauritania, in all which places there be both many Christian men and also Bishops, how can any man, being in his right mind, think such a Council to be a general Council? Or where so many parts of the world do lack, how can they truly say, they have the consent of the whole world? Or what manner of Council, ween you, was the same last at Trident? Or how might it be termed a general Council, when out of all Christian kingdoms and Nations, there came unto it but only forty Bishops, and of the same some so cunning that they might be thought meet to be sent home again to learn their Grammar, and so well learned that they had never studied Divinity?

Whatsoever it be, the truth of the Gospel of JESUS CHRIST dependeth not upon Councils, nor as St Paul saith, upon mortal creatures' judgments.[60] And if they which ought to be careful for God's Church will not be wise but slack their duty, and harden their hearts against God and his Christ, going on still to pervert the right ways of the Lord, God will stir up the very stones, and make children and babes cunning, whereby there may ever be some to confute these men's lies. For God is able (not only without Councils, but also will the Councils, nill° the Councils) to maintain and advance his own kingdom. Full many be the thoughts of man's heart (saith Solomon) but the counsel of the Lord abideth steadfast. There is no wisdom, there is no knowledge, there is no counsel against the Lord.[61] Things endure not, saith Hilarius, that be set up with men's workmanship: By another manner of means must the Church of God be builded and preserved,[62] for that Church is grounded upon the foundation of the Apostles and Prophets, and is holden fast together by one corner stone, which is Christ Jesu.[63]

---

[60] 1 Corinthians 4.3: 'As touching me, I passe very little to be judged of you, or of man's judgement: no, I judge not mine owne selfe.'

[61] Proverbs 19.21: 'Many devices *are* in a mans heart: but the counsell of the Lord shall stand.'

[62] Hilary of Poitiers, '*Domus ergo aedificanda per deum est. humanis enim operibus structa non permanet.*' (Hilary of Poitiers's commentary on Psalm 126). *Hilary, Episcopi Pictaviensis, Tractatus Super Psalmos, Recensit Antonius Zingerle* (Prague: F. Temsky, 1891), p. 618. Bacon captures the sense of Hilary's commentary with a developed contrast.

[63] **Marg.** Eph. ii. [Ephesians 2.20–21: 'And are built upon the foundation of the Apostles and Prophets, Jesus Christ himselfe being the chiefe corner stone, in

But marvellous notable and to very good purpose for these days be Hierom's words: Whosoever (saith he) the devil hath deceived, and enticed to fall asleep as it were with the sweet and deathly enchantments of the mermaids the Syrens, those persons doth God's word awake up, saying unto them: Arise thou that sleepest, lift up thyself, and Christ shall give thee light. Therefore at the coming of Christ, of God's word, of the ecclesiastical doctrine, and of the full destruction of Nineveh, and of that most beautiful harlot, then shall the people which heretofore had been cast in a trance under their masters, be raised up, and shall make haste to go to the Mountains of the Scripture, and there shall they find hills, Moses, verily and Joshua the son of Nun: other hills also which are the Prophets: and hills of the New Testament, which are the Apostles and the Evangelists. And when the people shall flee for succour to such hills, and shall be exercised in the reading of those kind of mountains, though they find not one to teach them (for the harvest shall be great, but the labourers few) yet shall the good desire of the people be well accepted, in that they have gotten them to such hills, and the negligence of their masters shall be openly reproved.[64] These be Hierom's sayings, and that so plain, as there needeth no Interpreter. For they agree so just with the things we now see with our eyes have already come to pass, that we may verily think that he meant to foretell, as it were by the spirit of prophecy, and to paint before our face the universal state of our time, the fall of the most gorgeous harlot Babylon, the repairing again of God's Church, the blindness and sloth of the Bishops, and the good will and forwardness of the people. For who is so blind that he seeth not these men be the masters, by whom the people, as saith Hierom, hath been led into

---

whom all the building coupled together, groweth unto an holy Temple in the Lord.'] **L**

[64] **Marg.** Hieron. in Maum. cap. iii. [Jerome composed his commentaries on the twelve minor prophets (39–392) at the request of Paula and Eustochium. Jewel and Bacon's texts mirror Jerome's Commentary on Nahum about the negligence of shepherds and the refuge of scripture: '*et ibit ad montes Scriptuarum, ibique inveniet montes Moyses et Jesum filium Nave; montes prophetas; montes novi Testamenti apostolos et evangelistas: et cum ad tales montes confugerit, et in hujuscemodi montium fuerit lectione versatus, si non invenerit qui eum doceat, tunc et illius stadium comprobabitur, quia confugerit ad montes, et magistrorum desidia coarguetur.' Commentariorum in Naum Prophetam, Patrologia Latina*, xxv (1845), III, vers. 18, col. 1272.]

AN APOLOGY OR ANSWER IN DEFENCE OF THE CHURCH

error, and lulled asleep? Or who seeth not Rome, that is their Nineveh, which sometime was painted with fairest colours, but now her vizer° being pulled off, is both better seen and less set by? Or who seeth not that good men being awaked as it were out of their dead sleep, at the light of the Gospel, and at the voice of God, have resorted to the hills of the Scriptures, waiting not at all for the Councils of such masters?

But by your favour, some will say, these things ought not to have been attempted without the Bishop of Rome's commandment, forsomuch as he only is the knot and band of Christian society: he only is that priest of Levi's order, whom God signified in the Deuteronomy, from whom counsel in matters of weight and true judgment ought to be fetched, and whoso obeyeth not his judgment, the same man ought to be killed in the sight of his brethren: and that no mortal creature hath authority to be judge over him whatsoever he do: that Christ reigneth in heaven and he in earth: that he alone can do as much as Christ, or God himself can do, because Christ and he have but one Council house: That without him is no faith, no hope, no church, and whoso goeth from him, quite casteth away and renounceth his own salvation. Such talk have the Canonists, the Pope's parasites surely, but with small discretion or soberness: for they could scant say more, at least they could not speak more highly of Christ himself.

As for us truly, we have fallen from the Bishop of Rome upon no manner of worldly respect or commodity, and would to Christ he so behaved himself, as this falling away needed not: but so the case stood, that unless we left him, we could not come to Christ. Neither will he now make any other league with us, than such a one as Nahas the king of the Ammonites would have made in times past with them of the city of Jabez, which was to put out the right eye of each one of the Inhabitants.[65] Even so will the Pope pluck from us the holy Scripture, the Gospel of our salvation, and all the confidence which we have in Christ Jesu. And upon other condition can he not agree upon peace with us.

For whereas some use to make so great a vaunt, that the Pope is only Peter's successor, as though thereby he carried the holy Ghost in his bosom and cannot err, this is but a matter of nothing,

---

[65] **Marg.** 1 Sam. xi. [1 Samuel 11.2: 'And Nahash the Ammonite answered them, On this condition will I make a covenant with you, that I may thrust out all your right eyes, and bring that shame upon all Israel.']

and a very trifling tale. God's grace is promised to a good mind, and to one that feareth God, not unto Sees and Successions. Riches, saith Hierom, may make a Bishop to be of more might than the rest: but all the Bishops whosoever they be, are the Successors of the Apostles.[66] If so be, the place and consecrating only be sufficient (why then) Manasses succeeded David, and Caiaphas succeeded Aaron. And it hath been often seen, that an Idol hath stand in the Temple of God. In old time Archidamus the Lacedaemonian boasted much of himself, how he came of the blood of Hercules, but one Nicostratus in this wise abated his pride: Nay, quoth he, thou seemest not to descend from Hercules, for Hercules destroyed ill men, but thou makest good men evil. And when the Pharisees bragged of their lineage, how they were of the kindred and blood of Abraham, Ye, saith Christ, seek to kill me, a man which have told you the truth as I heard it from God: thus Abraham never did. Ye are of your father the devil, and will needs obey his will.[67]

Yet notwithstanding, because we will grant somewhat to succession, tell us, hath the Pope alone succeeded Peter? And wherein I pray you in what Religion? In what office? In what piece of his life hath he succeeded him? What one thing (tell me) had Peter ever like unto the Pope? Or the Pope like unto Peter? Except peradventure they will say thus: that Peter when he was at Rome, never taught the Gospel, never fed the flock, took away the keys of the kingdom of heaven, hid the treasures of his Lord, sat him down only in his Castle in S. John Laterane, and pointed out with his finger all the places of Purgatory, and kinds of punishments, committing some poor souls to be tormented, and other some again suddenly releasing thence at his own pleasure, taking money for so doing: or that he gave order to say private Masses in every corner: or that he mumbled up the holy service with a low voice and in an unknown language, or that he hanged up the Sacrament in every Temple and on every Altar, and carried the same about

---

[66] Jerome, *Epistola Ad Euagrium*. '*Potentia divitiarum, et pauperitatis humilitas, vel sublimiorem, vel inferiorem episcopum non facit. Caeterum omnes Apostolorum successores sunt.*' *Patrologia Latina*, xxx (1846).

[67] John 8.40–41: 'But now ye goe about to kill mee, a man that have tolde you the trueth, which I have heard of God: this did not Abraham. Ye doe the works of your father. Then said they to him, We are not borne of fornication: we have one Father, which is God.'

before him whithersoever he went, upon an ambling Jennet,° with lights and bells: or that he consecrated with his holy breath, oil, wax, wool, bells, chalices, churches and altars: or that he sold Jubilees, graces, liberties, advowsons,° preventions, first fruits, Palls, the wearing of Palls, bulls, Indulgences and pardons: or that he called himself by the name of the head of the Church, the highest Bishop, Bishop of Bishops, alone Most holy: or that by usurping he took upon himself the right and authority over other folk's Churches: or that he exempted himself from the power of any civil government: or that he maintained wars, and set Princes together at variance: or that he sitting in his Chair, with his triple Crown full of labels, with sumptuous and Persian like gorgeousness, with his Royal sceptre, with his Diadem of gold and glittering with stones, was carried about not upon Palfrey,° but upon the shoulders of noble men. These things no doubt did Peter at Rome in times past, and left them in charge to his Successors as you would say, from hand to hand: for these things be nowadays done at Rome by the Popes, and be so done, as though nothing else ought to be done.

Or contrariwise peradventure they had rather say thus, that the Pope doth now all the same things which we know Peter did many a day ago: that is, that he runneth up and down into every Country to Preach the Gospel, not only openly abroad, but also privately from house to house: that he is diligent, and applieth that business in season and out of season, in due time and out of due time: that he doth the part of an Evangelist, that he fulfilleth the work and ministry of Christ, that he is the watchman of the house of Israel: receiveth answers and words at God's mouth: and even as he receiveth them, so delivereth them over to the people: That he is the salt of the earth: That he is the light of the world, that he doth not feed his own self but his flock, that he doth not entangle himself with the worldly cares of this life, that he doth not use a sovereignty over the Lord's people, that he seeketh not to have other men minister to him, but himself rather to minister unto others, that he taketh all Bishops as his fellows and equals: that he is subject to Princes as to persons sent from God, that he giveth to Caesar that which is Caesar's: and that he as the old Bishops of Rome did (without any question) calleth the Emperor his Lord: Unless therefore the Popes do the like nowadays, and Peter did the things aforesaid, there is no cause at all why they should glory so of Peter's name, and of his succession.

Much less cause have they to complain of our departing, and to call us again to be fellows and friends with them, and to believe as they believe. Men say, that one Cobilon, a Lacedaemonian, when he was sent ambassador to the king of the Persians to treat of a league, and found by chance them of the court playing at dice, he returned straightway home again, leaving his message undone. And when he was asked why he did slack to do the things which he had received by public commission to do, he made answer, he thought it should be a great reproach to his commonwealth to make a league with Dicers. But if we should content ourselves to return to the Pope, and to his popish errors, and to make a covenant not only with dicers, but also with men far more ungracious and wicked than any dicers be: besides that this should be a great blot to our good name, it should also be a very dangerous matter, both to kindle God's wrath against us, and to clog and condemn our own souls forever. For of very truth we have departed from him whom we saw had blinded the whole world this many a hundred year. From him who too far presumptuously was wont to say, he could not err, and whatsoever he did no mortal man had power to condemn him, neither Kings, nor Emperors, nor the whole Clergy, nor yet all the people in the world together, no and though he should carry away with him to hell a thousand souls. From him who took upon him power to command not only men but even God's Angels, to go, to return, to lead souls into Purgatory, and to bring them back again when he list himself: whom Gregory said, without all doubt is the very forerunner and standard bearer of Antichrist, and hath utterly forsaken the Catholic faith: from whom also those ringleaders of ours, who now with might and main resist the Gospel, and the truth which they know to be the truth, have ere this departed every one of their own accord and goodwill, and would even now also gladly depart from him, if the note of inconstancy and shame and their own estimation among the people were not a let° unto them. In conclusion, we have departed from him to whom we were not bound, and who had nothing to say for himself, but only I know not what virtue or power of the place where he dwelleth, and a continuance of succession.

And as for us, we of all others most justly have left him. For our Kings, yea even they which with greatest reverence did follow and obey the authority and faith of the Bishops of Rome, have long since found and felt well enough the yoke and tyranny of the

Pope's kingdom. For the Bishops of Rome took the Crown off from the head of our King Henry the second, and compelled him to put aside all majesty, and like a mere private man to come unto their Legate with great submission and humility, so as all his subjects might laugh him to scorn. More than this, they caused Bishops and Monks and some part of the nobility to be in the field against our King John, and set all the people at liberty from their oaths whereby they ought allegiance to their king: and at last, wickedly and most abominably they bereaved the king, not only of his kingdom, but also of his life. Besides this, they excommunicated and cursed King Henry the eighth, the most famous Prince, and stirred up against him sometime the Emperor, sometime the French King, and as much as in them was, put in adventure our Realm to have been a very prey and spoil. Yet were they but fools and mad, to think that either so mighty a Prince could be scared with bugs and rattles: or else that so noble and great a kingdom might so easily, even at one morsel be devoured and swallowed up.

And yet as though all this were too little, they would needs make all the Realm tributary to them, and exacted thence yearly most unjust and wrongful taxes. So dear cost us the friendship of the City of Rome. Wherefore if they have gotten these things of us by extortion through their fraud and subtle sleights, we see no reason why we may not pluck away the same from them again by lawful ways and just means. And if our kings in that darkness and blindness of former times gave them these things of their own accord and liberality for Religion's sake, being moved with a certain opinion of their feigned holiness, now when ignorance and error is spied out, may the kings their successors take them away again, seeing they have the same authority, the kings their ancestors had before. For the gift is void, except it be allowed by the will of the giver: and that cannot seem a perfect will, which is dimmed and hindered by error.

Thus ye see good Christian Reader, ye see how it is no new thing, though at this day the religion of Christ be entertained with despites and checks, being but lately restored and as it were coming up again anew, forsomuch as the like hath chanced both to Christ himself and to his Apostles: yet nevertheless for fear ye may suffer yourself to be led amiss and seduced with those exclamations of our Adversaries, we have declared at large unto you the very whole manner of our Religion, what our opinion is of God the Father, of his only son Jesus Christ, of the Holy Ghost, of the Church, of the Sacraments, of the ministry, of the Scriptures, of ceremonies, and of every part of Christian belief. We have said that we abandon and detest as plagues and poisons all those old Heresies, which either the sacred Scriptures, or the ancient Councils have utterly condemned: that we call home again as much as ever we can, the right Discipline of the Church, which our Adversaries have quite brought into a poor and weak case: That we punish all licentiousness of life and unruliness of manners by the old and long continued laws, and with as much sharpness as is convenient and lieth in our power: That we maintain still the state of kingdoms, in the same condition and plight wherein we have found them, without any diminishing or alteration, reserving unto our Princes their majesty and worldly pre-eminence safe and without impairing, to our possible power: That we have so gotten ourselves away from that Church which they had made a den of Thieves, and wherein nothing was in good frame or once like to the Church of God, and which themselves confessed had erred many ways, even as Lot in times past gat him out of Sodom, or Abraham out of Chaldea, not upon a desire of contention, but by the warning of God himself: And that we have searched out of the holy Bible which we are sure cannot deceive, one sure form of Religion, and have returned again unto the Primitive Church of the ancient Fathers and Apostles, that is to say, to the first ground and beginning of things, as unto the very foundations and headsprings of Christ's church. And in very truth we have not tarried for in this matter the authority or consent of the Trident Council, wherein we saw nothing done uprightly nor by good order: where also everybody was sworn to the maintenance of one man: where our Prince's Ambassadors were contemned: where not one of our divines could be heard, and where parts taking and ambition was openly and earnestly procured and wrought, but as the holy Fathers in former time, and as our predecessors have commonly done, we have restored our Churches by a Provincial Convocation, and have clean shaken off as our duty was, the yoke and tyranny of the Bishop of Rome, to whom we were not bound; who also had no manner of thing like neither to Christ nor to Peter, nor to an Apostle, nor yet like to any Bishop at all. Finally, we say that we agree amongst ourselves touching the whole judgment and chief substance of Christian Religion, and with one mouth and with one spirit do worship God and the Father of our Lord Jesus Christ.

Wherefore O Christian and godly Reader, forasmuch as thou seest the reasons and causes both why we have restored Religion, and why we have forsaken these men, thou oughtest not to marvel, though we have chosen to obey our Master Christ rather than men. Paul hath given us warning how we should not suffer ourselves to be carried away with such sundry learnings, and to fly their companies, in especial which would sow debate and variances, clean contrary to the Doctrine which they had received of Christ and the Apostles. Long since have these men's crafts and treacheries decayed and vanished and fled away at the sight and light of the Gospel, even as the owl doth at the sun rising. And albeit their trumpery be built up and reared as high as the Sky, yea even in a moment and as it were of the own self falleth it down again to the ground, and cometh to nought. For you must not think that all these things have come to pass rashly or at adventure: It hath been God's pleasure that, against all men's wills well nigh, the Gospel of Jesu Christ should be spread abroad throughout the whole world, at these days. And therefore men following God's biddings, have of their own free will resorted unto the Doctrine of Jesus Christ. And for our parts truly we have sought hereby neither glory nor wealth, nor pleasure nor ease. For there is plenty of all these things with our adversaries. And when we were of their side, we enjoyed such worldly commodities much more liberally and bountifully, than we do now. Neither do we eschew concord and peace, but to have peace with man, we will not be at war with God. The name of peace is a sweet and pleasant thing, saith Hilarius: But yet beware, saith he, peace is one thing, and bondage is another.[68] For if it should so be as they seek to have it, that Christ should be commanded to keep silence, that the truth of the Gospel should be betrayed, that horrible errors should be cloaked, that Christian men's eyes should be

---

[68] Hilary of Poitiers, an orthodox enemy of Arianism, devoted his *On the Trinity* to opposing the Arian view that the Son of God was not eternal but created by the Father. He wrote in praise of peace and unity and against the priests of antichrist: '*speciosum quidem nomen est pacis, et pulcra est opinion unitatis. [...] is est, impietatis suae unitate se jactant agentes se non up episcopos Christi, sed antichristi sacerdotes.*' *Sancti Hilarii Contra Arianos, vel Auxentium Mediolanensem, Patrologia Latina*, x (1845), col. 609.

bleared, and that they might be suffered to conspire openly against God: this were not a peace, but a most ungodly covenant of servitude. There is a peace, saith Nazianzen, that is unprofitable: again there is a discord, saith he, that is profitable.[69] For we must conditionally desire peace, so far as is lawful before God, and so far as we may conveniently. For otherwise Christ himself brought not peace into the world, but a sword.[70] Wherefore if the Pope will have us reconciled to him, his duty is first to be reconciled to God: for from thence, saith Cyprian, spring schisms and sects, because men seek not the head, and have not their recourse to the Fountain of the Scriptures, and keep not the Rules given by the heavenly teacher:[71] for, saith he, that is not peace but war: neither is he joined unto the Church which is severed from the Gospel.[72] As for these men they used to make a merchandise of the name of peace. For that peace which they so fain would have, is only a rest of idle bellies. They and we might easily be brought to atonement touching all these matters, were it not that ambition, gluttony and excess did let it: Hence cometh

---

[69] In his Oration on Peace, Gregory of Nazianzen declared in his title that not all peace was lovable and mastered: '*non omnis pax amanda et complectenda.*' He argued that it was fitting to bring together gentleness rather than quickness and tenderness rather than arrogance and stubbornness: '*tum vero lenitatem potius quam celeritatem, et indulgentiam potius quam arrogantiam et contumaciam adhibere convenit.*' *Orationes, accurantibus D.A.B. Caillau una cum D.M.N.S Guillon* (Paris: Parent-Desbarres, 1885), Oratio VI, sec. 20, p. 232.

[70] Matthew 10.34: 'Thinke not that I am come to sende peace into the earth, but the sword.'

[71] Cyprian, Bishop of Carthage (*c.* 200–258), disagreed with Pope Stephen on the validity of the baptism of heretics returning to the church. Roman practice recognized any baptism performed according to the correct formula with what was considered the correct intention. Cyprian associated the efficacy of the sacrament with the orthodoxy of the minister. In his letter to Pompey: 'And this the bishops of God ought to do now, observing the divine precepts, that, if truth has wavered or vacillated in anything, we should return both to the divine origin and to the evangelical and apostolical tradition and thence the reason for our acts should arise whence both our order and our origin have arisen.' Letter 74. To Pompey, *The Fathers of the Church: St. Cyprian, Letters 1–81*, trans. by Sister Rose Bernard Donna (Washington: Catholic University of America Press, 1964), p. 293.

[72] Cyprian, *On the Lapsed*, Parag. 16: 'They think that that is peace which some with deceiving words are blazoning forth: that is not peace, but war; and he is not joined to the Church who is separated from the Gospel.' *Ante-Nicene Fathers*, V (1888), 441.

AN APOLOGY OR ANSWER IN DEFENCE OF THE CHURCH

their whining, their heart is on their halfpenny. Out of doubt their clamours and stirs be to none other end, but to maintain more shamefully and naughtily ill gotten things.

Nowadays the Pardoners complain of us, the Dataries,[73] the Pope's Collectors, the Bawds, and others which take Gain to be godliness, and serve not Jesu Christ but their own bellies. Many a day ago and in the old world, a wonderful great advantage grew hereby to these kind of people, but now they reckon all is lost unto them that Christ gaineth. The Pope himself maketh a great complaint at this present, that Charity in people is waxen cold. And why so trow° ye? Forsooth because his profits decay more and more. And for this cause doth he hale us into hatred all that ever he may, laying load upon us with despiteful railings and condemning us for Heretics, to the end they that understand not the matter, may think there be no worse men upon earth than we be. Notwithstanding we in the mean season are never the more ashamed for all this: neither ought we to be ashamed of the Gospel: for we set more by the glory of God than we do by the estimation of men. We are sure all is true that we teach, and we may not either go against our own conscience, or bear any witness against God. For if we deny any part of the Gospel of Jesu Christ before men, he on the other side will deny us before his Father.[74] And if there be any that will still be offended and cannot endure Christ's doctrine, such say we, be blind, and leaders of the blind: the truth nevertheless must be preached and preferred above all: and we must with patience wait for God's judgment. Let these folk in the meantime take good heed what they do, and let them be well advised of their own Salvation, and cease to hate and persecute the Gospel of the son of God, for fear lest they feel him once a redresser and revenger of his own cause. God will not suffer himself to be made a mocking stock. The world espieth a good while agone what there is a doing abroad. This flame the more it is kept down, so much the more with greater force and strength doth it break out and fly abroad. Their unfaithfulness shall not disappoint God's faithful promise. And if they shall

---

[73] The Datary was a papal officer through whom petitions to the Pope had to pass. His name is derived from the fact he affixed the 'Datum Romae' to papal bulls.

[74] Matthew 10.33: 'But whosoever shall denie me before men, him will I also denie before my Father which is in heaven.'

refuse to lay away this their hardness of heart and to receive the Gospel of Christ, then shall Publicans and sinners go before them into the kingdom of Heaven.

GOD and the Father of our Lord JESUS CHRIST open the eyes of them all, that they may be able to see that blessed hope whereunto they have been called, so as we may altogether in one, glorify him alone, who is the true God, and also that same Jesus Christ whom he sent down to us from Heaven: unto whom with the Father and the holy Ghost be given all honour and glory everlastingly. So be it.

The end of the Apologie of the Church of England.

GLOSSARY

A

advowsons	the right of presentation of a candidate for a church or ecclesiastical benefice
appaire	to make or become worse
appeach	to accuse, to inform against
attached	affected, inclined, partial
avaunt	go away

B

benefice	permanent church appointment with property and income provided for pastoral duties
bewray	divulge, betray
boult	to examine and separate
brabler	clamorous, quarrelsome person
brablingly	clamorously
brast	burst
bye	situated to one side, out of the way, running in a side direction

C

clawbacks	recovery of money already disbursed
cloyed	disgusted or sickened with excess of sweetness, richness or sentiment
cockle	weed of grain fields, especially corn cockle and darnel
craked	boasted
cursed	accursed

D

darnel	weedy ryegrass
dusked	made dark or gloomy

E

eared	plowed
envy	ill-will
erst	long ago, formerly

F

factious	divided, discordant, schismatic
fainest	disposed, inclined, prepared
fet	fetch
force	care about
foreslowed	slowed down, hindered, impeded

G

glozing	specious or deceptive talk or action
Gyges' Ring	a mythical artifact mentioned in Plato's *Republic*, which allows its owner to become invisible at will

H

hucker mucker	the practice or policy of keeping secrets; also known as hugger-mugger

I

imbrued	stained

J

jennett	small Spanish horse
Juggler	sorcerer, usually implying deceit or trickery

L

league	covenant
let	hinder

M

made means	to come at anything by indirect practices

GLOSSARY

Mahometists	Mohammedans
malapertly	boldly, impudently, saucily
manqueller	murderer, homicide
marts	markets, trade centres
maugre	in spite of
meed	deserved share or reward

N

naughty pack	promiscuous activity
nill	to be unwilling

O

offscourings	refuse, rubbish, dregs
ousel	blackbird

P

packing	entourage or minions
palfrey	docile horse
palls	funeral cloths spread over coffin or hearse
pardy	interjection meaning literally by God, par Dieu
pattens	shoes or clogs with raised soles to raise feet above muddy ground
peason	peas
pinion	cut off the pinion of a wing or bird to prevent flight
profess	confess
proin	prune

Q

queans	prostitutes

S

shamefastness	state of being modest or being full of shame
shrewd	malicious

sibb	variant spelling of sib, blood relative, sibling
sithence	variant of sith, archaic for since
slowbellies	slothful persons, indolent gluttons
slug	sluggard, slow and lazy person
sooth	true
square	quarrel

T

tare	tore
trow	think or believe

U

ure	use, practice, exercise

V

vizard	mask or disguise

W

ween	believe
whelm	bury, engulf
whit	very small part or amount
wiss	know, understand
wot	what, in informal, dialectical use
wotteth	knows (third person singular)
wry	expressing mocking humour or disgust

WRITERS

A list of classical, patristic, papal, and early modern writers mentioned (excluding Anne Bacon, John Jewel, Thomas Harding, and citations from *The Geneva Bible*).

A

Aeneas Silvius *see* Pius II 70n.
Alliacensis, Pierre d'Ailly 88n.
Ambrose 57n., 66–67, 70–71, 74, 83–84, 163, 174
Anacletus 72n.
Andreas, Johannes 140n.
Argentine, Richard 8–9, 196
Aquinas, Thomas 19, 87–88, 90, 195, 199
Augustine 61, 63, 68, 70–71, 74, 77–80, 83–85, 87, 98, 109, 111, 122, 123, 131, 133, 135, 136, 163, 196

B

Bacon, Nicholas 12–13, 18, 202
Baldwin, William 10
Barker, William 6
Barnes, Robert 137n.
Beale, John xi, 18
Bernard of Clairvaux 96, 105, 118–19, 121–22, 138, 140, 196
Bèze, Théodore de 28
Bonaventure 80n.
Boniface VIII 102–03, 105n., 139n.

C

Cajetan, Thomas 88
Callistus 72n.
Campeggio, Lorenzo 95n.
Carletti, Angelo 145n.
Cassiodorus 160n.
Cecil, Mildred Cooke 7
Cheyne, Thomas xi, 20n.
Chrysostom, John 65, 68, 70, 72n., 74n., 76, 83, 84, 87, 107, 127, 128–29, 131, 134, 160, 163

Cicero 13, 47n., 59n. 144, 197
Clement V 104n., 105n., 106n., 138, 145
Cole, Henry 14, 134
Cooke, Anthony 6, 14, 38
Cranmer, Thomas 7, 9, 13, 89n., 152n., 155n., 158n., 197
Cyprian 6, 62–63, 76, 77n., 92, 93n., 131, 135, 153, 173, 184, 198

D

Durandus, William 140n., 157n.

E

Epiphanius 55n., 85, 87, 112, 134–36, 198
Erasmus 26, 132n.
Eusebius 47n., 52n., 66, 91, 115, 116n., 126n., 130, 131n., 161n.

F

Foxe, John 26, 103n., 104n., 197
Fulgentius 61n.

G

Gardiner, Stephen 89n., 90n., 198
Gelasius 73n., 74, 76n., 83–84, 138, 149
Gerson, Jean Charlier de 119, 120, 199
Giles of Viterbo 114n.
Gratian 57, 64n., 72n., 73n., 74n., 75n., 84n., 138n.
Gregory the Great 64, 107n., 118, 180

H

Harrington, John 6, 7n., 196
Hilary of Poitiers 117n., 175n., 183n., 199
Hierom *see* Jerome 51, 55, 57, 62, 70, 87, 131, 135, 155, 166, 176, 178
Hosius, Stanislaus 123–25, 158
Hostiensis 157n.
Huldericus 69n.
Humphrey, Laurence 5, 20

I

Irenaeus 171

J

Jerome 51n., 52, 55n., 57n., 62n., 135n., 155n., 166n., 176n., 178n.
Julius I 138
Justin Martyr 91n.
Justinian 137, 156, 169

L

Lefèvre, Jacques 69n.
Lombard, Peter 19, 88, 104n.

M

Magistris, Martinus de 94n.
Masso, Cornelius 157n.
Masson, Jacques 69n.

N

Nazianzus, Gregory 68–69, 87, 93, 152, 184, 199
Nicolas the Great 140n.
Nicholas of Lyra 156n., 201

O

Occam, William of 17, 88–89
Ochino, Bernardino 5–12, 23, 26n., 27, 29, 32–33, 203
Origen 52n., 70, 74–75, 78, 83–84, 86, 101n., 131n. 133–34, 166n.

P

Panormitanus *see* Tudeschi 69, 157n.
Parker, Matthew xi–xii, 13, 20, 26, 43, 204
Pausanias 145n., 204
Pighius, Albert 88n., 95, 120, 123n., 125–26, 133, 144, 159, 204
Platina, Bartolomeo 69n., 120n., 204
Pius II 69–70n.

Pius IV 23, 54n., 167n.
Plutarch 145n., 151n., 204
Prierus, Sylvester Mazzolini 144n.

R

Roberts, James xi
Roselli, Antonio 103n., 141n., 206
Rufinus, Tyrannius of Aquileia 52n., 161n., 166n., 197
Russell, Elizabeth Cooke Hoby 7

S

Sabellico, Marcantonio 106n.
Scholasticus, Socrates 86n., 136n., 161n.
Scotus, John Duns 17, 87–88
Segusio, Henricus de *see* Hostiensis 157n.
Sleidanus, Johannes 97n., 120n.
Sozomenus, Salaminias Hermias 68, 92, 112n.
Steuco, Agostino 102n.
Suetonius 49n., 205

T

Tacitus 46n., 205
Terence 94, 195
Tertullian 45n., 47–48n., 53n., 56n., 65–66, 68, 70, 93, 99–100, 108–09n., 127–28, 146, 171, 195
Textor, Johannes Ravisius 105n., 204
Theodoret 74, 83–84, 86n., 111, 133, 136n., 160n., 167
Theohylact of Ohrid 73–74, 127
Tudeschi, Niccolo de 69, 157n., 206

V

Vermigli, Peter Martyr 4, 61n.
Vigilius 61, 156n., 169

W

Whitaker, William 25
Wolfe, Reginald xi, 200

BIBLIOGRAPHY

The Adelphi of Terence, trans. by A. F. Burnet and J. H. Haydon (London: W. B. Clive, 1891)

Allen, Gemma, '"a briefe and plaine declaration": Lady Anne Bacon's 1564 translation of the *Apologia Ecclesiae Anglicanae*', in *Women and Writing, c. 1340–c. 1650: The Domestication of Print Culture*, ed. by Anne Lawrence-Mathers and Phillipa Hardman (York: York Medieval Press, 2010), pp. 62–76

——, *The Cooke Sisters: Education, piety and politics in early modern England* (Manchester: Manchester University Press, 2013)

André, James St, ed., *Thinking through Translation with Metaphors* (Manchester: St. Jerome Publishing, 2010)

The Ante-Nicene Fathers, ed. by Alexander Roberts, James Donaldson, and A. Cleveland Coxe, trans. by Robert Ernest Wallis, 10 vols (Buffalo, NY: Christian Literature Publishing Company, 1885–1896)

Apologia Ecclesiae Anglicanae (London, 1562), STC 555:02

The Apologia of Tertullian, trans. by William Reeve (London: Griffith, Farran, Okeden & Welsh, 1889)

An Apology for the Church of England, trans. by Stephen Isaacson (London: John Hearne, 1825)

An Apology of the Church of England, ed. by John E. Booty (Ithaca: Cornell University Press for the Folger Shakespeare Library, 1963)

The Apology for the Church of England, Translated from the Latin of Bishop Jewel, trans. by A. C. Campbell (Pontefract: B. Boothroyd, 1813)

Aquinas, Thomas, *Summa Theologica*, 5 vols (New York: Cosimo Classics, 2007)

Ariosto, Ludovico, *Orlando Furioso*, trans. by Sir John Harrington (1591), ed. by Robert McNulty (Oxford: At the Clarendon Press, 1972)

Augustine of Hippo, Selected Writings, ed. by Mary T. Clark (Mahwah: Paulist Press, 1984)

Bacon, Lady Anne, *The Letters of Lady Anne Bacon*, ed. by Gemma Allen (London: Royal Historical Society, Cambridge University Press, 2014)

Bacon, Francis, *Essays or Counsels Civil and Moral*, ed. by Charles W. Eliot (New York: F. P. Collier & Son, 1909)

Bacon, Sir Nicholas, *The Recreations of His Age* (Oxford: 1919)

Barker, William [pseud. Bercher], *The Nobility of Women (1559)*, ed. by W. Bond, Roxburghe Collection 142 (London: Chiswick Press, 1904)

Bernard of Clairvaux, *Sermons on Conversion*, trans. by Marie-Bernard Saïd, OSB (Kalamazoo, Michigan: Cistercian Publications, 1981)

Bernard, Saint, *On Consideration*, trans. by George Lewis (Oxford: Clarendon, 1908)

Bietenholz, Peter and Thomas Brian Deutscher, *Contemporaries of Erasmus: A Biographical Register of the Renaissance and Reformation*, 3 vols (Toronto: University of Toronto Press, 2003)

Binns, J. W., *Intellectual Culture in Elizabethan and Jacobean England: The Latin Writings of the Age* (Leeds: Francis Cairns, 1990)

Blatchly, J. M., 'Argentine, R (1510/11–1568)', *Oxford Dictionary of National Biography*, ed. by H. C. G. Matthew and Brian Harrison (Oxford: Oxford University Press, 2004)

Booty, John E., *John Jewel as Apologist of the Church of England* (London: S.P.C.K., 1963)

BIBLIOGRAPHY

British Library, MS Cotton Vitellius A XIII, f. 5ᵛ

Byrne, Muriel St Clare, 'The Mother of Francis Bacon', *Blackwood's Magazine* 236 (December 1934), 758–71

The Church Historians of England, Reformation Period: The Acts and Monuments of John Foxe, 8 vols (London: Seeleys, 1853–1868)

The Church History of Rufinus of Aquileia, trans. by Philip R. Amidon, S. J. (New York: Oxford University Press, 1997)

Cicero, trans. by W. A. Falconer, Loeb Classical Library, 30 vols (Cambridge, MA: Harvard University Press, 1912–1999)

Clarke, Danielle and Elizabeth Clarke, eds, *'This Double Voice': Gendered Writing in Early Modern England* (Basingstoke: Macmillan, 2000)

Claude, Jean, *A Defence of the Reformation*, trans. by T. B. (London: Hatchard, 1815)

Coldiron, A. E. B., 'Visibility now: Historicizing foreign presences in translation', *Translation Studies*, 5.2 (2012), 191–200

——, *Printers Without Borders: Translation and Textuality in the Renaissance* (Cambridge: Cambridge University Press, 2015)

Collinson, Patrick, *Godly People: Essays on English Protestantism and Puritanism* (London: The Hambledon Press, 1983)

——, *Richard Bancroft and Elizabethan Anti-Puritanism* (Cambridge: Cambridge University Press, 2013)

Cowell, Henry J., *The Four Chained Books* (London: Kingsgate Press, 1938)

Cranmer, Thomas, *Works*, ed. by John Edmund Cox for the Parker Society, 2 vols (Cambridge: Cambridge University Press, 1844–1846)

——, *Miscellaneous Writings and Letters*, ed. by John Edmund Cox for the Parker Society (Cambridge: Cambridge University Press, 1846)

Cyprian, *Corpus Scriptorum Ecclesiasticorum Latinorum, S Thasci Caecili Cypriani, Opera Omnia*, ed. by W. Hartel (Vienna: C. Geroldi Filium Bibliopolam Academiae, 1871)

——, *The Fathers of the Church: St. Cyprian, Letters 1–81*, trans. by Sister Rose Bernard Donna (Washington: Catholic University of America Press, 1964)

Decrees of the Ecumenical Councils, ed. by Norman P. Tanner, 2 vols (Washington: Georgetown University Press, 1990)

Demers, Patricia, '"Nether bitterly nor brablingly": Lady Anne Cooke Bacon's Translation of Bishop Jewel's *Apologia Ecclesiae Anglicanae*', in *English Women, Religion, and Textual Production, 1500–1625*, ed. by Micheline White (Farnham: Ashgate, 2011), pp. 205–17

Duffy, Eamon, *The Stripping of the Altars: Traditional Religion in England 1400–1580* (New Haven: Yale University Press, 1992)

Durand, Guillame, *Rationale divinorum officiorum*, 2 vols (Lyon: Jacobus Myt, 1518)

Epiphanius of Salamis, *The Panarion, A Treatise against Eighty Sects*, trans. by Frank Williams, 2 vols (Leiden: Brill, 1987–1994)

Erler, Mary C., *Reading and Writing during the Dissolution: Monks, Friars and Nuns 1530–1558* (Cambridge: Cambridge University Press, 2013)

Ferguson, Margaret W., *Dido's Daughters: Literacy, Gender and Empire in Early Modern England and France* (Chicago: University of Chicago Press, 2003)

Gardiner, Stephen, *A Detection of the devils sophistrie* (London: [n. pub.], 1546)

BIBLIOGRAPHY

Gee, Henry and William John Hardy, eds, *Documents Illustrative of English Church History* (New York: Macmillan, 1896)

The Geneva Bible: A Fascsimile of the 1560 Edition (Madison: University of Wisconsin Press, 1969)

Gerson, John, *Joannis Gersonii, Opera Omnia, Tomus secundus* (Antwerp: Sumptibus Societatis, 1706)

Gilson, Etienne, *History of Christian Philosophy in the Middle Ages* (New York: Random House, 1955)

Goodrich, Jaime, *Faithful Translators: Authorship, Gender, and Religion in Early Modern England* (Evanston, Illinois: Northwestern University Press, 2014)

Green, Ian, *Print and Protestantism in Early Modern England* (Oxford: Oxford University Press, 2000)

Gregory of Nazianzen, *Orationes, accurantibus D.A.B.* (Paris: Parent-Desbarres, 1885)

Hall, Alexander W., *Thomas Aquinas and John Duns Scotus: Natural Theology in the High Middle Ages* (London: Continuum, 2009)

Herde, Peter, 'The Empire: From Adolph of Nassau to Lewis of Bavaria, 1292–1347', in *The New Cambridge Medieval History: Vol 6 1300–c.1415*, ed. by Michael Jones (Cambridge: Cambridge University Press, 2000), pp. 515–50

Hermans, Theo, 'Images of Translation: Metaphor and Imagery in the Renaissance Discourse on Translation', in *The Manipulation of Literature: Studies in Literary Translation*, ed. by Theo Hermans (Beckenham, Kent: Croom Helm, 1985), pp. 103–35

Hilary, *Episcopi Pictaviensis, Tractatus Super Psalmos, Recensit Antonius Zingerle* (Prague: F. Temsky, 1891)

Hosington, Brenda M., 'Women Translators and the Early Printed Book', in *A Companion to the Early Printed Book in*

Britain 1476–1558, ed. by Vincent Gillespie and Susan Powell (Cambridge: D. S. Brewer, 2014), pp. 248–71

——, et al., ed., *Renaissance Cultural Crossroads: An Online Catalogue of Translations in Britain 1473–1640* <www.hri online.ac.uk/rcc>

Hughes, Philip, *The Reformation in England*, revised edition, three vols in one (New York: Macmillan, 1963)

Jardine, Lisa and Alan Stewart, *Hostage to Fortune: The Troubled Life of Francis Bacon 1561–1626* (London: Victor Gollancz, 1998)

Jenkins, Gary W., *John Jewel and the English National Church: The Dilemmas of an Erastian Reformer* (Aldershot: Ashgate Publishing, 2006)

Jewel, John, *An Apologie or answere in defence of the Churche of Englande, with a briefe and plaine declaration of the true Religion professed and used in the same* (London: Reginald Wolfe, 1564), STC 14591

——, *An Apologie or Aunswer in Defence of the Church of England, concerning the state of Religion used in the same 1562* (Menston, Yorkshire: The Scolar Press, 1969), STC 14590

——, *The Apology of the Church of England*, trans. by Lady Anne Bacon, rev. by Richard W. Jelf (Oxford: Oxford University Press, 1848)

——, *An Apology for the Church of England*, trans. and illustr. by Stephen Isaacson (London: John Hearne, 1825)

——, *The Apology of the Church of England and A Treatise of the Holy Scriptures*, trans. by William Rollison Whittingham (New York: New-York Protestant Episcopalian Press, 1831)

——, *Works*, ed. for the Parker Society by John Ayre, 4 vols (Cambridge: Cambridge University Press, 1845–1850)

BIBLIOGRAPHY

Ker, Neil, 'The Library of John Jewel', *Bodleian Library Record*, 9.5 (1977), 256–265

King, John N., *English Reformation Literature: The Tudor Origins of the Protestant Tradition* (Princeton: Princeton University Press, 1982)

King, John N. and Mark Rankin, 'Print, Patronage, and the Reception of Continental Reform: 1521–1603', *Yearbook of English Studies*, 38 (2008), 49–67

Kirsch, Johann Peter, 'Council of Trent' and 'Unam Sanctam', in *The Catholic Encyclopedia*, 15 vols (New York: Robert Appleton Company, 1907–1912), xv (1912)

Krey, Philip, 'The Apocalypse Commentary of 1329: Problems in Church History', in *Nicholas of Lyra: The Senses of Scripture*, ed. by Philip Krey and Lesley Smith (Leiden: Brill, 2000)

Kristeller, Paul Oskar, *Renaissance Thought II: Papers on Humanism and the Arts* (New York: Harper Torchbooks, 1965)

Lamb, Mary Ellen, 'The Cooke Sisters: Attitudes toward Learned Women in the Renaissance', in *Silent But for the Word: Tudor Women as Patrons, Translators, and Writers of Religious Works*, ed. by Margaret P. Hannay (Kent, Ohio: Ohio State University Press, 1985), pp. 107–25

Levy, F. J., *Tudor Historical Thought* (San Marino, California: The Huntington Library, 1967)

Loades, David, *Mary Tudor: A Life* (Oxford: Basil Blackwell, 1989)

Maas, Korey D., *The Reformation and Robert Barnes: History, Theology and Polemic in Early Modern England* (Woodbridge: Boydell, 2010)

MacCulloch, Diarmaid, *Reformation: Europe's House Divided 1490–1700* (London: Allen Lane, 2003)

——, *Silence: A Christian History* (New York: Viking, 2013)

Magnusson, Lynne, 'Widowhood and Linguistic Capital: The Rhetoric and Reception of Anne Bacon's Epistolary Advice', *English Literary Renaissance*, 31 (2001), 3–33

——, 'Imagining a National Church: Election and Education in the Works of Anne Cooke Bacon', in *The Intellectual Culture of Puritan Women, 1558–1680*, ed. by Johanna Harris and Elizabeth Scott-Baumann (London: Palgrave Macmillan, 2011), pp. 42–56

Mair, Katie, 'Material Lies: Anxiety and Epistolary Practice in the Correspondence of Anne, Lady Bacon and Anthony Bacon', *Lives and Letters* (2012), 59–74

McCutcheon, Elizabeth, *Sir Nicholas Bacon's Great House Sententiae* (Amherst, Mass.: English Literary Renaissance Supplements, 1977)

McGrath, Alister, *The Intellectual Origins of the European Reformation* (Oxford: Basil Blackwell, 1987)

——, *Iustitia Dei: A History of the Christian Doctrine of Justification*, second edition (Cambridge: Cambridge University Press, 1998)

McIntosh, M. K., 'Sir Anthony Cooke: Tudor humanist, educator, and religious reformer', *Papers of the American Philosophical Society*, 119 (1975), 233–50

Moretti, Franco, *Distant Reading* (London: Verso, 2013)

Morini, Massimiliano, *Tudor Translation in Theory and Practice* (Aldershot: Ashgate Publishing, 2006)

Nicene and Post-Nicene Fathers, ed. by Philip Schaff and Henry Wace, Series I, 14 vols (Buffalo: Christian Literature Publishing Company, 1886–1900)

Nicene and Post-Nicene Fathers, ed. by Philip Schaff and Henry Wace, Series II, 14 vols (Buffalo: Christian Literature Publishing Company, 1890–1899)

BIBLIOGRAPHY

Norton, David, *A History of the Bible as Literature* (Cambridge: Cambridge University Press, 2000)

Novesianus, Melchior, *Hierarchiae ecclesiaticae assertio* (1544)

Ochino, Bernardino, *Sermons of Barnardine of Sena godly, frutefull, and uery necessarye for all true Christians translated out of Italien into Englishe* (London: R. Carr for W. Reddell, 1548), STC 997:14

——, *Fouretene Sermons of Barnardine Ochyne, concerning the predestinacion and eleccion of god. Translated out of Italian in to our native tounge by A. C.* (London: John Day, 1551), STC 121:14

——, *Certayne Sermons of the right famous and excellente Clerk Master Barnardine Ochine. [...] Faythfully translated into Englyshe* (London: John Day, 1551?), STC 18766

——, *Prediche de Barnardino Ochino da Siena, Novallamente ristampate et con grande digientia rivedute et corrette. Con la sua Tavola nel fine.* Basilea, 1562

——, *Sermons of Barnardine Ochyne (to the number of 25) [...] Translated out of Italian into our native tongue by A. C.* (London: John Day, 1570), STC 18768

——, *Seven Dialogues*, trans. by Rita Belladonna (Ottawa: Dovehouse Editions, 1988)

O'Malley, John W., *Trent: What Happened at the Council* (Cambridge, MA: Harvard University Press, 2013)

Overell, M. A., 'Bernardino Ochino's Books and English Religious Opinion, 1547–80', in *The Church and the Book*, ed. by R. N. Swanson (Woodbridge, Suffolk: The Boydell Press, 2004), pp. 201–211

The Oxford Treatise and Disputation on the Eucharist, trans. and ed. by Joseph C. McLelland, *Sixteenth Century Essays & Studies*, 83 vols (Kirksville: Truman State University Press, 1983–2010)

Parker, Matthew, *The Correspondence of Matthew Parker, Archbishop of Canterbury*, ed. by John Bruce and Thomas Thomason Perowne (Cambridge: Cambridge University Press, 1853)

Patrologia Latina, ed. by Jacques-Paul Migne, 221 vols (Petit-Montrouge, Paris, Migne, 1844–1864)

Pausanias's Description of Greece, trans. by J. G. Frazer, 6 vols (London: Macmillan, 1898)

Pédeflous, Olivier, 'Textor's School Drama and Its Links to Pedagogical School Drama in Early Modern France', in *The Early Modern Cultures of Neo-Latin Drama*, ed. by Philip Ford and Andrew Taylor (Leuven: Leuven University Press, 2013)

Pelikan, Jaroslav, *The Christian Tradition: Reformation of Church and Dogma*, 5 vols (Chicago: University of Chicago Press, 1971–1989)

Pennington, Kenneth, *The Prince and the Law, 1200–1600: Sovereignty and Rights in the Western Legal Tradition* (Berkeley: University of California Press, 1993)

Pighius, Albertus, *Hierarchiae ecclesiasticae assertio. Coloniae Agrippinae* (Köln: *Apud Johannem Birckmannum*, 1558)

Platina, Bartolomeo, *De vitis ac gestis summorum pontificum* (Coloniae: Eucharius Cervicornius, 1540)

Plutarch, *Moralia*, ed. by T. E. Page, E. Capps, and A. Post for the Loeb Classical Library 245, trans. by Frank Cole Babbitt, 15 vols (Cambridge, MA: Harvard University Press, 1927–1969)

Rhodes, Neil, ed., with Gordon Kendal and Louise Wilson, *English Renaissance Translation Theory* (London: Modern Humanities Research Association, 2013)

Sacrosancta Concilia ad Regiam Editionem Exacta, ed. by Philippe Labbé and Gabriel Cossart, 23 vols (Venice: *Apud Jo. Baptistam Albrizzi Hieron. Fil. et Sebastianum Coleti*, 1728–1733)

BIBLIOGRAPHY

Schleiner, Louise, *Tudor and Stuart Women Writers* (Bloomington: Indiana University Press, 1994)

Setton, Kenneth M., *The Papacy and the Levant (1204–1571): The Sixteenth Century from Julius III to Pius V*, 4 vols (Philadelphia: American Philosophical Society, 1976–1984)

Sharpe, Kevin. *Selling the Tudor Monarchy: Authority and Image in Sixteenth-Century England* (New Haven: Yale University Press, 2009)

Southgate, Wyndham M., *John Jewel and the Problem of Doctrinal Authority* (Cambridge, MA: Harvard University Press, 1962)

Sterk, Andrea and Nina Caputo, eds, *Faithful Narratives: Historians, Religion, and the Challenge of Objectivity* (Ithaca: Cornell University Press, 2014)

Stevenson, Jane, *Women Latin Poets: Language, Gender, and Authority from Antiquity to the Eighteenth Century* (Oxford: Oxford University Press, 2005)

Stewart, Alan, 'The Voices of Anne Cooke, Lady Anne and Lady Bacon', in *'This Double Voice': Gendered Writing in Early Modern England*, ed. by Danielle and Elizabeth Clarke (Basingstoke: Macmillan, 2000), pp. 88–102

Sturiale, Massimo, *I* Sermons *di Anne Cooke: Versione "riformata" delle* Prediche *di Bernardino Ochino* (Catania: Quaderni del Dipartimento di Filologia Moderna, Università degli Studi di Catania, 2003)

Suetonius, *Lives of the Caesars*, ed. and trans. by J. C. Rolfe for the Loeb Classical Library 31 and 38, 2 vols (Cambridge, MA: Harvard University Press, 1914)

Tacitus, *Complete Works*, ed. by Alfred John Church, William Jackson Brodribb, and Sara Bryant for Perseus (New York: Random House, 1873, repr. 1942)

Theologiae Cursus Completus, ed. by Jacques Paul Migne, 28 vols (Paris: [n. pub.], 1840–1845)

Thomson, J. A. F., 'Papalism and Conciliarism in Antonio Roselli's *Monarchia*', *Mediaeval Studies*, 37 (1975), 445–58

Tudeschi, Niccolo de, *Abbatis Panormitani, Commentaria. Prima Partis in Primum Decretalium Librum* (Venice: *Apud Iuntas*, 1571)

Urwick, William, *Nonconformity in Herts: Being Lectures upon the Nonconforming Worthies of St. Albans* (London: Hazell, Watson, and Viney, 1884)

Venuti, Lawrence, *The Translator's Invisibility: A History of Translation*, second edition (New York: Routledge, 2008)

White, Peter, *Predestination, Policy and Polemic: Conflict and Consensus in the English Church from the Reformation to the Civil War* (Cambridge: Cambridge University Press, 1992)

INDEX

Aaron 50, 164, 178
Abiram 50
Abel 131
Abraham 110, 112–13, 126, 132, 147, 178, 182
Adam 115, 131
Adrian VI, Pope 120
Agesilaus, King 151
Ahab 100
Albert of Habsburg, Emperor 105
Alexander III, Pope 107
Allen, Captain Francis 29
Allen, Gemma 6, 8, 13, 27, 29, 35, 195–96
Ambrose 57n., 66–67, 70–71, 74, 83–84, 163, 174
Amos 48, 100, 147
Anabaptist 85, 103
Andreas, Johannes 140
Antaeus 113
Antichrist 64, 111, 116–17, 180, 183
Apollonius 136
Apologia Ecclesiae Anglicanae (*see* Jewel)
Aquinas, Thomas 19, 87–88, 90, 195, 199
  defending transubstantiation 19, 90
Archidamus 178
Argentine, Richard 8–9, 196
Articles of Convocation ix, 30
Assisi, Francis of 156
Athanasius 131, 160–61
Augustine *see* Writers
Ayre, John xi–xii, 14, 18, 20, 26, 51, 55, 64, 77, 119–20, 158

Babylon, harlot of 120
Bacchus 109

Bacon, Anne Cooke
  life:
    family background 6–7
    humanistic learning 3, 5–7
    lady-in-waiting 12
    marriage and children 7, 12–13, 29–30
    final decade 27, 37
    funeral 32
  letters:
    defence of preachers 30
    display of pedigree 28
    reported speech 29
    A Parte of a Register 31
  translations:
    of Jewel xi–xii, 1–5
    colloquial directness 2
    division into parts 18
    unacknowledged work xi–xii
    of Ochino 5–12, 38
    address to mother 8
    Certayne sermons 8–9
    Fouretene sermons 6, 8, 10–12
    Moral urgency 9
    Sermons of Barnardine Ochine 6–7, 11
    understanding of election 8–13
Bacon, Anthony 17, 27, 29–31
  charge of sodomy 29
Bacon, Francis 5, 31–33
Bacon, Nicholas 12–13
Bacon, Roger 119
Baldwin, William (Guilielmus) 10
Bancroft, Richard 1, 26
Baptista Mantuanus 121
Barker, William 6
Barnabas 86

Basil 68, 70, 101
Beale, John xi, 18
Benedict 69, 157
Bèze, Théodore 28
Booty, John xii, 14–18, 25–27,
    120n., 157n., 169n., 172n.
Bishop of Rome 50, 54, 67, 69,
    72n., 83n., 96, 104, 118,
    123, 127, 155, 166–67
  assumed titles 63–64, 107, 177
  tyranny of 86, 102, 106n.,
    120–21, 156n., 159, 180,
    182
Boniface VIII, Pope 103n.,
    105n., 139n.
brothelry 98
Bucer, Martin 9
Bulla celebrationis 54
Burghley, Lord (*see* Cecil,
    William)

Caesar 49n., 99–100, 126, 144,
    179
Cajetan, Thomas 88
Caligula 147
Calixtus 72
Camotensis 155–56
Campbell, A. C. xii, 18
Campeggio, Lorenzo 95n.
Caputo, Nina 34, 39
Catholic Church
  actions of 49, 108, 110, 112,
    122, 160
  authority of 50, 54, 56–57,
    64–65, 73, 77, 88, 102–04,
    124n., 126, 137–40, 144,
    151–55, 167–69, 179–82
  conciliarism 88n., 103n., 120n.
Catholicon 144
Carletti, Angelo 145n.
Cecil, Mildred Cooke 7
  translation 7
Cecil, William 5, 12, 18, 30, 33
Celestine III, Pope 106n.

Celsus 101, 130–31
Cephas 86
Ceres 109
Certayne sermons 8–9
Chard, Thomas 20n.
Charlemagne 104n.
Charles V, Emperor 7
Cheyne, Thomas xii, 18n.
Childeric III 104n.
Chrysostom *see* Writers
Church Fathers xi, 4, 19, 22, 24
Cicero 13, 47n., 59n., 144
Clement V, Pope 104–06n., 138,
    145
Clement VII, Pope 105n.
Clement, John 132n.
Coldiron, Anne 2, 35
Cole, Henry 14, 134
Collinson, Patrick 1
Colonna, Vittoria 6
Communion
  elevation of host 16
  reception in both kinds 73,
    125, 138n.
  reception in one kind 138
  words of consecration 16,
    74–75, 89–90n.
Constantine, Emperor 47n., 86,
    102n., 104n., 140n.,
    166–69, 174
controversy (Jewel-Harding) ix,
    xi, 5, 17, 24–25, 33
Cooke, Anthony 6
Corpus Christi, feast of 77n.
Councils:
  Aquileia 174
  Carthage 64, 137
  Chalcedon 63n., 74n., 91,
    111n., 166
  Constantinople 52n., 62–63,
    88n., 152n., 166
  Eliberine, Grenada 134
  Ephesus 63n., 74n., 166, 168n.
  Fifth Lateran 114n.

INDEX

Fourth Lateran 96n.
Gangra 137n., 173
Nicea 63n., 168n.
Rome 136
Trent ix, 19, 23–24, 51n., 54n., 63n., 139n., 157–58n., 167n.
Cowell, Henry J. 26
Cranmer, Archbishop Thomas *see* Writers
Cyprian 6, 62–63, 76–77, 92–93, 131, 135, 153, 173, 184
Cyril of Alexandria 111

Dandalus, Francis 106
Daniel 48, 110, 116–17, 148
Dathan 50
David, King 164
Day, John 4
Deuteronomy 7, 177
Devereux, Robert, Earl of Essex 32
Devil 45–46, 48, 52, 56, 69–70, 84, 89–90, 113, 118, 120–21, 124, 127, 131, 176, 178
Dietrich of Nieheim 145
Donatists 57, 174
Duffy, Eamon 15
Durandus, William 140

Edward VI, King 6, 132n.
Elijah 100, 115
Elizabeth I, Queen 132
  accession 1, 9, 12, 14–15, 25
  Act of Supremacy 14
  Act of Uniformity 15
Elizabethan Settlement 1, 3, 14, 17
English College, Douai 25
Epiphanius *see* Writers
Erasmus 26, 132n.
Erastianism 13n., 25
Eucharist 7, 16, 18–19, 61n., 71, 74n., 85n., 89–90, 105n.

Eusebius *see* Writers
Ewbank, W. W. xii

faith, gift of 23
Ferdinand, Emperor 167
fornication 94, 178n.
Foxe, John *see* Writers

Gelasius, Pope 73–74, 76n., 83–84, 138, 149
Geneva Bible xi
Gerson, Jean 119–20
Gidea Hall, Essex 6
Giles of Viterbo 114n.
Godhead 60–61, 111n., 168n.
Goodrich, Jaime 3, 36
Gorhambury 29, 31
Gospel of Christ 47n., 49, 53, 84, 186
Gracchus 111
Green, Ian 15
Gregory the Great 64n., 107n., 118n.
Gregory of Nyssa 68
Gregory VII, Pope 106

Hagar 112n.
Haggai (Aggeus) 57n., 172n.
Haman 100, 130–31
Harding, Thomas
  life:
    Devon background 24–25
    subscription and exile 12, 25
  disagreements on:
    married clergy 19, 68–69n., 133n., 136–37n.
    reception of Eucharist 149n.
    Pope Joan 22, 95
    interpretative authority 124n.
    concubinage 136n.
    reading scripture 45, 47, 65–66, 123–27

209

Answere to Maister Iuelles challenge 16
A Detection of sundrie foule errours 16
Harrington, John 6–7
Heathens 93, 109
Henry IV, Emperor 106
Henry II, King 181
Henry VIII, King 6, 132n., 181
Hercules 113, 178
Heresy 13, 19, 52, 55–58, 83–84, 94n., 156n., 161n. 174n.
heretics 49, 74n., 84–85, 87, 103n. 109, 111–12, 147, 168
Herod 90, 126
Hezekiah 165
Hickes, Michael 32
Hilary of Poitiers *see* Writers
Holy Ghost 24, 60–61, 67n., 84, 120, 154, 156, 158–59, 167, 182
Hosington, Brenda 2, 9–10, 36
Howard, Henry, Earl of Northampton 31
Hughes, Philip 21
Humphrey, Laurence 5

incest 47–48, 52, 97, 109
Interpretatio linguarum 5
Irenaeus 171
Isaacson, Stephen xii, 18n., 77n., 158n.
Isaiah 48, 112, 115, 122n., 142, 147, 154, 164

Jardine, Lisa 29, 32
Jehoshaphat, King 165–66
Jelf, Richard William xii, 18n., 26, 138n.
Jenkins, Gary 13–14n., 18, 25, 28
Jeremiah (Jeremy) 48, 80, 110, 142
Jeroboam 100, 143

Jerome (Hierom) *see* Writers
Jewel, John
life:
    education 13–14
    subscription and recantation 14
    mentorship by Peter Martyr 4, 13–14, 20
    roles in Elizabethan England 14
    vestments controversy 28
Challenge Sermon (The Copie of a Sermon) 16
Epistola 16–17
Apologia Ecclesiae Anglicanae 1, 13, 15–22, 26, 32–33
A Replie unto M. Hardinges Answeare 16
A Defence of the Apologie 16, 18, 26
Joachim of Fiore 121n.
Joan, Pope 22, 95
John, King 105, 181
John XXII, Pope 156n.
Joshua 164, 176
Josiah 165
Julius I, Pope 138n.
Julius III, Pope 54n., 167n.
justification by faith 23, 69n.
Justin martyr 91n.
Justinian, Emperor 137, 156n., 169

Kenninghall palace 12

Lamb, Mary Ellen 9n., 27
Lambeth Conference 30
Lawson, Thomas 29–31
Leo III, Pope 104n.
Levi 177
Liberius, Pope 155, 169
Libertines 85, 103
Loades, David 12n.
Lombard, Peter 88n,

INDEX

Lord of Lords 102, 141
Lot 147
Lucifer 64
Luther, Martin 69n., 87–88,
    101–02, 145n.
Lutherans 7, 106, 167n.
Lyra, Nicholas of 156n.

MacCulloch, Diarmaid 1n., 17
Magdalen College 4–5
Magnusson, Lynne 21, 31
Mair, Katy 29
Mammetrectus 144
Marcion 47n., 66n., 124
Martinengo, Girolamo 23
Martyr, Peter
    letter of congratulation xi, 20
Mary Tudor, Queen 12
Marsilius of Padua 121
Mass
    Massing priests 21, 66
    Private mass 71, 73, 83, 141,
        148–49, 173, 178
Maurice, Emperor 63
McGrath, Alister 1, 9–10
meritum condigni 87
meritum congrui 87
Menonians (Mennonites) 85
Micah 153–54
Ministers in church 62, 65,
    67–69, 77n., 89n., 93
Moses 46, 50, 103n., 131–32,
    146, 164–65, 172, 176
Mühlberg, battle of 7

Nahum 176n.
Nazianzen, Gregory *see* Writers
Nestorius 74n., 76., 111
Nicholas the Great, Pope 69n.
Nicodemites 17
Nicostratus 178
Noah 110
Norton, John 26
Novellae 137n.

obedience to papal authority
    103, 107–08
Ochino, Bernardino
    life 5, 7
    appeal to Anne Cooke 8–9
    Prediche 6, 8, 10–11
    Sermons translated by Anne
        Cooke and Richard
        Argentine *see* Writers
Ockham, William of 17, 88–89
Origen 52n., 70, 74–75, 78,
    83–84, 86, 101n., 131n.,
    133–34, 166n.
Overell, M. Anne 9

Panarion 112n., 135n.
Pandects of civil law 137n.
Paphnutius 160–61
Parker, Archbishop Matthew xi,
    13, 20, 26
    prefatory letter 43–44
Parkhurst, Bishop 26
Paul 46–48, 51–52, 56–58, 66,
    68–70, 72n., 79–81, 86,
    91, 116, 118, 119n.,
    124–25, 128, 130, 132,
    147, 149, 152, 172, 175,
    183
Paul III, Pope 96–97, 167n.
Paula 166, 176n.
Pelagians 174
Peter 47, 51, 62, 86, 91, 97–98,
    102n., 107, 115–16, 152,
    169, 177–79, 182
Petrarch, Francesco 121
pharisees 52, 67, 90, 98, 110,
    113, 115, 143, 147, 156n.,
    159, 172, 178
Phocas 63
Pighius, Albert 88n., 95, 120,
    123n., 125–26, 133, 144,
    159
Pilate 90, 122
Pius II, Pope 69–70n.

Pius IV, Pope 23, 54n., 167n.
Platina, Bartolomeo Sacchi 69n., 120n.
Pole, Cardinal 159
Porphyrius 101
polemic 1, 15, 23n., 25, 27, 130n., 137n.
Polycarpus 91
predestination 8–9, 23
print technology 2–3
procession of Corpus Christi 77–78
purgatory 19, 78–79, 141, 178

Raphael, archangel 131
Reformation 1, 4, 14, 16, 17–19, 27, 30, 103n., 132n., 137n.
Roberts, James xi
Rhodes, Neil x, 2n., 4
Roselli, Antonio 103n., 141n.
Rufinus 52, 161n., 166n.
Russell, Elizabeth Cooke Hoby 7

Sabellico, Marcantonio 106
sacraments 15, 18–19, 23–24, 57n., 63, 67n., 70–78, 83, 88–90, 105, 111n., 133, 137–38n., 141–43, 148–49, 171, 173, 178, 182, 184n.
sacrilege 46, 56n., 73, 83, 138, 149
Sadducees 90
Samaritan 46, 56, 112
Sapor, Persian King 107
Saul 164
Savonarola, Girolamo 121
schism 14, 49, 57n., 84, 88n., 103n., 138n., 145n., 147, 184
Schleiner, Louise 8–9, 27
Schmalkaldic league 7
Scotus, Duns 17, 87–88

Seat of Rome 53
Seres, William 4
slander 18, 45–46, 50–52, 75, 101, 108–09, 158n.
Sleidanus, Johannes 97n., 120n.
Socrates 86, 136n., 161n., 167–68
Solomon 162, 165, 172, 175
Sophocles 22, 58–59
Southgate, Wyndham 1n., 14n., 25
Sozomenus 68, 92, 112n.
Spencer, Edward 27
Spiridion 68
Standen, Anthony 30
Stephen, martyr 46, 48
Sterk, Andrea 34
Steuco, Agostino 102n.
Sturiale, Massimo 10
Stewart, Alan 20, 29n., 32
Supremacy, Act of 14
Sylverius, Pope 169
Symmachus 101

Tamerlane 107
Terence 94
Tertullian *see* Writers
Textor, Joannes Ravisius 105
Theodoret *see* Writers
Theophylact 73–74, 127
Three Articles 30
Throckmorton, Nicholas 16
translation
 as authorial multiplicity 2
 dialogue with sources 4
 opportunity for women 3, 21, 33
 reconstruction 3
 visibility 21
transubstantiation 19, 76n.
 defined by Aquinas and at Trent 19, 90n.
 opposed by Jewel and Bacon 90n. 133n.

INDEX

Trent, Council of (Trident)
  Documents 23, 51n., 139n.
  exclusion 23
  sessions 51n., 54n., 63n., 157–58n. 167n.
Truth 7, 18–19, 24, 34, 45–46, 49, 62, 71, 84–87, 90. 100, 108–10, 115–17, 127–28, 130, 144–45, 151–52, 158–61, 175, 178, 180–85
Tudeschi, Niccolo de 69, 157n.
tyranny of pope 86, 102, 106n., 121, 156n., 159, 180

Valla, Lorenzo 121n.
Victor III, Pope 105–06n.

Vigilius 61, 156n., 169
Virgin Mary 81n.

Whittingham, W. R. xii, 18n., 95n., 105n. 114n. 117n., 119–20n., 122n., 133n., 137n., 156–57n.
Word of God 16, 57, 66–67, 73–75, 77, 110, 113, 123–25, 128, 134n., 142, 147–48, 157–58, 164

Zachary, Pope 104n.
Zadok 165
Zosimus, Pope 155–56
Zwenckfeldians 84, 124–25
Zwinglius, Hulderic 87, 101–02, 121

www.ingramcontent.com/pod-product-compliance
Lightning Source LLC
Chambersburg PA
CBHW061444300426
44114CB00014B/1820